VIDEO NASTIES!

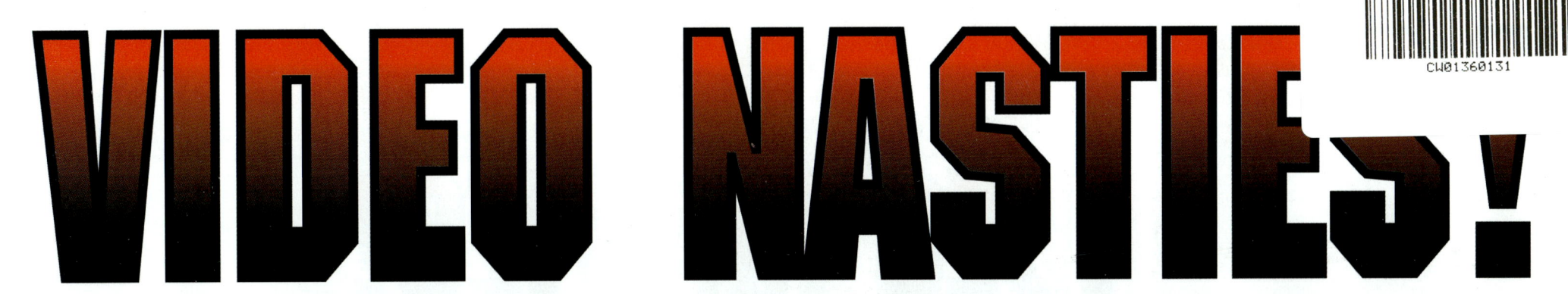

From Absurd to Zombie Flesh-Eaters - A Collector's Guide To The Most Horrifying Films Ever Banned!

By Allan Bryce

The Dark Side
The Magazine of the Macabre and Fantastic

Stray Cat Publishing Limited

VIDEO NASTIES!

ISBN 0-9533261-6-0

Published By Stray Cat Publishing Ltd.
PO Box 36, Liskeard, Cornwall. PL14 4YT. England

© 2004 Allan Bryce

This book is sold subject to the condition that it shall not by way of trade or otherwise, be lent, re-sold, hired out or otherwise circulated without the publishers prior consent in any form of binding or cover other than that in which it is published and without a similar condition including this condition being imposed upon the subsequent purchaser.

Design & Typeset by Ebony Media Ltd
This Volume © Stray Cat Publishing Ltd 2004

Authors Acknowledgments

I would like to thank Marc Morris for supplying the credit details on all of the movies and Matthew Hopkins, Richard Marshall and Norman Taylor for illustrations from their collections.
I would also like to thank Kevin Coward for the cover re-design.

VIDEO NASTIES!

CONTENTS

Official Nasties List.....................4

Introduction................................5

Censorship Scandal.....................6

Dark Side Of The Boom................8

Nice 'N' Nasty............................10

Return Of The Video Nasties......12

The Films....................................13

SCOTLAND YARD'S OFFICIAL LIST OF VIDEO NASTIES

- Absurd
- Anthropophagous The Beast
- Beast In Heat
- The Beyond
- Blood Bath
- Bloody Moon
- The Bogey Man
- The Burning
- Cannibal Apocalypse
- Cannibal Man
- Cannibal Terror
- Contamination
- Dead And Buried
- Death Trap
- Deep River Savages
- Delirium
- Don't Go In The Woods Alone
- Don't Go Near The Park
- Driller Killer
- The Evil Dead
- Expose
- Faces Of Death
- Forest Of Fear
- Frankenstein (Andy Warhol)
- Gestapo's Last Orgy
- House By The Cemetery
- House On The Edge Of The Park
- I Spit On Your Grave
- Last House On The Left
- The Living Dead (At The Manchester Morgue)
- The Madhouse
- Mardi Gras Massacre
- Nightmare Maker
- Nightmares In A Damaged Brain
- Night Of The Bloody Apes
- Night Of The Demon
- Possession
- Pranks
- Prisoner Of The Cannibal God
- The Slayer
- Snuff
- SS Experiment Camp
- Tenebrae
- Terror Eyes
- The Toolbox Murders
- Unhinged
- The Witch Who Came From The Sea
- Zombie Creeping Flesh
- Zombie Flesh-Eaters

Introduction

Home video recorders first came on the market in the late 70s, and the so-called 'video nasties' arrived very soon afterwards. While the major studios dithered about whether or not to put their recent blockbusters out on tape, enterprising distributors filled the shelves of the newly-opening video rental shops with lurid shockers that would never have stood the remotest chance of getting a cinema release. In fact in the early days the only movies you could rent on video were low budget sex and horror titles. For fans of exploitation cinema, it was a Golden Age!

At the start the sudden popularity of the new medium caught the authorities out. There was no law on the statute books to say that video movies had to be certificated, and there was even some doubt as to whether films on video were covered by the Obscene Publications Act. I vividly remember wandering round Epsom Market in the early 80s and suddenly being confronted by a newly-opened video library stall, decorated with large posters of *I Spit On Your Grave* and *Driller Killer*, both of them movies that I had read about but never expected to get to see.

I later got quite friendly with the guy who ran the stall and used to recommend good horror titles to him. He probably cursed me when the 'nasties' purge got under way because he must have had to get rid of half his stock. But of course anybody with any sense knew that the bubble would burst sooner or later. As it happened, the bad publicity generated by a gory back page ad for *Driller Killer* in January 1982's issue of *Television And Video Retailer* was the very first rumbling of a landslide that would eventually bury countless small distributors and change the face of the UK video industry forever.

In May of the same year, *The Sunday Times* carried a feature headlined *How High Street Horror Is Invading The Home*, which reported: "These videos, called 'nasties' in the trade – are rapidly replacing sexual pornography as the video trade's biggest money-spinner. The 'nasties' are far removed from the suspense of the traditional horror film. They dwell on murder, rape, sado-masochism, mutilation of women, cannibalism and Nazi atrocities." The same month *The Daily Express* identified 'nasties' as "films which show castration, sadistic attacks on women, and violence including the use of chainsaws or electric drills."

We all know that the media decide government policy in this country, and once they'd got their teeth into the 'video nasties' they were not going to let them rest. Nor were the police, who started raiding video shops and distributors left, right and centre. In June of 1983 *The Daily Mail* launched a "Ban the sadist video's" campaign to coincide with the publishing of an official list of 52 'nasties' by the Director of Public Prosecutions.

This list quickly became a shopping guide for horror buffs anxious to grab their gory vicarious thrills while they could, and there were still plenty of video shop owners ready to take a chance on stocking the movies while the demand was there. In many cases horror fans were in for a severe disappointment, since the only thing truly horrific about many of the films on the list was that anyone had the nerve to release them the first place. In that respect the list had the adverse effect of giving undeserved stature to films that frankly did not deserve it.

As the press kept the pressure on, one Graham Bright, Conservative MP for Luton South, announced his intention to introduce a private member's Bill on the control of video nasties. Actually instigated by then Home Secretary Leon Brittan, the Bill was rushed through to become law in July 1984, with a 12 month grace period to clean all non-certificated tapes out of the system. Since it would now cost quite a large sum to certificate a movie, many of the smaller distributors decided to close their doors once the grace period was over, leaving the field to the major players with Hollywood backing.

A lengthy chronology of the nasties phenomenon is provided by John Martin in his excellent book, *The Seduction Of The Gullible*, and it is not my intention here to document (as John does so well) the never-ending series of tabloid scare stories, prosecutions and acquittals that have led us to our present sorry state. This aspect of the book is covered by a number of articles which I originally wrote for video magazines at various key points during the nasties period.

The Bright Bill has been with us for 13 years now, and we have the most heavily censored video industry in Europe, maybe even the world. And it's not over yet, folks. The Video Standards Council recently felt obliged to react to a threat of even further censorship by publishing a paper entitled, *If It Ain't Broke, Don't Fix It*, reminding us of all the good things about the video industry. This was prompted by a recent report that came to the conclusion if you show violent videos to violent criminals they will be more "readily influenced" than their peers. Is this news? I think not.

But supposing we do accept this as "earth-shattering news," the question then is do we want all videos, movies and television to be made to suit the needs of a few violent delinquents? I think not, again. It is not such a baffling or unusual problem. We know that some children, and perhaps adults too, will be harmed or even killed every year if weedkiller, bleach and sharp kitchen knives remain on sale to the public. They could be banned, but we accept that this is a tough world and there is a price to pay for having such things available. It is not unreasonable, therefore, to argue that freedom of expression, including the freedom to depict violence, should remain available despite the risks – which are undoubtedly less significant than those attaching to weedkiller, bleach and knives.

You'll find a few anti-censorship articles here, but in the final analysis all sensible grown-ups realise that censorship of any kind is not really possible in today's information technology world. So this book's main purpose is to provide reviews and credits for 74 movies that at one time or another found themselves on the nasties list. The first nasties list of 52 titles was published in June 1983. 11 more titles were added in in August 1984 after the passing of the Video Recordings Act, and many more titles were added and dropped in the following years, leaving a final 'definitive' 39 titles that were successfully prosecuted. ut we figured you'd like to have the full number, since you're hardly likely to find them on the shelf at *Blockbuster* nowadays!

Glancing through this colourful and lurid tome, the average middle-class, middle-aged *Daily Mail* reader might feel increasing nausea and the return of a nearly-two-decade-old anxiety that society is once more collapsing round their ears. But I am pretty certain that most horror buffs of a certain age will merely experience a twinge of nostalgia, and a longing to revisit those halcyon days of the early 1980s, when the blood ran in rivers and you had to keep repeating to yourself.... it's only a movie.... it's only a movie.... But then we always knew that they were only movies. Nastiness, like everything else, is purely in the eyes of the beholder.

Allan Bryce

Video Nasties:
The Censorship Scandal

Having been a horror fan for many years before video ever came on the scene, I was delighted when it opened the floodgates to a lot of material that the British censor would otherwise not have allowed me to see. I sat through them all: *Driller Killer* (pretty boring), *Last House On The Left* (amateurish) and *I Spit On Your Grave* (a well-made female *Death Wish*).

But then along came the vocal minority and the so-called video nasty scare was born. Sensational articles appeared in the tabloids, the powers-that-be started to ban titles such as the above, and dealers were fined for stocking them. All of this was a great disappointment to me. Even watching *Snuff* had not turned me into a drooling psychopath (well, not in my opinion anyway) - in fact the fuss made over that movie was ridiculous, because anybody who took the trouble to watch it would have known that the "real-life murder" that took place at the end was just a phony ploy to sell a film which was otherwise too poorly made to find an audience.

Initially, it appeared that police were banning on video material that was unavailable in cinemas. But they then began to confiscate titles which carried a legally-obtained British Board of Film Censors (BBFC) certificate, stating that what was permissible in the controlled environment of a cinema was not necessarily so in the home. If dad's at the pub, they reasoned, and mum's down the bingo hall, what's to stop junior watching *The Texas Chainsaw Massacre*? I find this presumption on the part of the authorities that parents cannot be trusted to take care of their own children insulting and ridiculous. They may as well ban beer or cigarettes from the home on the same premise - will off-licences, I wonder, be next to have their stocks confiscated. But to me, the most intriguing thing is the term 'video nasty.' Nasties, if we are to believe the popular press, seem to have been responsible for ninety percent of the violence in this country since the advent of home video. But as we await the arrival of Graham Bright M.P.'s famous Video Recordings Bill aimed at controlling them, no one has come forward yet to give us a clear idea as to what nasties are! To clarify the situation I think it is a good idea to look at some films currently under threat of police confiscation according to a "hit list" recently drawn up by Scotland Yard.

This list puzzles me. It is understandable that movies depicting realistic rape and carnage - such as *The Last House On The Left* and *I Spit On Your Grave* could, at a stretch of the imagination, have a perverse effect on already sick minds. But what about the zombie films that are dubbed nasties? In general these are cheaply made schlocky horror pics which are more likely to amuse than deprave and corrupt!

One title on the hit list, for instance, is *Zombie Creeping Flesh* (Merlin Video), a movie with dubbing of the sort that leaves characters' mouths flapping like stranded fish while their dialogue half-heartedly attempts to follow. The story depicts a world taken over by glassy-eyed creatures who like to amble up to people and take huge bites out of them while the soundtrack goes potty with unsynchronised slurping noises. Pretty reporter Margit Evelyn Nelson tracks down the cause of this epidemic of bad acting to a chemical research laboratory somewhere up the Amazon, encountering lots of zombies en-route.

It seems ludicrous that such a daft movie as this could ever be the subject of police prosecution, and, seeing it included on the hit list leads me to suppose that the police are pretty uninformed and indiscriminate in the titles they are choosing to seize.

Quite often it seems videos are being confiscated largely on the evidence of their covers and, in particular, their titles. For instance, there is on the hit list a number of tapes which include the word 'cannibal' in the title. *Cannibal Apocalypse* (Replay Video) for example, which was originally known as *The Cannibals Are In The Streets*. This admittedly does serve up the gore with a trowel. John Saxon stars as an ex-Vietnam war hero who returns with a taste for human flesh. Undeterred by the VAT on take-away food, he sets off with two like-minded war buddies to sample the citizens of Atlanta, Georgia. This is an extremely violent exercise which stood little chance of getting past the censor. It's nevertheless very well made and puts across the potent message that not only is war hell - but that it can also give you indigestion!

The most horrid cannibal title around is *Cannibal Ferox* (Replay). This is another Italian-made epic and it takes a hardy constitution to sit through it. The story is purportedly based on fact and tells of a group of young people who fall foul of a tribe of cannibals deep in the jungles of the Amazon. Scenes of awful mutilation are graphically depicted, and the film seems designed merely to test audience endurance. Both it and *Cannibal Apocalypse* are very gory films, which a lot of people would not want to see anyway. They do, however, appeal to horror buffs who, if they cannot get their meat on video legally, will surely seek it out illegally and create a sizeable black market for this sort of product.

The cannibal titles, however, are the thin end of the wedge – anonymous foreign productions released by small companies obviously prepared to take a risk to make a profit. But what about Thorn/EMI, who have had their fingers burned with *The Burning*? To be fair, they withdrew all copies of the film originally when it was discovered that seven seconds snipped out by the censor had been accidentally restored in the tape version. But even the BBFC-approved version has been causing them trouble. I can't understand why this particular title seems to have been singled out for so much attention. It's just another variation on the *Friday The 13th* stalk-and-slash genre, with a badly burned lunatic murdering kids at a summer camp as a way of getting back at the juveniles who caused his scarring. The best thing about the film is Tom Savini's gruesome make-up work – otherwise it's dull and predictable.

Another Thorn/EMI release to make the list is the excellent and highly underrated *Dead And Buried*. Set in the sleepy seaside town of Potter's Bluff in California, the imaginative story tells of police chief James Farentino investigating mysterious deaths which seem to have a bizarre connection with the behaviour of the townspeople. The twist ending is a cracker, and though there is a fair amount of gore on display, the film is not swamped with it. In fact it mainly relies on good performances and direction to give it its chilling impact. It went the rounds of provincial cinemas a couple of years ago and didn't cause any controversy at all, so it would be a shame if it was lumbered with a nasty status just because of its appearance on this blacklist.

Another, perhaps more famous, case of indiscriminate and arbitrary seizure by police is *The Evil Dead*. Most people will remember that this schlock-horror film directed by Sam Raimi came out in the cinema in January 1983 with a BBFC 18 certificate. It played on over 190 screens around the country, to an audience of more than two million people, and proved popular on video too (it was released on tape in February 1983), being awarded Best Rental Title of 1983.

Notwithstanding this obvious public approval, however, and ignoring the film's legally awarded certificate, the Manchester police seized *The Evil Dead* in February 1983, and ever since that first seizure (when it was returned with apologies), the video has been subject to seizure and now turns up on the hit list of cassettes which police suggest dealers withdraw from their shelves.

Understandably Palace Video, who handle the *Evil Dead* cassette, are angered by this unfair treatment, maintaining that "sections of the press have misrepresented the film" and that there has yet to be a successful prosecution of *The Evil Dead* where a defence has been made. So strongly do they feel about it that they are giving their full support to Barker's Video Tape Centres of Leeds, who are being prosecuted for a number of films, including *The Evil Dead*. Palace Video are also awaiting a date for their own defence of *The Evil Dead* to come to court. (*Note: Barkers were acquitted of all charges, with the films being found "not obscene."*)

This spirited defence is not to be found everywhere, however. I went to see my local dealer the other day and he was busy removing horror titles from his shelves. "I'd rather not stock any at all than get done for having nasties," was his comment. I could see his point.

But the question remains, just what is a nasty? On the evidence of this article, it seems that 'nastiness,' like beauty, is in the eye of the beholder. What appears nasty to the Manchester Police Force, for instance, receives hearty approval from the management of London's Scala Cinema (who recently ran a legal night-long cinema session of films confiscated on video). It remains to be seen what changes the proposed Bright Bill brings about, but I know one thing – if I can't get hold of decent horror movies on video any more, then I shall simply have to start going back to the cinema again!

Originally published June 1984

The Dark Side of the Boom

The Nasties – the adult movies you can't see!

Everybody knows what a video nasty is nowadays. Exposure to one is liable to turn even the most timid of souls into a rabid cannibal, wielding an axe in one hand and a chainsaw in another. Fortunately for society (and unfortunately for the axe and chainsaw industry) we now know what titles fall within this category and are extremely unlikely to encounter them at our local video shop thanks to the tireless efforts of the more sensational tabloids, Mary Whitehouse and co. – and the boys in blue!

There's no doubt that video nasties got the video industry a bad naame. In the early days BB (Before Bright) you could see just about anything on video and the floodgates were open for a lot of quite offensive material that would never have otherwise been allowed past the British censor. Because video shop owners were dealing with a product that was possibly "likely to deprave and corrupt," they began to be lumped in with the traditional porn merchants in the eyes of the police and a large section of the general public.

Of course the truth was that most video shop owners had no more idea of what they were renting out than their customers. One horror film sounds very much like another as far as the man in the street is concerned – the blood may "run in rivers" in *Driller Killer*, but it does in the most harmless of Hammer Dracula pics too, and a title like *The Last House On The Left* doesn't sound at all like the catalogue of sadism it actually is.

Video shop owners don't particularly like being raided by the police every five minutes and so most of them have removed all suspect products from their shelves. The list of semi-official video nasties prepared by Scotland Yard has been their guideline. But is it a fair one? Probably the most infamous title on the list is *Snuff* – a movie that ends with the supposedly real-life killing of an actress on camera. In fact the American producer Allen Shackerton bought a very dull 1971 Argentinian film called *Slaughter*, tacked on the bloody climax (which is obviously faked), and made a fortune from morbid thrill-seekers. The sickest thing about it is the way that most people seem to want to believe that a person was killed for their entertainment.

Real death on camera, as opposed to the pathetic faking of *Snuff*, can be found in another hit list entry, the Japanese documentary, *Faces of Death*. Its collection of newsreel footage graphically depicting beheadings, shootings, maimings and natural disasters makes it extremely disturbing viewing. But it also reminds us that few of the horrors we encounter in the make-believe world of movies can be as upsetting as the grim reality encountered, often unexpectedly, on *The News At Ten*.

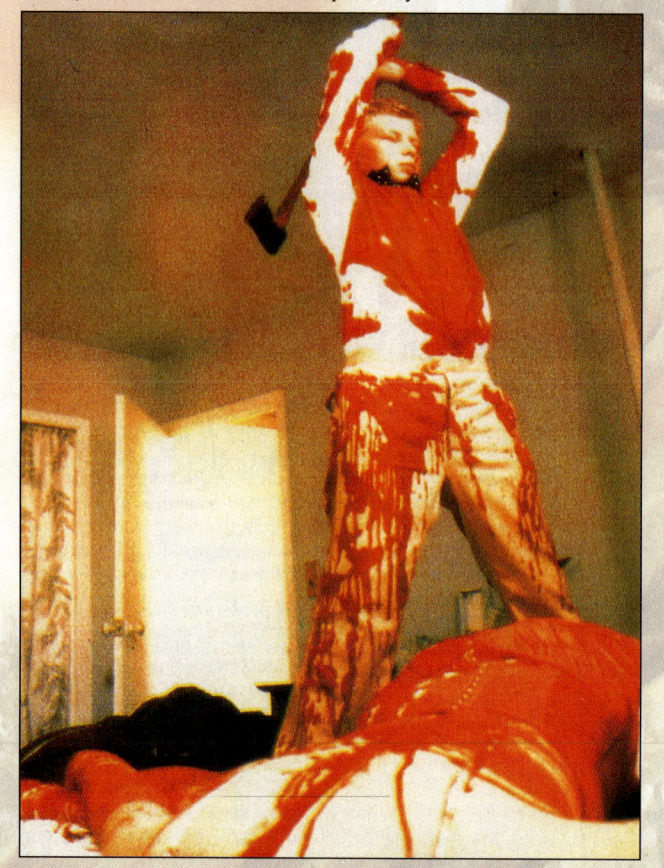

Real life horror certainly has no place in the films of American gore master Herschell Gordon Lewis. His *Blood Feast* made the nasties list with its patently fake bloodletting and atrocious acting despite the fact that it was made as far back as 1963. Lewis was inspired by a visit to a French Grand Guignol theatre, and became interested in duplicating the graphic gore he saw on stage in low budget movies. *Blood Feast*, which tells of an exotic Egyptian caterer named Fuad Ramses who murders women to get the ingredients for his cooking pot, is the most successful of his films – and it's still lousy!

The gore in the film certainly isn't convincing by today's makeup standards, but we must remember poor H.G. was working on a very low budget. There's an amusing story about the making of *Blood Feast*. It was shot in Miami, an area where there are no earthworms. H.G. needed some for a "tasteful" shot of a wormy corpse and was fortunate enough to discover a local citizen who had a worm-farm! He paid for the hire of 30 of them for a day's shooting, but afterwards when they went round gathering them up they discovered one was missing. The owner had threatened all sorts of trouble if anything untoward happened to his "pets" and so they looked for hours. Finally the resourceful Mr Lewis had a brainwave: he cut one in half!

At the end of Lewis' *Blood Feast*, the villainous Fuad Ramses meets a suitably grisly demise by falling into the squasher of a rubbish collector's lorry, while one law-abiding onlooker comments: "He died a fitting death for the garbage he was!" No such thing happens to the disturbed hero of *Driller Killer* though, another hit list entry that is far more unsettling because it actually has some basis in reality.

Made by the talented but wayward Abel Ferrara, *Driller Killer* is a nightmare exploitation pic about a psychotic character on the loose in New York City armed with a power drill. The violence is unflinchingly shown as our crazed hero goes around drilling into the skulls of derelicts, watching in fascination as the blood jets out. No reason is given for his anti-social behaviour (he doesn't own a video, so it can't be down to watching too many nasties), and the film concentrates on depicting ever-more-brutal slayings in a disturbing semi-documentary fashion. The killer is not even apprehended at the climax – a grim fadeout shows him about to claim his own sleeping girlfriend!

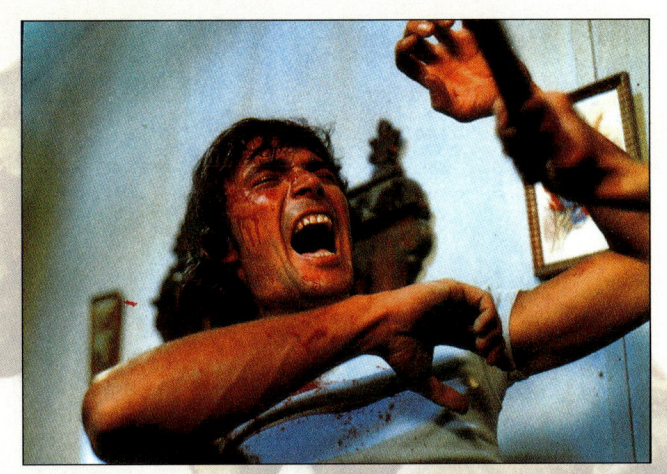

Many people would find a movie like *Driller Killer* disturbing because it could actually happen in real life. No such claim could be made for something like *The Living Dead At The Manchester Morgue*, which is a gory but well-made zombie picture shot in - of all places - the Lake District by an Italian crew. It originally went out as a second feature back in 1974, though cuts were made in it to get an "X" certificate. Needless to say, scenes such as a bunch of zombies feeding on a policeman and the inmates of a hospital, which were removed from the cinema version, found their way back into the video cassette release - which is why it made the nasties list. It's actually one of the better zombie movies around (or not around, that is) and one that makes good use of some stunning English locations.

I personally find nothing offensive about zombie movies. The plots of them are all so far removed from reality that any gore they contain tends to be offset by the sheer ridiculousness of their plotting. A good example can be found in *Zombie Flesh-Eaters*, the uncut tape of which offers up a very grisly moment where a girl has a wooden splinter thrust into her eye. The laughs here come from the fact that the zombies move so slowly that it is necessary for the rest of the cast to stand rooted to the spot, looking as though they have forgotten their lines, while the glassy-eyed creatures shamble up to them to take a bite. It is now a well-known bit of zombie lore that a spell six foot under gives a chap a hell of an appetite for his fellow man, but I've yet to read of a real-life funeral where the dear departed has leapt up and started munching on the mourners!

More believable are the realistic horrors of hit list entries *Cannibal Holocaust* and *Cannibal Ferox*, which offer up a parade of revolting detail in their slim stories concerning explorers falling foul of hungry, flesh-eating natives deep in the Amazon jungle. The way these savages go about preparing for their meal is enough to give Egon Ronay heart failure. In fact some of the scenes in *Ferox* in particular are almost unwatchable, seemingly designed solely to test audience endurance. Such moments as a very real-looking (though obviously not) castration, and somebody having the top of their skull sliced open like a breakfast egg are far removed from what most well balanced individuals would refer to as entertainment.

Equally gross is the moment in the Italian-made chiller *Anthropophagous The Beast* where seven-foot cannibal George Eastman rips open a pregnant woman and devours her baby. Big George has a hell of an appetite, and at the end of this gore-feast he even snacks on his own entrails as they spill out of his mutilated body.

A lot of the films on the banned list are pretty harrowing stuff. But at the other end of the scale it also contains many titles that are so lacking in incident it seems amazing that anyone should want to ban them other than on the grounds that they could cause extreme boredom. *Love Camp 7*, for example, has a bunch of Americans masquerading as Nazis and inflicting bad acting on all and sundry. It's an awful load of rubbish, completely lacking in gore and laughable in its ineptitude. I can only assume it was banned because the British find exploitation pics involving concentration camps extremely distasteful - and certainly no laughing matter.

Similarly banned, possibly on the grounds of incompetence, is a Mexican-made horror flick called *Night Of The Bloody Apes*, which has a plot torn from today's headlines: "SCIENTIST PUTS HEART OF GORILLA INTO DEAD SON!" It's obviously very serious stuff, packed with poor photography and acting so bad as to make your teeth ache. At one point one of the characters drops a rubber knife, and it bounces!

As we can see, the titles that make up the Scotland Yard list are an odd assortment. When the Bright Bill fully takes effect we can be certain that many of them will be weeded out to take their rightful place in society, where bad movie afficionados can seek them out should they so desire. As for the rest of the hard-core nasties, well they will still be around on the black market, keeping the boys in blue occupied for many more years to come..

Originally published in 1985.

Nice 'N' Nasty

Are you worried about the troubles in Yugoslavia? Losing sleep over the ongoing recession? Concerned about losing your job and having your house repossessed? The message from the men in grey suits is not to fret over such trivialities. Instead they want us to worry about something really important for a change, like the return of the dreaded video nasties!

Yes it's open season on video violence once more as all the blame for society's ills is conveniently laid at the door of our old friend, the so-called video nasty. Questions have been asked in the house, and Mr. Plod and his pals have been put on red alert. Even Mrs Whitehouse has a new spring in her step. Any day now we're going to be told that Normy Lamont used his Access card to rent an uncut version of *Zombie Creeping Flesh*.

Aren't you glad the fearless British press are on the case? Asking such pertinent questions as: Did the whacko from Waco, David Koresh, take some time off from reading The Bible to watch *Nightmares In A Damaged Brain*? Or was he inspired to get his matches out by glimpsing the title of Dario Argento's *Inferno*? We'll never know. Let's just hope nobody at *The Daily Mail* comes to the conclusion that it was reading The Good Book that put all those mad thoughts into his head, or they may start campaigning to get that banned as well!

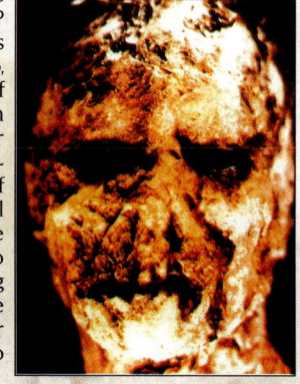

The media got the scent of blood with the kidnap and murder of two-year-old Jamie Bulger, an horrific act carried out by two ten-year-old boys. Nobody managed to lay the blame for their evil actions on any particular video release, but society's constant demand for carnage-packed column inches (a strange double standard, this) immediately led the howling hypocrites of our tabloid press to lay the blame at the door of violent videos as a whole. I don't expect that made Jamie's poor parents feel any better.

Whenever there's a debate about the effects of violent films or videos, you can bet your life some trained shrink and/or terribly concerned social worker type will start rattling on about the harm such material does to children. Now I don't know many parents who would be happy to let their kids settle down for the evening with *The Texas Chainsaw Massacre*, but I suspect that most children in their early teens are quite able to deal with such entertainment without being brainwashed into going on a power tool rampage. I first started getting into 'X' films when I was 13 and by that age quite a percentage of today's kids have worked their way right through the nasties list with no mental damage whatsoever!

Nobody ever asks how many of these social worker types are parents themselves, but then theory is always so much more comfortable than practice. Just look at the misguided individuals who took a bunch of Orkneys children away from their parents and almost ruined the lives of these youngsters because of some pie-in-the-sky fancy that they had been playing human sacrifice round a bonfire...

What these holier-than-thou types are really saying is that most of we parents are not fit to control what our children watch, so the responsibility should be taken out of our hands. Fair enough. Perhaps the state should take this one step further and make some stipulation as to what sort of people are allowed to have children in the first place?

We've now been informed that particularly violent movies like *Reservoir Dogs* and *The Bad Lieutenant* will be joining the likes of political hot potatoes like *The Exorcist*, *A Clockwork Orange* and *Straw Dogs*, and will not be made available for home video consumption. There's also a question mark hanging over *Mikey*, a forthcoming Columbia Tristar release about a devilish child. I suppose they're too late to do anything about *The Omen*.

All this proves is that the more things change, the more they stay the same. Back in the lawless days before the 1984 Video Recordings Act made it compulsory for all video films to be certificated, Mr Plod and the gang at 999 Letsby Avenue were kept busy booting down doors and clapping handcuffs on anything with *Cannibal* or *Zombie* in the title. They certainly didn't employ film buff officers for the task. Coppola's *Apocalypse Now* was seized by a silly constable who mistook this classic Vietnam epic for *Cannibal Apocalypse*, and one raw recruit even put the irons on Sam Fuller's acclaimed war drama *The Big Red One* - goodness knows what he expected it to be about, but it was released after questioning, undoubtedly leaving the plod concerned with a big red face.

The video industry has since bent over backwards to promote a wholesome family image and get away from the more popular public conception of their trade as being populated by back street Arthur Daley types doing most of their business "under the counter." But in the process they have let the government walk all over them. Profits have got thinner and the pirates have got fatter and fatter.

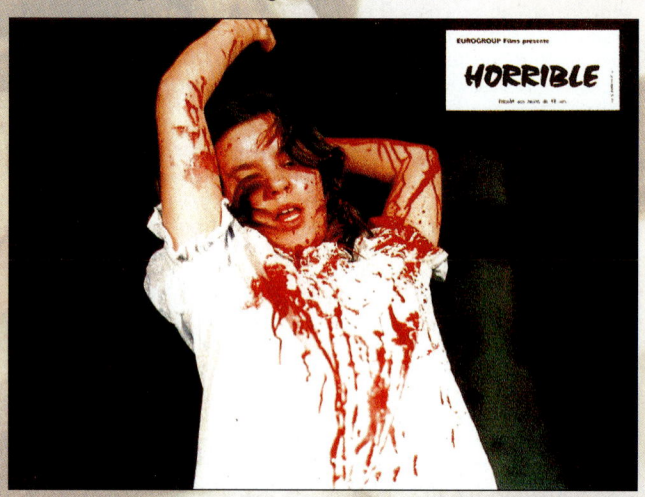

As if bowing and scraping to the BBFC wasn't enough, the video industry has also set up a ridiculous organisation to police its own members. Called the Video Packaging Review Committee it's their terribly important job to cast a jaundiced eye over all video packaging to prevent distributors selling their exploitation movies in an exploitative manner (perish the thought!).

Among the more ludicrous decisions made by the VPRC (without whose approval a tape can only receive limited distribution in UK shops and rental outlets) was their refusal to allow the movie *Hollywood Chainsaw Hookers* to be released with that title. Instead the distributors (Colourbox) had to call it *Hollywood Hookers* and insert a picture of a chainsaw in the hope that punters would get the drift! Just last month the VPRC reached new heights of silliness rejecting the first draft cover of the Kurt Russell thriller *Unlawful Entry* because they felt a picture of Kurt aiming a gun was too threatening. And this is the 90s?

What the moaning minnies of the pro-censorship lobby would really like to do is dis-invent video altogether. Then they would go on to dis-invent satellite and maybe after that they'd stamp out violent video games as well. And why not? After all haven't we all been better people since they took the golliwogs out of Enid Blyton books?

The real troublemakers here are the media who have never been known to let the truth get in the way of a good story. Take this ridiculous article that appeared in the *Express* and *Star* recently. I quote:

"**A violent snuff video, allegedly featuring real murders is to be sent to the Federal Bureau of Investigation after its seizure by trading standards officers at the Birmingham comic fair. This gruesome film was spotted alongside pirate copies of classic children's films. Other banned videos featuring mutilation, decapitation and violent sex, were also taken from the Birmingham Comic Mart and Film Fair at the Midland Hotel on Saturday. The alleged snuff video shows an Amazon tribe chasing and killing a film crew. Principal trading standards officer Dennis Cronin said it was thought this section of the film was taken by a genuine documentary crew who were killed In the process..."**

In a word: Bullshit!

I should imagine a fair percentage of horror buffs will have seen the above movie, which is of course the Italian-made *Cannibal Holocaust*. The director is Ruggero Deodato, who is still working in the film industry and has never to my knowledge been eaten alive by cannibals. The whole point of *Cannibal Holocaust* is that it pretends to be a snuff movie while anyone who has seen it can easily tell that the stomachs being ripped open are made of foam latex. Unless of course you are the sort of person who can't sort fantasy from reality – in which case there's a job waiting for you in newspapers!

Let's just pause to tackle this snuff movie business for a moment. I'm sure that if I had murdered somebody I would want to make a home movie of it and go and flog it at a car boot sale for a tenner. What a good idea that would be! The press have rattled on about the existence of snuff movies ever since the heady days of the Charles Manson gang, but to their eternal frustration they have never been able to unearth any.

Most of the titles that made it onto the DPP's shopping list were boring rip-offs that failed to live up to the lurid promise of their video jackets. Any horror fan worth his salt will be able to tell you that even your old Aunt Ethel would fall asleep during them. Quite a few have been reissued lately with minimal cuts

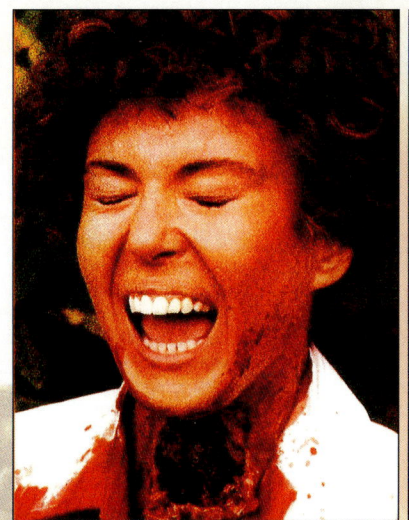

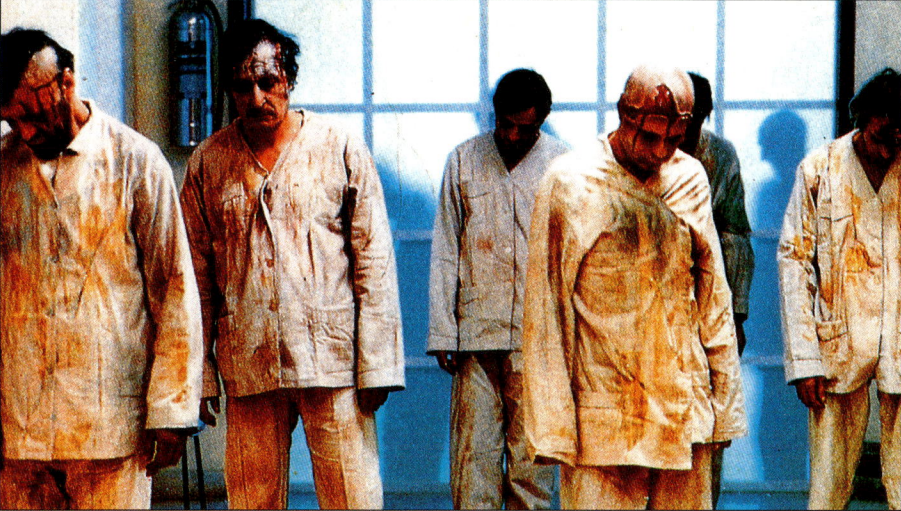

(*Inferno*, *The Slayer*, *The Burning*, *Zombie Flesh-Eaters*, *Killer Nun* etc), and – surprise, surprise – the fabric of our society has not split asunder.

Luckily, society is constantly changing anyway, and what will happen now that we're all being dragged kicking and screaming into Europe? The Mary Whitehouse brigade can censor everything in sight, but what good is it going to do them when people can breeze through customs with a suitcase full of *Texas Chainsaw* and *Ilsa* movies, or for that matter order them direct from the States on NTSC? Who cares that *Reservoir Dogs* and *The Exorcist* have been banned? Most of my friends have got them on laser disc anyway. You want hard porn? Get a satellite decoder and watch Filmnet or Red Hot Dutch. These are broadcast from countries where porn is legal, and put plainly, the government can do sod all about it.

My own conclusion is that those of us who are against censorship should make as much noise as those who are for it seem to do. Why should we be ashamed for wanting to see movies that are violent and/or sexy? Far from there being too many violent movies around, I believe that most of them are not violent enough! Let's face facts and admit that films that deglamourise violence, presenting it in all its gory reality, do society less harm than the fantasy world mayhem of *The A-Team*. Burt Reynolds piles a car up at 100 mph in *Smokey And The Bandit* and steps out of the wreckage with a smile on his face – so tell me if that's not likely to encourage some of the real life horrors that teen joyriders cause every day on our streets?

Having said that, though, I don't think Burt's movies should be banned (apart from *A Cop And A Half*, that is. . . .). You see, the trouble with censorship is that the people doing the censoring never know when to stop. One minute they're saintly individuals who genuinely believe they are working for the common good, and the next they turn into Adolf Hitler. What makes one person feel they have the right to say what another can or cannot watch, or indeed the way they think? It's the thin end of a very deadly wedge that not so long ago caused one of the worst holocausts in living memory.

In the final analysis though, all censorship is doomed to fail, because people will always get what they want. You may have to pay a little more for your pirate copy of *Reservoir Dogs*, but that's par for the course. In the meantime, tomorrow's chip wrappings will keep rattling on about non-existent snuff movies, social workers will keep taking innocent children into protective custody because they've seen the latest Freddy movie, and car boot sales will continue to do a roaring trade in all those video nasties that have supposedly been stamped out by the intrepid 'untouchables' of trading standards.

Of course we're all horrified by the all too frequent press reports of murder and mayhem committed by disturbed individuals, but let's for goodness sake get them in perspective. Nobody has ever been able to prove a direct connection between violent movies and real-life acts of violence – and believe me they've tried bloody hard! Movie drama, like life, is all about conflict. Take the major conflicts of violence and sex out of our entertainment and we'll all be left watching the Disney channel.

So my message to all those anti-violence busybodies is: keep your nose out of our entertainment. If you don't like it, reach for the off switch, like we all have the right to do. We've got to stick up for ourselves now, otherwise we may well end up as meek and brainwashed as the followers of a certain Mr David Koresh, waiting for the madman in charge to strike the final match....

Originally published in 1992

Return Of The Video Nasties

Now pay attention kiddies, because here's a grim fairy tale for you. Once upon a time, a minor, bible-bashing politician named David Alton dreamed up an absurd provision banning videos and films which might present "an inappropriate model for children." Most sensible folk thought the whole thing was a bit of a joke. After all, with this kind of law on the statute books, the government could appoint itself as our nanny and ban just about everything with an adult theme, including a large percentage of the works of Dickens and Shakespeare!

But through a cunning bit of political chicanery designed to strike at the heart of an already weak government, the publicity-seeking Mr Alton managed to get a result on this one (after his equally misguided anti-abortion bill bit the bullet). He got a bunch of back-stabbing Tory backbenchers on side, conjured up a silly 'non report' from a child psychologist pal who said that she couldn't deny a link between video violence and violent behaviour in children (nor could she actually prove one, but there you go!). Then he withdrew his fantasy world agenda at the last minute in return for a panicky promise from Home Secretary Michael Howard that stricter measures would be brought in for the control of so-called "video nasties."

The following amendments to the Criminal Justice Bill will now be presented in the House of Lords:
1. A maximum sentence of two years jail for dealing in uncertificated videos.
2. A maximum six months jail for supplying age restricted videos to minors
3. "More rigorous" censorship of video films. More 15-rated films will suffer cuts or be uprated to 18. More 18-rated films will be cut for video release.
4. More explicit guidelines issued to the BBFC which will in future have to take into account possible psychological effects on children.

We wouldn't argue with the steeper fines, though I wouldn't fancy being a video dealer having to judge the age of every older teenager who presents himself at the counter. As for the increased censorship, well it's not quite certain at this point exactly what that means - or even if it means anything different at all. We've had draconian censorship laws for long enough already, and it's difficult to see how they could get much worse.

Certainly there can be few horror fans who didn't chuckle over the neither liberal or democratic David Alton's victorious TV speech about films like *Child's Play 3* being banned under the new laws, because this is plainly not so. Shortly afterwards, BBFC head James Ferman stated that *Child's Play* 3 and mild films like it would still be available, and this is the way it should be in what purports to be a free country. Certain movies, like *Reservoir Dogs* and *The Exorcist* will probably not be released on video, but then what else is new?

The least unexpected thing here is the fact that the government have apparently once more agreed to do exactly the opposite of what they once said. Those all-wise and impeccably moral men who sit in Parliament have decided that The Great British public cannot be trusted to bring up its own children. When it was getting into such a muddle over basics the government should have thought about the basic areas it should leave to individual good sense and judgement. But as we become more and more of a nanny state, so we play into the hands of people who would impose their own hidden political agenda on us. History has shown where this leads. They start by burning videos and end with burning people who don't agree with them....

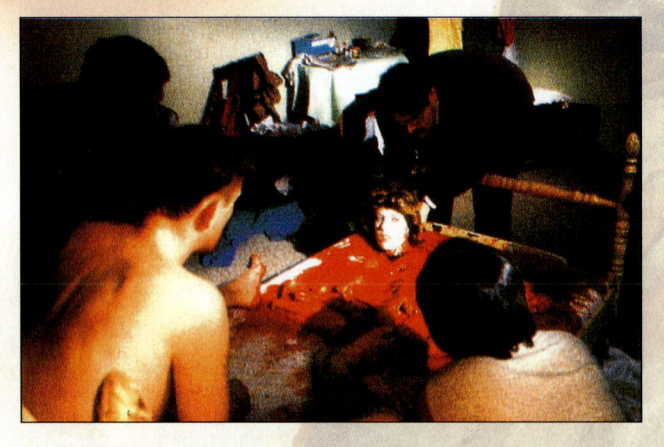

Censorship of nasty videos can soon turn into censorship of controversial videos, and then videos that don't subscribe to the current political agenda. From there on it's but a short step to the censorship of books and newspapers. The saddest thing about all this nonsense is that it has effectively diverted the public's attention from the real problems that plague our society. Wouldn't it be better for the government to provide some hope of decently paid jobs to make children feel that life may offer more excitement than watching gory videos and pinching cars?

In the end, censorship can be simply defined as somebody not wanting you to read or see what they don't want to read or see themselves. Alton and co obviously don't like horror movies. Tough luck! Horror has long been one of the most popular film genres, and passing laws to outlaw them will make them more popular than ever. The joke is that hardcore horror fans consider *Child's Play 3* to be more like a Disney movie. Thousands of collectors in this country have copies of films like *Cannibal Holocaust*, *Men Behind The Sun*, *Nekromantik* and others. These are the real video nasties, and Alton's crusading won't have any effect upon them. Okay, so people can now go to jail for supplying uncertificated videos. But we all know that people will always find a way to get what they want, no matter what the law says.

We're not condoning these movies, just stating the simple fact that even if every horror movie in the country is banned, nothing can be done about the millions of copies circulating in private collections, and on satellite and and cable. How can any law wipe them out? In the light of this you begin to realise how toothless the Alton proposals really are. This man is a bit like a modern day King Canute, dipping his toe in the surf of a huge, unstoppable tide of information technology. Let's hope for his sake he has some effective scuba diving gear!

You don't really need to ask where we stand on this issue. We're firmly on the side of common sense. No proof has ever been put forward that violent videos cause people of any age to behave violently. In fact a recent German report on the subject discovered that watching such films is liable to cause the viewer to empathise with the *victims* rather than the aggressor, and therefore shy away from violent behaviour. If this is true, then the violence we are being denied on screen may well spill over into real life. If I was an MP, I wouldn't want that on my conscience....

I can see the parent's point of view. I have two very young daughters myself, and of course I wouldn't let either of them watch horror movies. I'm ultra-careful to keep my video collection under lock and key, and in that respect I'm just the same as millions of other responsible parents all over the UK. But I object very strongly to the government treating me like I treat my children, particularly as we all know that cabinet ministers hardly behave like exemplary parents in other ways.

Finally, here's a story you won't read in the papers. Hordes of national press hacks descended on the city of Gloucester recently and did the tour of video shops in the vicinity of 25 Cromwell Street. Their task was to find out what sort of films a certain builder (and mass murderer) chappie named Frederick West watched in his spare time "Yes, he's one of my customers," said one shopkeeper. "He rents a lot of Disney movies." Makes you think, doesn't it?

Originally published in 1994

ABSURD

BRUTAL! ...SHOCKING! ...VIOLENT! ...SAVAGE!

...NOT FOR THE SQUEAMISH!

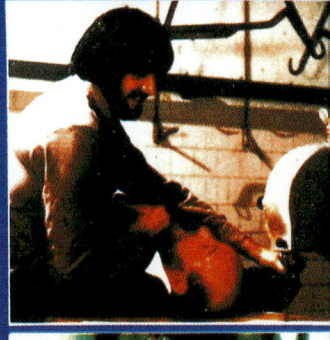

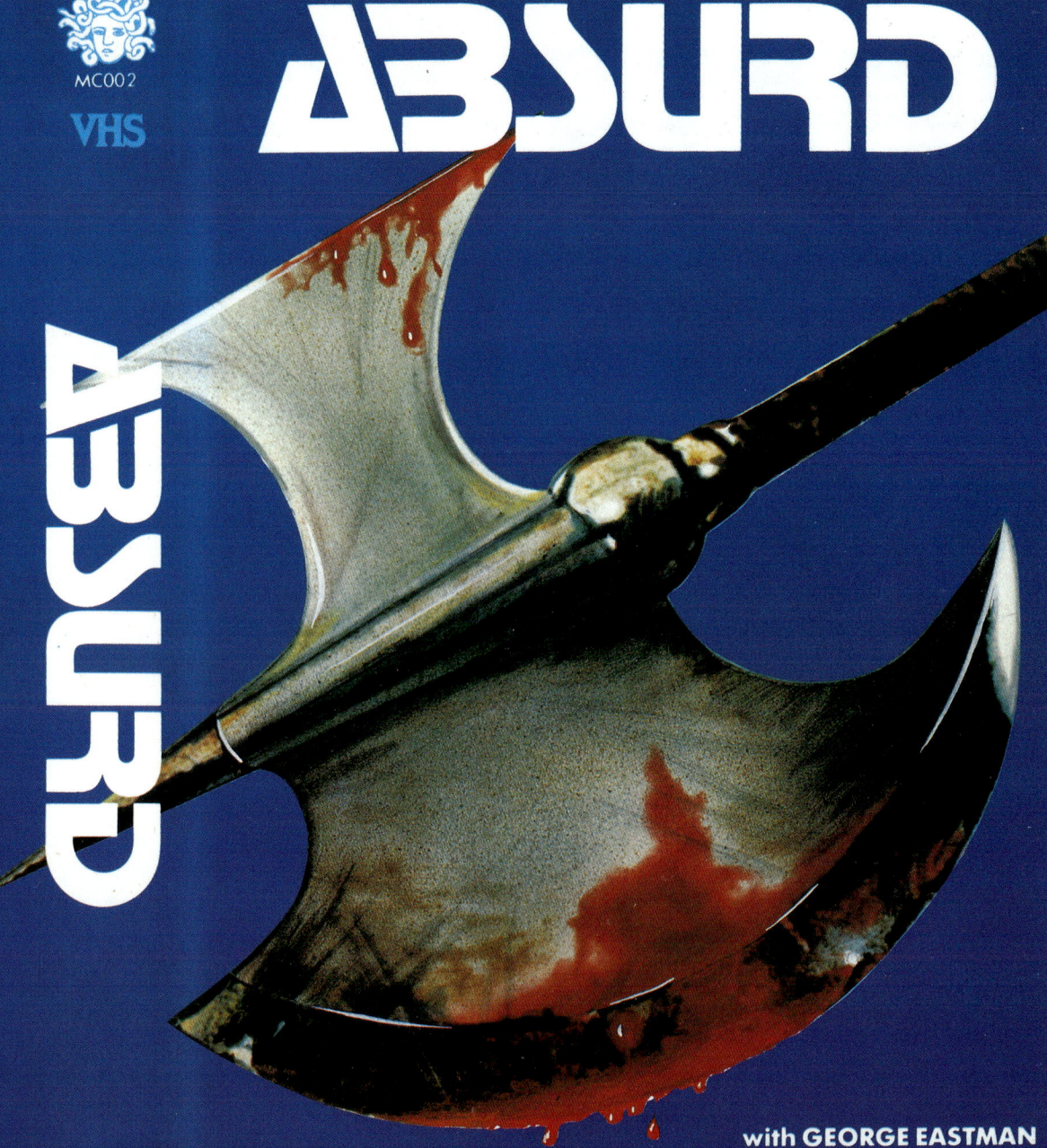

MC002
VHS

MEDUSA
WARNING: Copyright protected. All rights reserved. © Medusa Communications Ltd.

Sleeve design by
IMPRESSIONS
01-722 3939

R WARNING X RATED
This film must not be sold or rented to minors.

Running time:
96 minutes approx. Colour

with GEORGE EASTMAN
ANNIE BELLE – CHARLES BORRONEL
and IAN DANBY
story and screenplay by JOHN CART
directed by PETER NEWTON

REVIEW

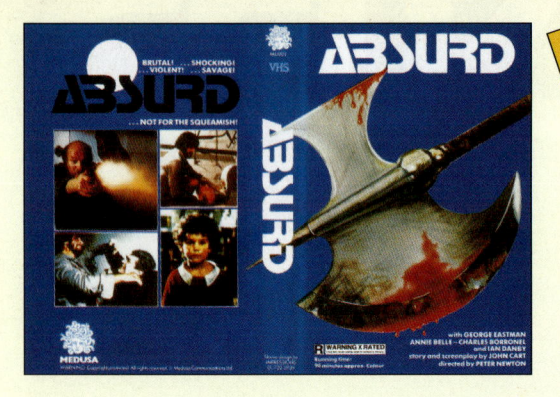

Originally entitled **Anthropophagous II**, this brutal Italian gore-fest has a plot that lives up to its title. Big George Eastman is back as a cannibal killer who escapes from an asylum and promptly rips his stomach open climbing a spiked fence. Fatally injured, he becomes the guinea pig in an operation to test a new drug that regenerates body tissue. This brings him back to full strength and he goes on the rampage through the hospital, stuffing people in ovens and sticking hypodermics in their eyes. Not much of a visual stylist, director Joe D'Amato comes into his own during the well-telegraphed gore sequences - you can detect a change for the better in the lighting as the camera moves in close to showcase the next bit of ghastly bloodletting. The most grisly sequence involves a hospital orderly having his hair parted in a dramatic fashion, with a bandsaw. Shame about that putty forehead though... In the end our boy has his head chopped with an axe and his eyes popped out with a geometric compass. Don't try this at home, kiddies. Joe apparently wanted to make **Anthropophagous III**, but his untimely death saved us from that!... Look out for Michele Soavi, director of **Stagefright** and **The Sect**, as one of Eastman's victims.

TITLE	ABSURD
AKA	Rosso sangue; The Monster Hunter; Horrible (France); Ausgeburt der Hölle (Germany); Terror sin Limite (Spain)
DIRECTOR	Aristide Massaccesi (as Peter Newton)
COUNTRY	IT
SOURCE	Medusa (UK)
YEAR	1981
TIME	90m06s
CAST	George Eastman (Luigi Montefiori), Annie Belle, Charles Borromel (Cristiano Borromei), Katya Berger, Kasimir Berger, Hanja Kochansky, Ian Danby, Ted Rusoff, Edmund Purdom. [and uncredited] Michele Soavi, Mark Shannon (Manlio Certosini), Dirce Funari.
PRODUCTION	The Metaxa Corp. presents... [prod] Aristide Massaccesi & Donatella Donati (uncredited). [prod man] Jack Bush. Filmirage - Metaxa Corporation. © 1981 Metaxa Corporation.
PHOTOGRAPHY DIRECTOR	John Cart (Aristide Massaccesi)
MUSIC	Carlo Mario Cordio
EDITOR	George Morley (Giorgio Moriani)

DVD Review

Absurd was originally released to UK cinemas with a small number of cuts – imagine this playing at your local multiplex alongside the latest Disney! Though quite a grisly movie, it would undoubtedly get past the BBFC uncut these days because none of its violence is sexually related, and to be honest the special effects are looking increasingly naff in comparison with what's on offer today. However, as with its predecessor, **The Anthrophagous Beast**, the rights reside with a big time Italian company who are asking so much for them that an American (or UK) release is not likely in the near future. There are DVD-Rs kicking around, but they are poor quality rip-offs from the original Medusa VHS. The only version worth having is a German language disc that unfortunately doesn't have subtitles, though this is not too much of a problem since it's not the kind of movie you watch for the dialogue!

ANTHROPOPHAGOUS THE BEAST

A deserted beach. A bloodcurdling scream. A decapitated head. So ends another tourist's holiday. So begins Anthropophagous The Beast as it gallops through shock after bloody shock. Probably one of the most frightening films you will ever see, it will leave you wondering if deep inside us all, there may lurk the cannibal. Watch it, if you dare!

VHS FORMAT

VFP001

ANTHROPOPHAGOUS THE BEAST

WATCH IT IF YOU DARE!

WARNING
"The copyright proprietor has licensed the film contained in this video cassette for private home use only. Any other use including making copies of the film, causing it to be seen or heard in public or broadcasting it or causing it to be transmitted to subscribers to a diffusion service, letting on hire or otherwise dealing with it in whole or in part is strictly prohibited. Any breach of the above conditions renders the offender liable to prosecution."
© Video Film Promotions Ltd.

Sleeve design by
IMPRESSIONS
01-722 3939

VFP
VIDEOFILM PROMOTIONS

VFP
VIDEOFILM PROMOTIONS

A film by JOE D'AMATO
starring GEORGE EASTMAN and TISA FARROW
Running time 1 hr. and 30 mins. approx. Colour.

REVIEW

The prolific Joe D'Amato (Aristide Massaccesi) struck gold with this grisly gore epic concerning the cannibalistic activities of a Robinson Crusoe-like fellow who has turned to eating human flesh as a means of survival. As played by George Eastman, the monster is a shipwrecked man who has eaten his wife and son, and then - obviously quite taken with the flavour of human nosh - sets about adding a group of tourists to the menu. Inept direction takes the sting out of some potentially supenseful scenes, and the gore is mainly of the, 'pull-entrails-out-from-under-the-jumper' variety seen in most cheapie cannibal movies. But the film hits new heights of grossness in the disgusting scene where Big George rips a pregnant woman apart to scoff her unborn foetus. In the final sequences the monster gets a taste of his own medicine and has his stomach split open with a pickaxe. He then proceeds to scoff his own intestines - now that's what we call one hell of an appetite! Star Tisa Farrow is Mia's sister - she also appeared in **Zombie Flesh-Eaters**. Apparently she's been working as a cab driver in New York and in an eerie parallel to her gore movie career recently lost one of her eyes in an accident!

TITLE ANTHROPOPHAGOUS THE BEAST

AKA Antropophagus; The Man Eater; The Grim Reaper; Maneater-Der Menschfresser; Gomia, The Savage Island; Anthropofago.

DIRECTOR Aristide Massaccesi (as Joe D'Amato)

COUNTRY IT
SOURCE VFP (UK)
YEAR 1980
TIME 88m14s

CAST Tisa Farrow, George Eastman (Luigi Montefiore), Zora Kerova, Saverio Vallone, Vanessa Steiger (Serena Grandi), Margaret Donnelly, Mark Bodin, Bob Larsen, Rubina Rey, Simone Baker, Mark Logan.

PRODUCTION P.C.M. Int - Filmirage. [prod man] Oscar Santaniello. None.

PHOTOGRAPHY DIRECTOR Enrico Biribicchi.

MUSIC Marcello Giombini
EDITOR Ornella Micheli

DVD Review

The rights of **Anthropophagous** are owned by a large Italian company who want quite a lot of money to release it. Meanwhile though there are a few American companies that are sub-licensing the heavily cut US cinema version, called **The Grim Reaper**. Hollywood Video released a bog standard DVD under this title and it's pretty awful in every way. An incredible nine minutes has been slashed, reducing the running time to 81 minutes. Most of the big gore scenes have been trimmed or removed completely, and the quality of the image is appalling. You're better off sticking with the original VHS until someone forks out for a remastered version of the original. You'll also find fully uncut DVD-R bootlegs if you trawl the net, and having seen these I can recommend them with the usual reservations – they were obviously taken straight from a VHS tape source, but they're watchable enough (if you have the stomach for it) and cheaper to buy than the original tapes these days. Be warned that some players may have trouble with DVD-Rs, and my own copy has problems fast-forwarding on some of these.

# HOME VIDEO MOVIE

V.R.O.

AXE

"AXE" stars Jack Canon as a man on the run from the police. He and his gang hid out in a peaceful-looking farmhouse where a little girl lives with her crippled grandfather.

The young child is forced to use an axe to defend herself from the three killers. A spellbinding performance by Leslie Lee as the 13-year-old axe murderer adds to the realism and suspense.

The man responsible for bringing "AXE" to the screen is the talented Fredrick R. Friedel, who not only wrote the movie's screenplay, but also directed "AXE" and acted in it. He plays one of the three killers who meet a violent death.

COPYRIGHT NOTICE

The Copyright proprietor has licensed these films contained in these video cassettes for private home use only and other use including making copies of the films, causing them to be seen or heard in public or broadcasting them or causing them to be transmitted to subscribers to a diffusion service or selling, letting on hire or otherwise dealing with them in whole or in part is strictly prohibited.

VIDEO NETWORK
DISTRIBUTORS OF VIDEO MOVIES

MADE IN EUROPE

HARRY NOVAK presents

AT LAST... TOTAL TERROR!

AXE

Starring JACK CANON
RAY GREEN • FREDERICK R. FRIEDEL
And Introducing LESLIE LEE as LISA with DOUGLAS POWERS
FRANK JONES • CAROL MILLER • HART SMITH • GEORGE J. MONAGHAN • SCOTT SMITH
Music by GEORGE NEWMAN SHAW and JOHN WILLHELM
Produced by J.G. PATTERSON, JR. Written and Directed by FREDERICK R. FRIEDEL
EASTMANCOLOR • a BOXOFFICE INTERNATIONAL PICTURES release

R RESTRICTED

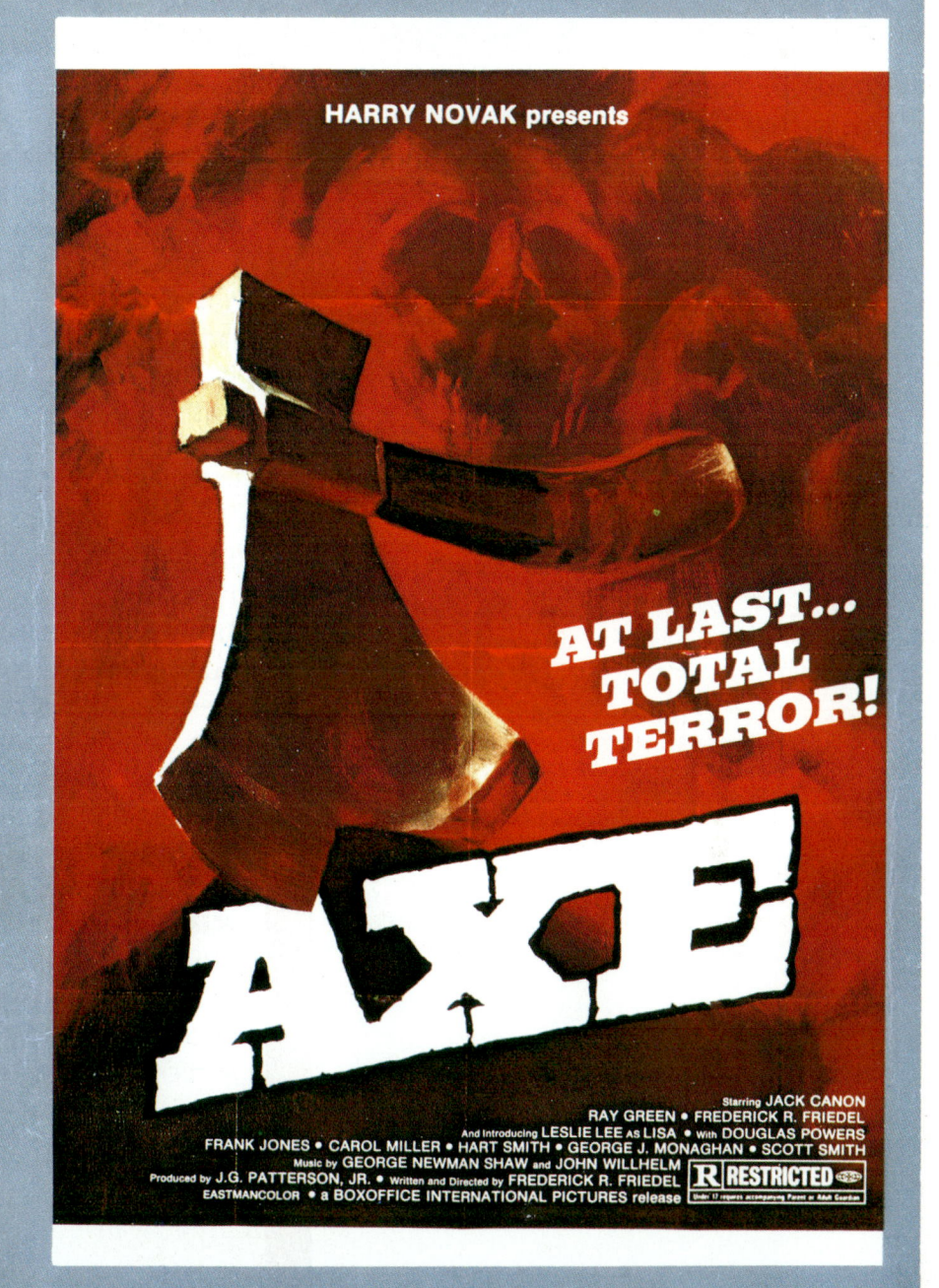

© VIDEO RELEASING ORGANIZATION

REVIEW

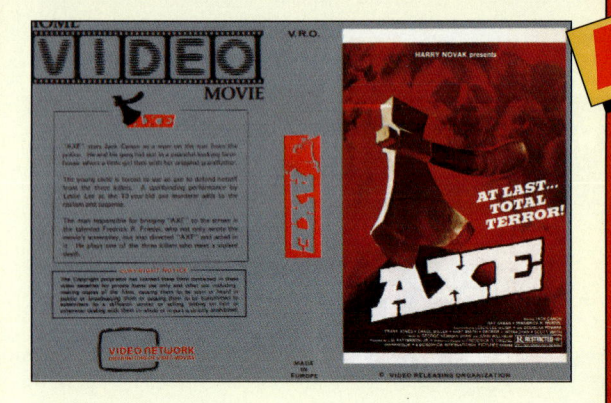

This cheapo effort achieved its fifteen minutes of stardom by briefly featuring on the nasties list before the authorities came to their senses. Frederick R. Friedel wrote, directed and also turns up as the youngest of a trio of psychos who terrorise the cashier of a small town store, stripping her down to her undies and forcing her to play a nerve-wracking game of 'William Tell.' They then hole up in a lonely house inhabited by moody Southern belle Lisa (Leslie Lee) and her crippled grandfather. Two of the nutters rape Lee, which drives her over the edge in **I Spit On Your Grave** fashion and causes her to retaliate with axe and razor. In the early scenes the three gangsters terrorise a pair of homosexuals, forcing one to consume a lighted cigar before they execute them both. It's certainly nasty in tone, but the gore is as amateurish as the acting here, and the film hardly lives up to its alternate title of **The California Axe Massacre**, since only one guy actually gets offed with a chopper.

DVD Review

Something Weird has released an uncut disc of **Axe**, which is region free. The same company's VHS was missing two of the most contentious scenes, one in which the criminals pour a bottle of Coke onto a scantily-clad sales clerk, the other being the brutal axe murder of Steele. Luckily they were able to source a complete print for the DVD. It's a pretty good transfer in general, though there are a number of speckles and it's grainy in places – probably a fault of the original camerawork. The only real damage is shown at reel changes, otherwise colours are strong and the transfer is pleasing. As always SWV offer a treasure trove of extras: a handful of trailers for other Novak-distributed horror flicks (including **Toys Are Not For Children, Behind Locked Doors** and **Kidnapped Coed**). There's also an educational short ("Mental Health: Keeping Mentally Fit"); Martia Cortez swallowing swords in "We Still Don't Believe It"; a gallery of exploitation art with radio spots; and an entire extra b/w feature, **The Electric Chair**, which fits in with the redneck horror feel of **Axe**.

TITLE	AXE
AKA	California Axe Massacre; Lisa Lisa; The Virgin Slaughter
DIRECTOR	Frederick R. Friedel
COUNTRY	US
SOURCE	Video Network (UK)
YEAR	1977
TIME	64m49s
CAST	Leslie Lee, Jack Canon, Ray Green, Frederick R. Friedel, Douglas Powers, Frank Jones, Carol Miller, George J. Monaghan, Hart Smith, Scott Smith, Jeff MacKay, David Hayman, Don Cummins, Jaqueline Pyle, Lynne Bradley, Richie Smith, George Newman Shaw, Ronald Watterson, Beverly Watterson, Graddie Lane, Suzy Bertoni.
PRODUCTION	Frederick Productions presents... [prod] J. G. Patterson, Jr. [exec prod] Irwin Friedlander. © None.
PHOTOGRAPHY DIRECTOR	Autin McKinney
MUSIC	George Newman Shaw & John Willhelm
EDITOR	Frederick R. Friedel & J. G. Patterson, Jr.

The Beast in Heat

In a remote village in occupied Europe, the SS pursue their inhuman treatment of captured partisans in efforts to force them to betray their comrades.... while Fraulein Krast, a sadistic biologist, concentrates her efforts on the womenfolk with refined tortures and humiliation, leaving them to the mercy of a sex-crazed half-man, half-beast she has created with experimental injections....
And as advancing Allied forces approach the village, Krast herself becomes a victim of her own fiendish rituals....

86 minutes

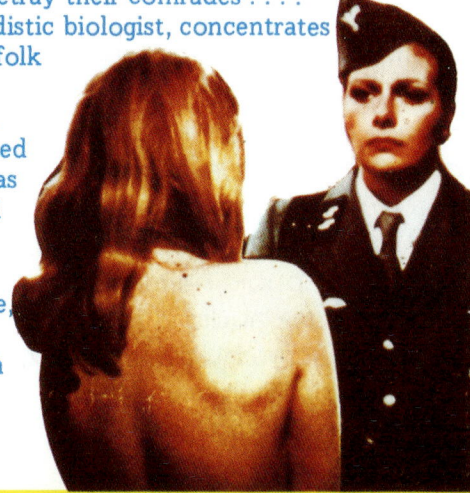

The film contained in this video cassette is fully protected by copyright and the video rights vested in JVI Video Films. It is for home video use only. Any other manner of broadcasting or exhibition is an infringement of those legal rights.

J.V.I. VIDEO FILMS. UNIT 2, 31 MILKSTONE ROAD, ROCHDALE, LANCS.
Tel: (0706) 47980

The Beast in Heat

JVI 006

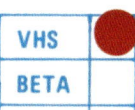

VHS	●
BETA	
V2000	

The Beast in Heat

HORRIFYING EXPERIENCES IN THE LAST DAYS OF THE S.S.

WARNING: This cassette contains disturbing scenes and is not suitable for viewing by children. **STRICTLY ADULTS ONLY.**

REVIEW

One of the most elusive of so-called video nasties, this Italian-made concentration camp exploitationer contains the usual round of sadistic titillation, plus a few new wrinkles to please those who were getting concerned that they might have seen it all. The thin plot concerns a beautiful but evil female SS officer (Macha Magall) who has created a human Beast to carry out some sort of strange genetic experiment. As played by the grotesque Sal Boris (a regular in this genre), the Beast has little to do apart from screwing a choice selection of terrified-looking young women to death - not that this isn't nice work if you can get it! At one point he chews off a girl's pubic hair - now there's something we didn't see in **The Lover's Guide**. One woman is apparently eaten alive by guinea pigs, while another has her fingernails pulled out with pliers. Meanwhile, the slinky Magall carries on like **Ilsa, She Wolf Of The SS**, prick-teasing the POWs and then cutting them off in their prime - ouch! Despite one or two memorable torture sequences this manages to be quite dull, and is frequently interspersed with boring stock footage of battle scenes taken from Italian pot boilers that are even more anonymous than this. The same director made **Perversions Of The Third Reich**, which was also rubbish.

TITLE BEAST IN HEAT, THE (as Horrifying Experiments of S.S. Last Days)

AKA La Bestia In Calore; SS Hell Camp; Holocaliste Nazi; SS Experiment Camp 2

DIRECTOR Luigi Batzella (as Ivan Katansky)

COUNTRY IT
SOURCE JVI (UK)
YEAR 1977
TIME 85m59s

CAST Macha Magall (Ellen Kratsch), John Braun, Kim Gatti, Sal Boris (Salvatore Baccaro) [and uncredited] Xiros Papa (Ciro Papa), Alfredo Rizzo.

PRODUCTION An Eterna Film production. [prod] Eterna Film. © None.

PHOTOGRAPHY DIRECTOR Ugo Brunelli (uncredited)

MUSIC Giuliano Sorgini (uncredited)
EDITOR Paolo Solvay (Luigi Batzella)

DVD Review

This sickest of all Nazi exploitation films is easily the rarest of the Video Nasties, and the situation remains the same in the age of DVD. It's very unlikely that this film will ever be made legally available in the UK, even with cuts, and therefore it's hardly surprising that VHS tapes still change hands for quite large sums - check out the situation on e-bay! The only DVD release to date is a bootleg DVD-R which features a very nice (for a bootleg) uncut widescreen 1.85:1 transfer. Well, I say it's uncut, but this has been taken from a Japanese tape source and has optical censoring of pubic hair and genitalia. It also has the original Japanese subtitles, non-removable, and the audio is in Spanish only! The disc is predictably lacking in extras too, with only a rather scratchy trailer. But if you're after completing your nasties collection on DVD, this is currently the only option - nobody's in a bidding war for the US rights!

THE BEYOND

KATHERINE McCOLL   DAVID WARBECK
SARAH KELLER   ANTOINE SAINT JOHN
VERONICA LAZAR

in

The run down, eerie Louisiana hotel was Liza's inheritance. She planned to renovate it and reopen it as a going concern.

It was her last chance to build a new life for herself.

She didn't know then that the hotel was built on one of the Seven Gates of Hell!

She didn't know that in 1927, a warlock, the Sentinel of the Undead, had been tortured and crucified, unlocking this doorway to Hades!

She didn't see the stirrings of the cadavers in the neighbouring morgue!

And she didn't heed the warnings of the mysterious, blind stranger, Emily.

Until it was too late — and the zombies rose to violently claim victims for eternal damnation in The Beyond.

The latest film from director Lucio Fulci, whom horror buffs have crowned the new "Master of Terror".

"Lucio Fulci's best film."
STARBURST magazine.

Running Time : 89 mins

A VIDEOMEDIA RELEASE
VIDEOMEDIA LIMITED
70 WARDOUR STREET, LONDON W1V 3HP

All rights of the producers and owners of the recorded work reserved. The film contained in this video cassette is protected by copyright and use of this recording is restricted to private home use only. Any other manner of exhibition and any broadcast public performance, diffusion, copying, re-selling, hiring or editing constitutes an infringement of copyright unless the previous written consent of the copyright owner thereto has been obtained.

Designed by SATORI Graphic Applications.

CERT - X
COLOUR
HVM 1021
VHS PAL

VAMPIX

A VIDEOMEDIA RELEASE

THE BEYOND

Produced by FABRIZIO DE ANGELIS
Directed by LUCIO FULCI

Vampix
a Videomedia release

REVIEW

One of the best of the Italian zombie epics sparked by the success of Romero's **Dawn Of The Dead**, this grisly affair apes the plot of Michael Winner's **The Sentinel** (1976) to good effect. It's an atmospheric tale about a hotel in Louisiana which stands on one of the seven entrances to hell - a gateway that eventually opens and provides the place with a horde of unwelcome zombie guests. Regular Lucio Fulci heroine Catriona MacColl inherits the haunted hotel along with her helpmate, David Warbeck, and she has to endure a number of frightening supernatural manifestations before the ambiguous climax. The eerie end scenes see MacColl and Warbeck (both British performers, by the way) trapped in hell itself, a landscape foreshadowed in the painting which the former manager of the hotel was working on when he was crucified as a satanist - a gory event shown in the prologue. The plot doesn't really hang together, but there are some gory moments to treasure: a plumber has his eyes gouged out, a maid gets an acid facewash, a charlady's head is punctured by a nail that exits through her face, pushing her eye out, and a seeing-eye dog rips its mistress's throat out. Best of all, though is the bit where an army of venomous spiders appear from nowhere to strip a unfortunate guest's flesh from his bones. Possibly Fulci's finest movie.

TITLE BEYOND, THE

AKA L'aldila; Seven Doors of Death; Die Geisterstadt der Zombies

DIRECTOR Lucio Fulci

COUNTRY IT
SOURCE Videomedia/Vampix (UK)
YEAR 1981
TIME 81m59s

CAST Katherine MacColl (Catriona MacColl), David Warbeck, Sarah Keller, Antoine Saint John, Veronica Lazar, Anthony Flees, Giovanni De Nava, Al Cliver (Pier Luigi Conti), Michele Mirabella, Giampaolo accarola, Maria Pia Marsala, Laura De Marchi.

PRODUCTION Fulvia Film srl (Rome). [prod] Fabrizio De Angelis. © None.

PHOTOGRAPHY DIRECTOR Sergio Salvati

MUSIC Fabio Frizzi
EDITOR Vincenzo Tomassi

DVD Review

Lucio Fulci's movie was originally released to UK cinemas, cut, and with an X-certificate. That version was still banned on video for a while. In 2001 common sense finally prevailed - there's no sexual violence in the film - and VIPCO got a video 18 for the uncut version. You can get German and Dutch discs of this, plus an American one from Diamond Entertainment. The best version to date, though, is Anchor Bay's 2000 release, which features an excellent quality 2.35:1 anamorphic widescreen transfer, sound that's remastered in Dolby Digital 5.1, a commentary track from stars David Warbeck and Catriona MacColl, a short 'Making of' piece, a music video, production stills, a trailer, plus some interesting (though very poor quality) footage of Fulci at work directing a gore scene from one of his later movies, **Demonia**. There's also an alternate German pre-credits sequence. The VIPCO version presents us with just the movie, a trailer, and a small stills gallery. It's non-anamorphic 2.35:1 but has decent enough picture quality if you want to pick up a copy on the cheap. At least you know you won't have any trouble importing this one though.

BLOOD BATH

Starring:
Isa Miranda
Claudine Auger
Luigi Pistilli
Laura Betti

Running time 82 mins approx
Certificate "18"
Copyright: Hokushin Audio Visual Ltd
2 Ambleside Avenue
London SW16 6AD

Produced by Giuseppe Zaccariello
Directed by Mario Bava

The day a group of pleasure-seeking teenagers wander into a deserted leisure centre coincides with the callous murder of the widow owner of the property. Her death is just the beginning of a blood bath.

VHS

They came seeking pleasure, they found death

Blood Bath

VIDEO MOVIES™ from Hokushin VM 75 **VIDEO MOVIES™ from Hokushin**

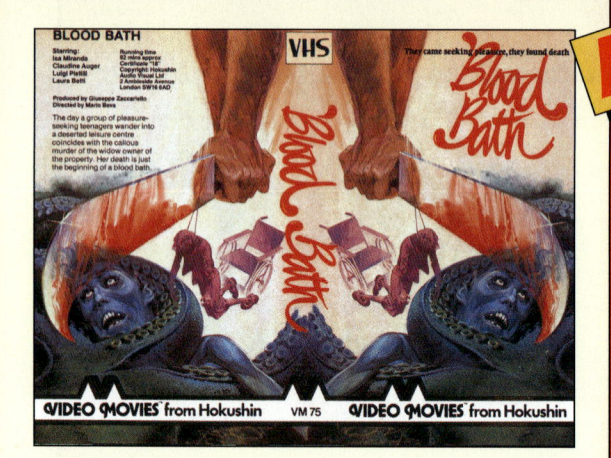

REVIEW

Some years before **Friday The 13th**, Italian horror stylist Bava (**Black Sunday**) made this **Ten Little Indians**-style stalk and slash shocker about a bunch of grasping relatives who all murder each other, one by one, in the hopes of owning a very pleasant and desirable country mansion. The film can be looked upon as a gory black comedy, the punchline coming when the last two survivors are playfully shot dead by their own two children. The '13 periods of intense shock' advertised by the makers takes in graphic sequences of people getting axes in the face and being stabbed repeatedly. In one scene two lovers are impaled on a spear that suddenly shoots up through the bed (a scene that was definitely pinched by the makers of **Friday The 13th**). Bava does his own camerawork and achieves some striking images of misty, pastel-coloured landscapes. One scene has a woman swimming in a lake and bumping into a floating corpse - Dario Argento used a similarly chilling sequence at the beginning of **Inferno**, a film which Bava also assisted on. Not one of Mario's best pictures, **Blood Bath** is nevertheless an interesting work that deserves to be seen.

DVD Review

When the British-based Redemption Films submitted this to the BBFC in 1994 they received an 18 certificate with cuts. Their disc was a nice job apart from this, but we all want the full monty of course so the way to go is with Image's **Twitch Of The Death Nerve**, the US retitling of the movie. Released in the USA as part of Image's Mario Bava Collection, the film is presented in anamorphic 16x9 framed at 1.77:1. Image throws in a 'murder menu' where you can go straight to the grue, a funky trailer for the film under the title **Carnage**, two cheesy radio spots, a biography and filmography of Mario Bava, and trailers for six other Bava films released under the Image banner. But the audio for the film is among the worst ever heard on a DVD. Dialogue is tinny, drops out with cringing regularity, and then swells up again. It's most annoying. There is another uncut **Bay of Blood** DVD released under the Scimitar label that has much better audio, but the picture quality on that disc is mediocre. What a shame.

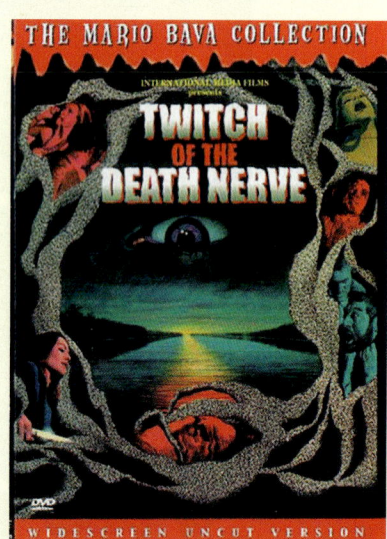

TITLE BAY OF BLOOD, A (as Blood Bath)

AKA Reazione A Catena; Ecologia Del Delitto; Antefatto; Twitch Of The Death Nerve; Carnage; A Bay of Blood

DIRECTOR Mario Bava

COUNTRY IT
SOURCE Hokushin (UK)
YEAR 1971
TIME 80m54s

CAST Claudine Auger, Luigi Pistilli, Iaudio Volonté, Anna Maria Rosati, Chris Avram, Leopoldo Trieste, Laura Betti, Brigitte Skay, Isa Miranda, Paola Rubens, Guido Boccaccini, Roberto Bonanni, Giovanni Nuvoletti [and uncredited] Nicoletta Elmi.

PRODUCTION Nuova Linea Cinematografica. [prod] Giuseppe Zaccariello. [prod man] Ferdinando Franchi. © None.

PHOTOGRAPHY DIRECTOR Mario Bava

MUSIC Stelvio Cipriani
EDITOR Carlo Real

NOTHING SO APPALLING IN THE ANNALS OF HORROR!

BLOOD FEAST

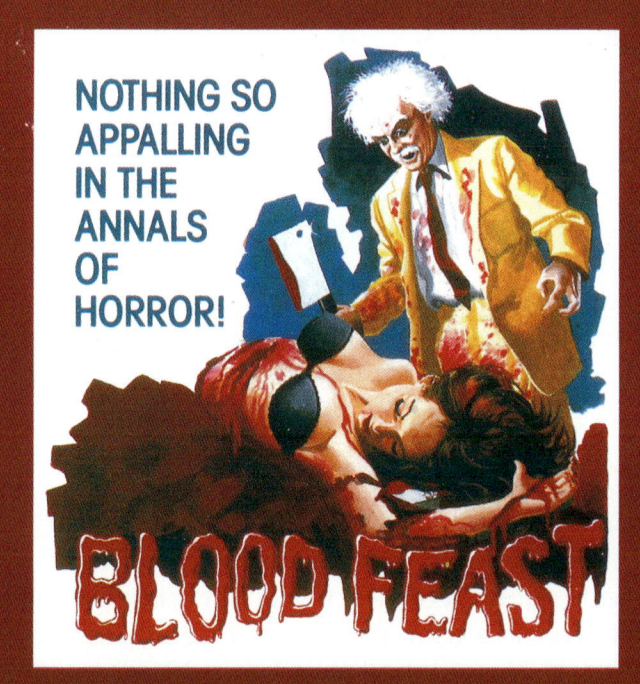

Released in 1963 to large crowds of shocked and horrified people, "BLOOD FEAST" has acquired an incredible cult following as the "first full fledged splatter movie"! Produced, directed, photographed, and scored by Herschell Gordon Lewis, the "godfather of gore," "BLOOD FEAST" tells the story of a modern day Doctor Frankenstein who wants to bring a dead Egyptian princess back to life! But to satisfy his lust, he goes much further into the depths of moral depravity. Our hero doesn't even bother to wait for his victims to die before "dis-assembling" one part of the body to reach another! See "BLOOD FEAST," a veritable orgy of blood and gore!

CULTVIDEO

The copyright proprietor has licensed the film contained in this videocassette for private home use only. Any other use including making copies of the film, causing it to be seen or heard in public or broadcasting it or causing it to be submitted to subscribers to a diffusion service is strictly prohibited. Any breach of the above conditions render the offender liable to prosecution by Astra Video Ltd.

PRINTED IN THE U.S.A.

ASTRA VIDEO

VHS VIDEO CASSETTE

CULTVIDEO

BLOOD FEAST

ASTRA VIDEO

You'll Recoil and Shudder as You Witness the Slaughter and Mutilation of Nubile Young Girls — in a Weird and Horrendous Ancient Rite!

NOTHING SO APPALLING IN THE ANNALS OF HORROR!

BLOOD FEAST

CultVideo Presents A Box Office Spectaculars Release
Starring Connie Mason
Produced by David F. Friedman
Directed by Herschell G. Lewis
COLOR   RUNNING TIME 70 MINUTES

CULTVIDEO

CULTVIDEO DISTRIBUTED EXCLUSIVELY IN THE U.K. BY

ASTRA VIDEO

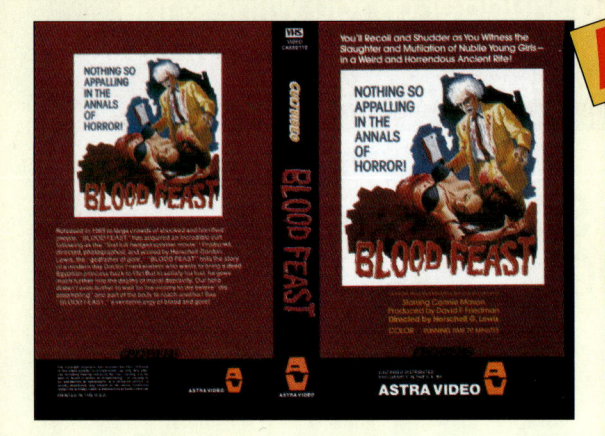

REVIEW

This notorious nasty from HG Lewis has the dubious distinction of being the first film to openly wallow in gratuitous gore - there weren't many movies as sick as this around in 1963! Of course the gore effects aren't exactly believable by today's standards, but the film still has a number of devotees - all of whom should seek psychological assistance. The insipid plot details the activities of an insane caterer named Fuad Ramses (Mal Arnold). He prowls about hacking the limbs, tongues and brains of his female victims in bloody close-up (the tongue he pulls out of one looks about five times too big for her mouth!). In the end the crazed Ramses falls into the blades of a rubbish truck, leaving stolid copper Thomas Wood to comment: "He died a fitting death for the garbage he was!" If you can take bad acting, awful dialogue and lots of inappropriate music just to get to the gore scenes then you're welcome to this. I prefer to pass. The doom-laden soundtrack music was composed by Lewis, and it's available on CD!

DVD Review

When you consider the fact that this was made thirty years ago and has some of the phoniest-looking gore effects you will ever see, it's amazing that it still hasn't been passed in the UK totally uncut. Metro Tartan's disc (on their Tartan Terror label) is missing 23 seconds of footage, and though otherwise it's an excellent quality release one has to say that this makes the uncut US version the stronger option. Released in America as a region free disc by Something Weird, the 1.33:1 (virtually full screen, the way it was shot) image is great. This looks like it was taken from a 35mm vault master. You also get an audio commentary from producer David Friedman and director H.G. Lewis, which is a lot of fun. There's nothing particularly revealing in the commentary, but it's still great to hear these exploitation legends discuss their work. You get the full film, outtakes, a gallery of exploitation art, a Carving Magic featurette (instructing you how to best carve a joint of meat!), and a theatrical trailer.

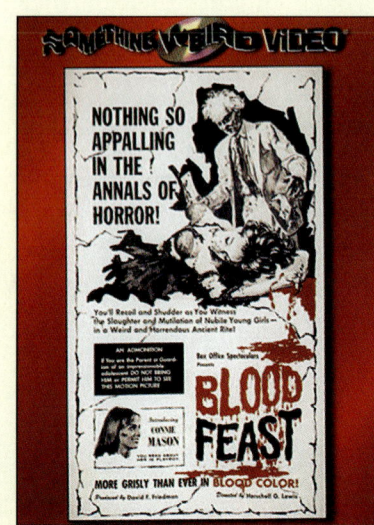

TITLE BLOOD FEAST

AKA NONE

DIRECTOR Herschell Gordon Lewis

COUNTRY US
SOURCE Astra (UK)
YEAR 1963
TIME 64m10s

CAST Thomas Wood, Mal Arnold, Connie Mason, Lyn Bolton, Scott H. Hall, Toni Calvert, Astrid Olsen, Sandra Sinclair, Gene Courtier, Louise Kamp, Al Golden.

PRODUCTION Box Office Spectaculars, Inc. presents... A Friedman - Lewis Production. [prod] David F. Friedman. © 1963 Box Office Spectaculars, Inc.

PHOTOGRAPHY DIRECTOR Herschell Gordon Lewis

MUSIC EDITOR Herschell Gordon Lewis
Robert Sinise & Frank Romolo

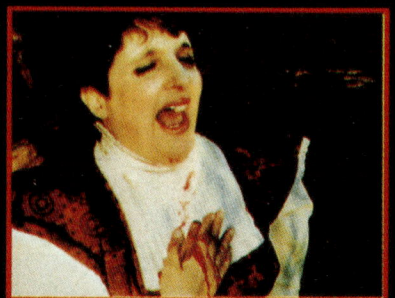

Blessed are the meek for they shall inherit...

BLOOD RITES

STARRING

VERONICA RADBURN • HAL BORSKE RICHARD ROMANOS

Three sisters and their husbands are forced to stay at their late Father's house in order to inherit his fortunes.

But their stay quickly turns into a never ending nightmare as the evil force within the house unleases it's savage fury against them.

As the unwelcome guests are dispatched in a variety of gruesome ways the house finally yields it's sinister secrets – can anyone survive long enough to learn them!

Blessed are the meek for they shall inherit...

DIRECTED BY JEROME-FREDERIC

COLOUR ● 'X' RATED

BLOOD RITES

SCORPIO VIDEO

REVIEW

Anyone who's ever had the misfortune of sitting through an Andy Milligan movie will know that moviemakers don't come any more inept than this (now - deceased) Staten island horror 'auteur.' Milligan churned out countless crap no-budgeters in the 60s and early 70s, and nobody ever took them seriously apart from those misguided souls who nominated this for the nasties list. **Blood Rites** is the UK video title for Milligan's **The Ghastly Ones**, and the film tells of three sisters and their husbands who turn up at their late father's house in the hopes of collecting an inheritance. Instead they get served up severed heads on plates and pitchforks in the neck by a loony retard who doesn't like visitors. The gore is extremely unconvincing, the acting is incredibly amateurish, and as usual Milligan always seems to put the camera where it can only see half of what's going on. The main psycho is called Colin, by the way, and he eats baby rabbits, fur and all!

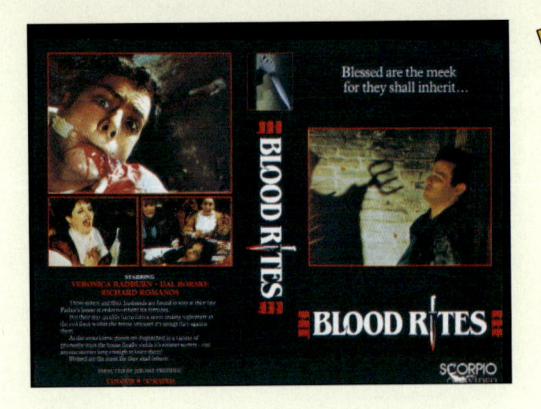

TITLE	GHASTLY ONES, THE (as Blood Rites)
AKA	The Ghastly Ones
DIRECTOR	Andy Milligan
COUNTRY	US
SOURCE	Scorpio (UK)
YEAR	1967
TIME	67m22s
CAST	Veronica Radburn, Maggie Rogers, Hal Borske, Anne Linden, Fib La Blaque, Carol Vogel, Richard Romanos, Eileen Haves, Don Williams, Hal Sherwood, Niel Flanagan, Ada McAllister, Robert Adsit.
PRODUCTION	[prod] Jerome - Fredric. © 1967 J.E.R. Pictures, Inc.
PHOTOGRAPHY DIRECTOR	Andy Milligan
MUSIC	Not credited
EDITOR	Gerald Jackson

DVD Review

Now the very idea of putting an Andy Milligan movie on DVD seems totally ridiculous, and therefore it's not surprising to discover that **Blood Rites** has never legally been issued on disc anywhere in the world. One or two other Milligan movies (**Guru The Mad Monk**, **The Body Beneath**) have been put out by Image in the States, but the only way you're going to get your sticky mitts on **The Ghastly Ones** is to go the bootleg tape or DVD-R route. You'll also have to seek it out under its original release title of **The Ghastly Ones**. A company called Cinefear put out a decent quality uncut tape, while the DVD can be purchased from the Something Weird folks in the USA. Taken from a slightly scratchy 35mm print and presented full screen, this isn't bad at all considering how awful the film looked in its original incarnation as a Video Nasty. And if you survive **The Ghastly Ones**, you should definitely check out SWV's disc of **Seeds of Sin**, shot the same year, in which another family reunion ends in everyone getting killed. It also stars Maggie Rogers, the very same house and, in particular, that same godawful wallpaper!

Panic and hysteria hit the Spanish resort of Costa del Sol when a language school loses its pupils in a series of blood thirsty murders.

OLIVIA PASCAL
CHRISTOPH MOOSBRUGGER
ALEXANDER WAECHTER

BLOODY MOON

© This pre-recorded Video Tape Cassette is protected by Copyright. Any unauthorised broadcasting, public showing or copying in all or part is strictly prohibited.

Running Time 95 mins

ILV 107

Inter-Light Video

REVIEW

This typical Jess Franco abomination made it into the DPP hit list because of its lurid mix of sex and horror. But does Jess know how to make 'em any other way? The yawn-inducing plotline tells of a murderous couple (Moosbrugger and Gerganoff) who are out to sadistically slaughter attractive girl students at a Euro language school. Sex movie regular Olivia Pascal is the woman in peril, around whom the corpses pile up. Among the gore scenes on offer are scissor murders committed by a guy in a Mickey Mouse mask (we bet Disney didn't get any royalties!), and a real, live snake being decapitated by a pair of shears. Contrived and unimaginative, the film has lots of those horrid zooms and jump-cuts that signify the work of this nutty Spanish 'auteur.' It exists merely to showcase endless scenes of bared breasts and mutilated corpses. The most famous splatter image is of a girl being fed through a sawmill, but that's not shown in any convincing detail. One of the more boring of the nasties, though Franco fans will no doubt find some redeeming value in it.

TITLE BLOODY MOON

AKA Die Säge Des Todes; Colegialas Violadas; ProFonde Tenebre

DIRECTOR Jesús Franco

COUNTRY WG
SOURCE Inter-Light (UK)
YEAR 1980
TIME 81m35s

CAST Olivia Pascal, Christoph Moosbrugger, Nadja Gerganoff, Alexander Waechter, Maria Rubio, Otto W.Retzer, Jasmin Losensky, Corinna Gillward, Ann-Beate Engelke, Antonio Garcia, Peter Exaccoustos, Jesús Franco.

PRODUCTION [prod] Wolf C. Hartwig. Lisa Film (MUNICH) - Metro Film (Munich) - Rapid Film (Munich). © None.

PHOTOGRAPHY DIRECTOR Juan Soler

MUSIC EDITOR Gerhard Heinz
Karl Aulitzky & Christine Jank (uncredited)

DVD Review

This title remains unavailable in the US, and VIPCO's UK version is cut and of poor quality, plus it's in fullscreen, which is a dead giveaway that it was mastered up from their old VHS tape. The only worthwhile DVD release so far comes from Holland on the European Shock label. Letterboxed at 1.85:1 with anamorphic enhancement, the transfer is perhaps a shade dark in places but generally it's quite pleasing - even if the film as a whole isn't! Fully uncut, the movie is accompanied by a small slide show of front-of-house images, posters and video covers, plus a trailer for **Bloody Moon** and another for **Linda**, one of Jess Franco's 70s sex movies which the company also released on DVD as part of their Jess Franco Collection. This trailer is quite raunchy, in fact, and some parts of it might even earn an R-18 in the UK! The disc has English audio with removable Dutch subtitles.

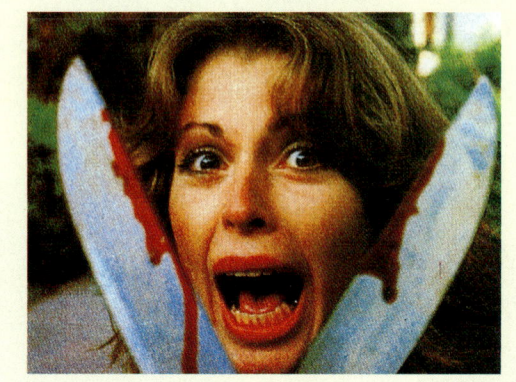

THE BOGEY MAN

It begins with a horrifying killing and then starts to get bloody!!

"The Bogey Man" is the chilling story of concentrated evil and its gruesome effect on a small American farming community. The evil is so great that even exorcism cannot stop the blood bath. Pray before you next look in a mirror!!

WARNING
"The copyright proprietor has licensed the film contained in this videocassette for private home use only. Any other use including making copies of the film, causing it to be seen or heard in public or broadcasting it or causing to be transmitted to subscribers to a diffusion service, letting on hire or otherwise dealing with it in part or any kind of exchange scheme is strictly prohibited. Any breach of the above conditions render the offender to prosecution by Video Instant Picture Company Limited".

VIPCO
Video Instant Picture Company Limited

VHS VIDEO CASSETTE

THE BOGEY MAN

VIPCO present

Suzanna Love   Ron James   John Carradine
also starring
Nicholas Love   Raymond Boyden   Felicite Morgan

Written, Directed and Produced by Ulli Lommel
Executive Producer Wolf Schmidt   Music by Tim Krog

SEE WARNING ON REVERSE

Running Time 84 Minutes

REVIEW

This strange mixture of stalk and slash and art house movie made the nasties list but was later reissued with a few slight cuts. It's an imaginative effort from the director of **Tenderness Of The Wolves**, which begins with a **Halloween** -style flashback (complete with tinkly music) showing a youngster stabbing his mum to death with a carving knife. The youngster grows up to be a mute, while his sister (who is played by Suzanna Love, the wife of the director) has psychological problems of her own. Under hypnosis she starts imitating Linda Blair in **The Exorcist**, spitting out curses and threatening dire dangers in a croaky voice. The mute guy has now come to the conclusion that he was influenced by an evil mirror, so he goes around the house painting them all black. But Suzanna smashes one of the mirrors and a shard of glass finds its way into her handbag. We know from the fact that it's glowing red and there's a thumping heartbeat on the soundtrack that this can only mean bad luck - seven years' worth at least. Three kids bite the big one in typically contrived death scenes: one is guillotined by a falling window, one is battered by an item of furniture, and another is stabbed repeatedly with scissors. The best gore is saved for the old screwdriver-through-the head routine, though there's also a nifty pitchfork killing if you're fond of that sort of thing. John Carradine turns up in a small role as a doctor - trust him! Pretty good of its type.

TITLE BOOGEYMAN, THE (as The Bogeyman)
AKA The Bogeyman
DIRECTOR Ulli Lommel
COUNTRY US
SOURCE Vipco (UK)
YEAR 1980
TIME 79m24s
CAST Suzanna Love, Ron James, John Carradine, Nicholas Love, Raymond Boyden, Felicite Morgan, Bill Rayburn, Llewelyn Thomas, Jay Wright, Natasha Schiano, Gillian Gordon, Howard Grant, Jane Pratt, Lucinda Ziesing, David Swim, Katie Casey, Ernest Meier, Stony Richards, Claudia Porcelli, Catherine Tambini.
PRODUCTION [prod] Ulli Lommel. [assoc prod] Terrell Tannen. [exec prod] Wolf Schmidt. © 1980 Interbest American Inc, ,
PHOTOGRAPHY DIRECTOR David Speling & Jochen Breitenstein
MUSIC Tim Krog
EDITOR Terrell Tannen

DVD Review

This movie was passed uncut for UK release in the year 2000. Apart from the fact that we call this **The Bogey Man** and the yanks call it **The Boogeyman**, there's not much difference between the UK and US discs, quality-wise. In the US, Anchor Bay have it in 1.85:1 non anamorphic NTSC in Dolby Digital Mono. It's on a Double Feature disc with **The Devonsville Terror**, which is also directed by Ulli Lommel. That film is in 1.33:1 non-anamorphic NTSC, though the packaging states that the aspect ratio is 1.85:1. The UK version is from VIPCO and contains a theatrical trailer and photo gallery. It's in 1.85:1 non anamorphic PAL. There's also a R2 German disc on the CMV Laservision label, which is uncut, and one from Astro/Best Entertainment which is supposedly cut. The Anchor Bay double disc offers the best value, but VIPCO's disc is cheaper and just as worthwhile a purchase. You can see why nobody would double this up with its sequel - the followup is largely comprised of footage nicked from the original!

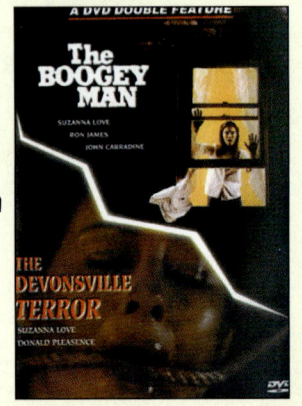

Don't look he'll see you.
Don't breathe he'll hear you.
Don't move you're dead.

JEAN UBAUD, MICHAEL COHL and CORKY BURGER
present a MIRAMAX Production of

THE BURNING

THE BURNING x

JEAN UBAUD, MICHAEL COHL and CORKY BURGER present
A MIRAMAX Production of "THE BURNING"
Starring BRIAN MATTHEWS, LEAH AYERS, BRIAN BACKER,
LARRY JOSHUA and LOU DAVID as Cropsy
Music composed and performed by RICK WAKEMAN
Screenplay by PETER LAWRENCE and BOB WEINSTEIN
Created and Produced by HARVEY WEINSTEIN
Directed by TONY MAYLAM

On a moonlit evening many years ago, a group of young campers played a trick on Cropsy, the camp caretaker. The trick backfired, and Cropsy became a horribly disfigured maniac, a mutilated killer with a thirst for revenge. This is the terrifying account of Cropsy's return and of the trail of blood he leaves in the dark woods...

Starring
BRIAN MATTHEWS
LEAH AYERS
BRIAN BACKER
LARRY JOSHUA
and LOU DAVID
as Cropsy

© Cropsy Venture 1981

VHS
87 MINS
PAL COLOUR

WARNING: FOR PRIVATE DOMESTIC USE ONLY. ANY UNAUTHORISED COPYING, HIRING, LENDING OR PUBLIC PERFORMANCE OF THIS VIDEOGRAM IS PROHIBITED.

TVA 90 0836 2

The most frightening of all maniac films

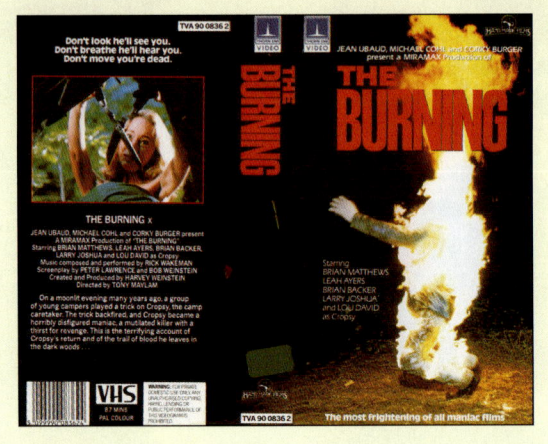

REVIEW

It's difficult to think of a more derivative stalk and slash movie that this thoroughly predictable **Friday The 13th** clone featuring a horribly burned camp counsellor who comes back to kill and maim as many promiscuous teens as he can find. A caring hospital orderly describes the madman as "a fucking Big Mac, overdone!"). Early on it looks like the movie might give us a decent bit of sleaze in a scene where Lou David's "Cropsy" goes to visit a prostitute. Not surprisingly she takes one look at his melted cheese fizzog and suddenly develops a blinding headache. So he stabs her and throws her through a window. This one got itself included on the nasties list because of one scene where our demented hero snips off a teen's fingers with a pair of garden shears. The effects are generally very good, but one would expect that from Tom Savini. What's not good about the film is its boring script, inept direction (by Tony Maylam, who went on to be fired from Rutger Hauer's **Split Second**), and overdone Rick Wakeman sound track music. See **Friday The 13th** again instead.

DVD Review

This stalk and slash favourite was re-released on video here in 1992 with a few seconds of cuts to a scene in which the maniac shears off a victim's fingers. VIPCO resubmitted it last year and the film was passed completely uncut with this footage restored. The down side is the fact that VIPCO's disc is a bare bones release that looks like it was sourced from an old tape master. The image is full screen and very obviously cropped - it's apparent that a lot of picture information is missing from the edges. The colours are also very bright, unnaturally so in places, and the image has lots of grain. Dragon Entertainment's German release is marginally better, but also a fairly bog standard full frame release. You get slightly more picture info that with the VIPCO title, but it's far from satisfactory. Ironically the best version is on tape only, from MGM in the USA. Also full frame, this presents us with a sharply colourful and satisfying picture and a nicely remastered stereo soundtrack. MGM have no current plans to release this on disc, but my bet is they will eventually, so hang on.

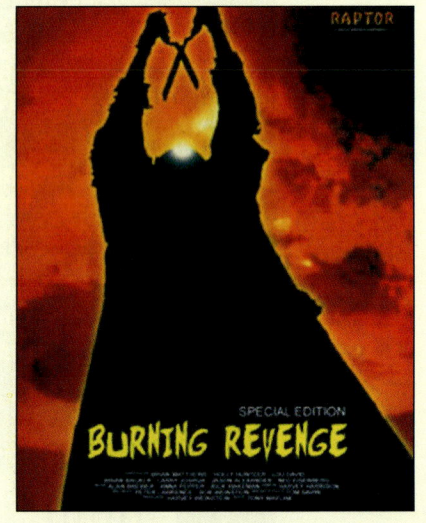

TITLE	BURNING, THE
AKA	NONE
DIRECTOR	Tony Maylam
COUNTRY	US
SOURCE	Thorn EMI (UK)
YEAR	1980
TIME	87m26s
CAST	Brian Matthews, Leah Ayres, Brian Backer, Larry Joshua, Jason Alexander, Ned Eisenberg, Carrick Glenn, Carolyn Houlihan, Fisher Stevens, Lou David, Shelley Bruce, Sarah Chodoff, Bonnie Deroski, Holly Hunter, Kevi Kendall, J. R. McKechnie, George Parry, Ame Segull, Jeff De Hart, Bruce Kluger, Keith Mandell, Jerry McGee, Mansoor Najee-Ullah, Willie Reale, John Roach, Reid Rondell, K. C. Townsend, John Tripp, James Van Verth.
PRODUCTION	Jean Ubaud, Michael Cohl & Corky Burger present... A Miramax Production. [prod] Harvey Weinstein. [assoc prod] Dany Ubaud. [exec prod] Jean Ubaud, Michael Cohl & Andre Djaoui. [exec in charge of prod] Corky Burger. © 1980 Cropsy Venture.
PHOTOGRAPHY DIRECTOR	Harvey Harrison
MUSIC	Rick Wakeman
EDITOR	Jack Sholder

R 1015 **REPLAY**

CANNIBAL APOCALYPSE

JOHN SAXON in CANNIBAL APOCALYPSE

STARRING

JOHN SAXON · ELIZABETH TURNER
CINDY HAMILTON · JOHN MORGHEN

Released from captivity in Vietnam, two American Army officers return to civilian life and discover they have acquired an insatiable taste for human flesh.

A city is terrorised… as they stalk the inhabitants to satisfy their primitive appetites.

Based on an original story by Jimmy Gould
Directed by **ANTHONY M. DAWSON**
© New Fida Organisation 1980

COLOUR ● 90 MINUTES ● CERT 'XX'

THIS FILM IS NOT RECOMMENDED FOR VIEWING BY PERSONS UNDER 18 YEARS OF AGE

WARNING: The copyright proprietor has licensed the film contained in this video cassette for private home use only, and any other use including making copies of the film, causing it to be seen or heard in public or broadcasting it or causing it to be transmitted to subscribers to a diffusion service or otherwise dealing with it in part, is strictly prohibited without the prior written permission of REPLAY VIDEO LTD.

VPD

VIDEO PROGRAMME DISTRIBUTORS LIMITED
G.E.C. ESTATE, EAST LANE, WEMBLEY,
MIDDX HA9 7FF

VHS

CANNIBAL APOCALYPSE

POW's in Vietnam…starved in captivity…
released with a taste for human flesh.

REVIEW

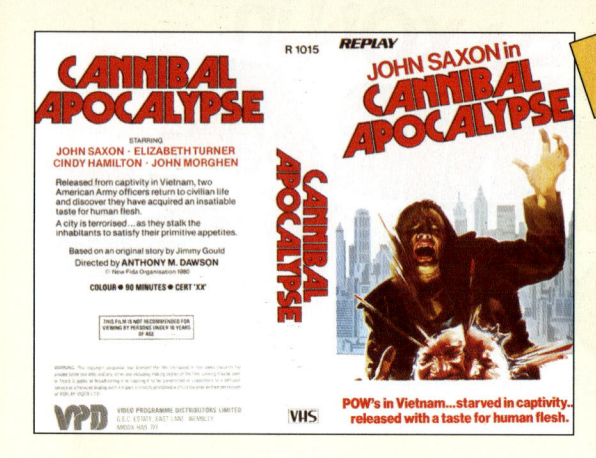

This grim and gory horror tale crossbreeds the Vietnam war and cannibal movie genres to potent effect. Shot in Atlanta by an Italian crew, the storyline opens in Vietnam, where American officer John Saxon leads a low-budget skirmish into enemy territory and rescues two of his men from a bamboo trap. To his disgust he notes that the lads have been feeding from the flesh of a Vietnamese peasant. Rather foolishly he reaches down to help them out of their hole in the ground and is rewarded by one of them taking a nasty chunk out of his arm. Of course we all know what *that* means in this kind of movie, and sure enough, much later, back in Atlanta, Saxon discovers he has also developed a taste for human munchies. He meets up with his two old cannibal buddies, and they set off on an orgy of violence, nibbling on nurses and snacking on a motorcycle gang. This is a movie for hardcore gore freaks, and features eyeballs being squished, stomachs being ripped out, plus an unforgettable scene where John Morghen (a regular victim in this genre) is shotgun-blasted in the stomach. The camera then gives us a nice view of the daylight that you can see through the football-sized hole in his gut! Scenes like this earned the movie an X-rating in the States and a place on the video nasties list in the UK. The make-up (by **Zombie Flesh-Eaters** man Gianetto De Rossi) is excellent. Pandering to the public's conception of Vietnam vets as homicidal time bombs just waiting to explode, this nevertheless delivers the goods as a hard-edged blood and guts action thriller. One of Margheriti's best movies.

TITLE   CANNIBAL APOCALYPSE

AKA   Apocalipse domani; Invasion of the Flesh Hunters; Cannibals in the Streets

DIRECTOR   Antonio Margheriti

COUNTRY   IT
SOURCE   Replay (UK)
YEAR   1980
TIME   92m06s

CAST   John Saxon, Elizabeth Turner, John Morgen (Giovanni Lombardo Radice), Cindy Hamilton, Tony King, Wallace Wilkinson, Ray Williams, John Gerosen, May Heatherley, Ronnie Sanders, Vic Perkins, Jere Beery, Joan Riordan, Laura Dean, Lonnie Smith, Don Ruffin, Benjamin Rogers, William H. Gribble, George Nikas, Doug Dillingham, Ralph Vaughn.

PRODUCTION   Edmondo Amati presents... [prod] Maurizio Amati & Sandro Amati. A New Fida Organisation - Josè Frade Production. © 1980 New Fida Organisation (Rome)..

PHOTOGRAPHY DIRECTOR   Fernando Arribas

MUSIC   Alexander Blonksteiner
EDITOR   George Serralonga

DVD Review

Unavailable for quite some time, this was eventually released uncut by Image in the USA as a Region 0 disc as part of their rather haphazard Euroshock Collection. The disc is a revelation, which presents the film in an immaculate 1.66:1, anamorphic transfer. It has a bright, colourful (though grainy in places) image, and the sound's good too. It's also well worth checking out the extras that come along with the movie, especially **Cannibal Apocalypse Redux**, an interesting short documentary that interviews two of the stars and the (now sadly deceased) director about how the movie was handled and so forth. We even get Quentin Tarantino explaining why he thinks of this as one of his favourite movies ever, and you can chuckle over John Saxon saying he didn't realise he was starring in a cannibal flick! It also shows us an alternate version of the movie that was edited for its US video release - obviously we Brits aren't the only nation that has censorship to contend with. Last but not least there's a text feature covering the butchering of **Cannibal Apocalypse**, though you will need good eyesight to read the very small print.

CANNIBAL FEROX

COLOUR • 89 MINUTES • CERT 'XX'

R 1016

CANNIBAL FEROX

STARRING

JOHN MORGHEN

LORRAINE DE SELLE

BRIAN REDFORD

DUE TO THE SPECIFIC AND HORRIFIC NATURE OF THIS FILM THIS AREA IS NOT GRAPHICALLY ILLUSTRATED TO AVOID OFFENCE

NOT RECOMMENDED FOR PERSONS UNDER 18 YEARS OF AGE

WARNING: The copyright proprietor has licensed the film contained in this video cassette for private home use only, and any other use including making copies of the film, causing it to be seen or heard in public or broadcasting it or causing it to be transmitted to subscribers to a diffusion service or otherwise dealing with it in part, is strictly prohibited without the prior written permission of REPLAY VIDEO.

VPD

VIDEO PROGRAMME DISTRIBUTORS LIMITED
G.E.C. ESTATE, EAST LANE, WEMBLEY,
MIDDX HA9 7FF.

VHS

REPLAY Video

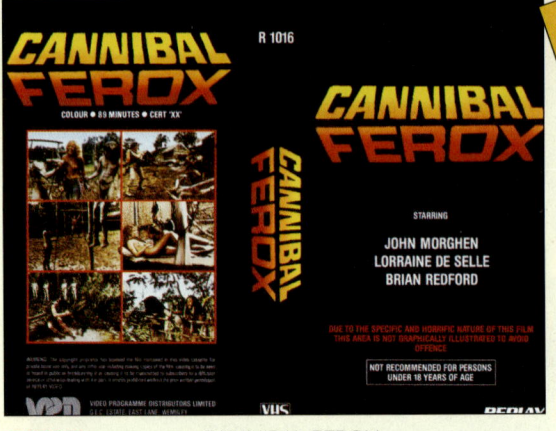

REVIEW

This gruesome yarn is actually in **The Guinness Book Of Records** as having been "banned in 31 countries," and one of them is the UK! The movie follows the traditional formula for jungle gut-crunchers, with lots of cruelty to animals and people. It tells of two attractive college girls and a boyfriend who go to Columbia in search of evidence that cannibalism is a mere myth perpetrated by whites. Not too good a guess, as it happens. Once there they end up as the dish of the day on the cannibal menu after joining forces with a demented drug dealer who has brutally tortured the locals. The ghastly gourmets take revenge by hanging one of the gals up by her breasts in a grisly reverse on **A Man Called Horse**, and chopping bad guy John Morghen's arm and dick off before slicing open the top of his skull like a breakfast egg. They then scoop out the brains, of course - sunny side up. The film tries to avoid accusations of racism by presenting the whites as more brutal and depraved than the cannibals, who after all are only following the dictates of their diet. Almost on a par with **Cannibal Holocaust** in the graphic gore stakes, this is gruelling stuff that is most assuredly not for the squeamish.

TITLE CANNIBAL FEROX

AKA Make Them Die Slowly; Let Them Die Slowly; Woman from Deep River; Die Rache der Kannibalen; Canibal Feroz

DIRECTOR Umberto Lenzi

COUNTRY IT
SOURCE Replay (UK)
YEAR 1981
TIME 89m08s

CAST John Morghen (Giovanni Lombardo Radice), Lorraine De Selle, Bryan Redford, Zora Kerowa, Walter Lloyd, Meg Fleming, Robert Kerman, John Bartha, Venantino Venantini, "El Indio" Rincon.

PRODUCTION A Dania Film - Medusa Distribuzione - National Cinematografica production. [exec prod] Antonio Crescenzi. [prod organiser] Giovanni Masini. © 1981 Dania Film - Medusa Distribuzione - National Cinematografica.

PHOTOGRAPHY DIRECTOR Giovanni Bergamini

MUSIC EDITOR Budy Maglione Enzo Meniconi

DVD Review

When the original distributors realised that **Cannibal Ferox** was going to be classed a Video Nasty they took fright and lopped 7 minutes out of it - this was even before the Video Recordings Act became law. However, the film was still refused a certificate and prosecuted in a number of cases. Flash forward to the year 2000, and this hacked-up version was re-presented to the BBFC by the stalwarts at VIPCO. It was then passed, but with a further 6 seconds of cuts for animal cruelty. Obviously this UK disc is to be avoided. There are a number of European versions of this, but the way to go is with the NTSC Region O disc from Grindhouse Releasing, which presents the film in its original Italian language with English subtitles in a splendid anamorphic 1.85:1 print. The disc also contains a commentary by long-suffering star John Morghen and director Umberto Lenzi, who tries to wriggle out of accusations of animal cruelty! There are also production stills and trailers, an on-camera interview with Lenzi, and some grisly Easter Egg surprises!

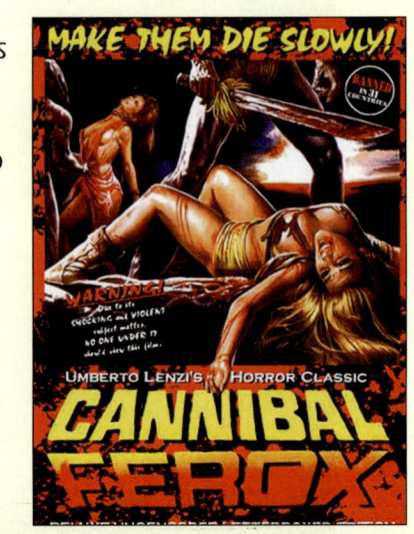

Cannibal Holocaust

The story concerns the disappearance of an expedition and film crew in the depths of unexplored jungle. A rescue expedition finds no survivors, but they do recover the film taken by their doomed predecessors.
The sickening contents reveal a terrifying catalogue of life — and horrific death — among the cannibal tribe which still inhabits the jungle...

WARNING
This film contains scenes of horrific nature and should not be viewed by those of a nervous disposition.

GO VIDEO LTD.,
P.O. BOX 4BT, 35-37 WARDOUR STREET, LONDON W1A 4BT.
WARNING: All rights of the Producer and the Owner of the work reproduced reserved Unauthorised Copying, Hiring, Lending Public Performance, Radio or T.V. Broadcasting of this Video Cassette prohibited. CERT X

GO 121

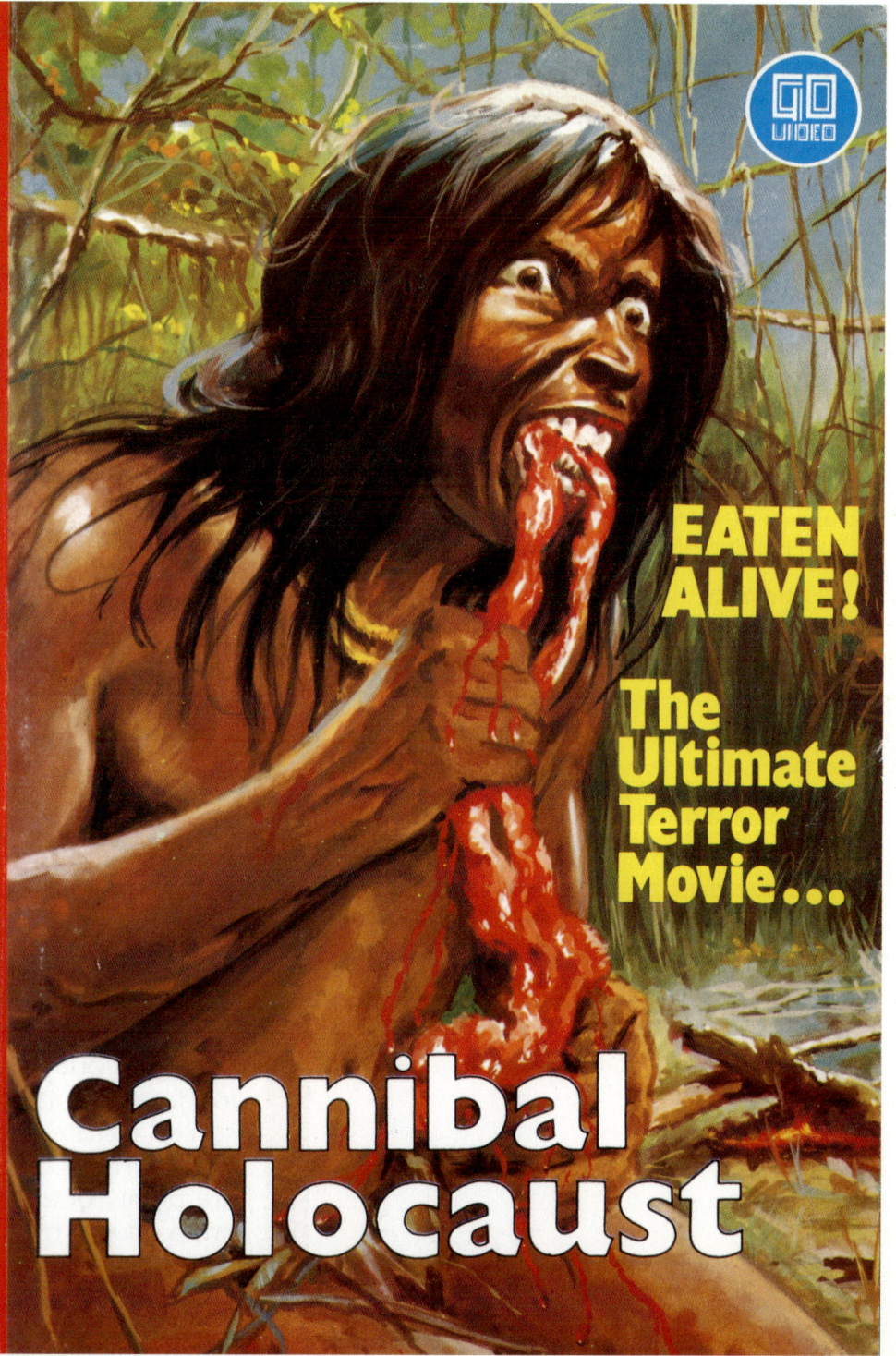

EATEN ALIVE!

The Ultimate Terror Movie...

Cannibal Holocaust

REVIEW

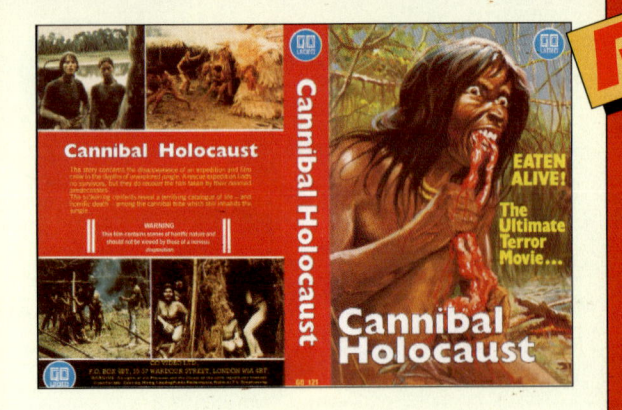

One of the first and most effective of all cannibal gut-crunchers, this grim movie tries to increase the viewer's sense of dread by pretending that it's a documentary consisting of "found" footage depicting the brutal fate of a camera crew ventured too deep into cannibal country. This fake "snuff" movie (complete with scratches, jumps and awkward zooms) makes up the bulk of the film's running time. It also shows the makers of the film-within-a-film to be smug, snotty, spoiled and sporting a very mean streak which is generally directed at helpless animals. In an early scene they drag a huge turtle to shore and summarily behead it, ripping it apart in close-up. We also get to see pigs being shot, a muskrat getting a hunting knife through his gut and out of the top of his head, and of course we are treated to the obligatory feasting on a monkey's brains. On the human cruelty front, we witness a choice scene where a foetus is ripped out of a woman's womb and buried in mud, and the torching of a native village with women and children trapped in the flames. ("Beautiful It's beautiful" cry the thrill-hungry filmmakers as they photograph the carnage). The gore is extreme and ranges from the amputation of somebody's penis to a hacking off of a leg with a machete, and all the usual disembowellings and eye-gougings that make you wonder why cannibals never get told off for playing with their food. There is also a very gross shot of a woman impaled on a stake with its sharpened point exiting her mouth. But in many ways the gore is easier to stomach than Deodato's mealy-mouthed, "who are the real savages?" lament, so he can pretend to condemn what he is really exploiting. Undeniably very effective, but like cannibalism itself it leaves a bad taste.

TITLE CANNIBAL HOLOCAUST

AKA Cannibal Massaker; Holocausto Cannibal; Nackt und Zerfleischt

DIRECTOR Ruggero Deodato

COUNTRY IT
SOURCE Go (UK)
YEAR 1979
TIME 85m14s

CAST Robert Kerman, Francesca Ciardi, Perry Pirkanen, Luca Giorgio Barbareschi, Salvatore Basile, Ricardo Fuentes, Gabriel Yorke, Paolo Paoloni, Pio Di Savoia (Pio Lionello Di Savoia), Luigina Rocchi.

PRODUCTION Franco Palaggi & Franco Di Nunzio present... An F.D. Cinematografica production. [in charge of prod] Giovanni Masini. © None.

PHOTOGRAPHY DIRECTOR Sergio D'Offizi

MUSIC Riz Ortolani
EDITOR Vincenzo Tomassi

DVD Review

There are a couple of different versions of **Holocaust** out there. The best known is EC Entertainment's region free European disc, which sports an anamorphically enhanced 1.85:1 transfer. Considering the age of the film, it looks quite good. Colours look accurate, and the print appears relatively free of damage aside, of course, from the damage that Deodato purposefully inflicted upon the documentary footage to give it an air of realism. But if you're looking for the ultimate DVD edition of **Cannibal Holocaust**, it's to Italy you must cast your sights! A brand new Italian Special Edition gives us the best version of the film we could ever hope for, but with one small problem - for some reason there are a couple of seconds missing from the infamous Last Road To Hell documentary showing real-life executions by firing squad! Picture quality is stunning to say the least, easily the best I've ever seen this film look. The fly in the ointment here is the non-removable Italian subs over the English track. There are plenty of extras here, but you need to speak Italian to get the most out of them. There are a couple of trailers and a radio spot (English) in addition to a 3-minute piece on the restoration of the film, with no dialogue, just music. There's also an hour-long documentary, only in Italian, and an audio commentary featuring Deodato, Italian only as well.

THE CANNIBAL MAN

Marcos works in a canning plant attached to the local slaughterhouse. Every day he must wade through rivers of blood, down seemingly endless rows of dissected animal corpses, to pick up the meat his plant processes.

One evening he kills a taxi driver in self defense, and then desperate with fear, strangles his own girl friend, the only witness to the crime. When the girl's friend tries to find her he kills her as well, and before he knows it, he has the blood of several victims on his hands. He disposes of their bodies in a manner he had learned at work, cutting them to pieces and stuffing them into the plant's meat grinder.

This one week in the life of a murderer is a fascinating character study of a frightened man whose chain of horrid crimes is more worthy of our pity than our condemnation.

Running time: 98 minutes

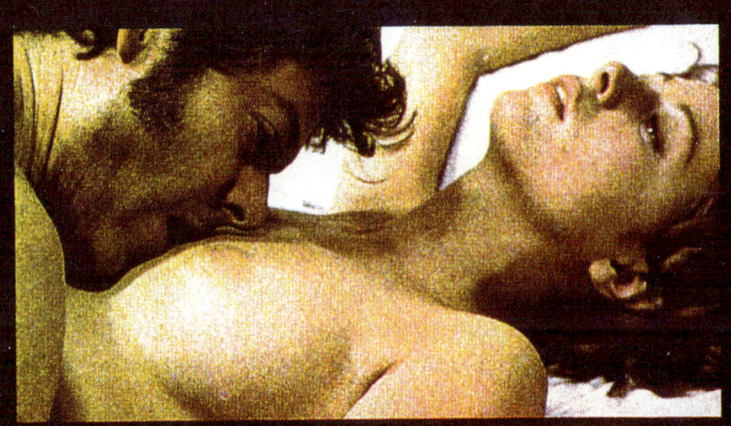

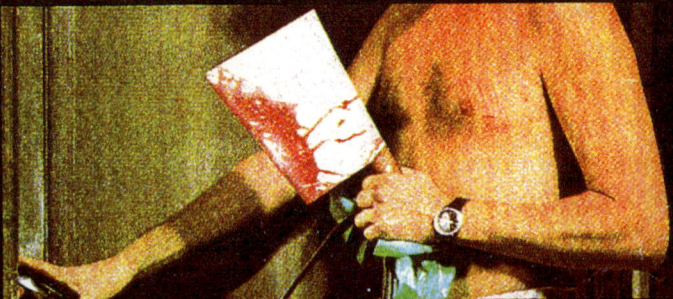

INTERVISION VIDEO LIMITED
1, McKAY TRADING ESTATE, KENSAL ROAD, LONDON, W10

© INTERNATIONAL COPYRIGHT PROTECTION. Warning: Copyright subsists in all recordings issued under this label for private home use only and prohibits any other use. Unauthorised broadcasting, public performance, copying or re-recording in any manner whatsoever is prohibited, not to be re-sold, hired out, exchanged, or leased without the prior written permission of Intervision Video Limited.

DESIGNED BY GRAFFITI PRODUCTIONS LIMITED
Printed by Popper & Company Ltd

WHEN THE BUTCHER GOES BERSERK....

ATLAS INTERNATIONAL presents
ELOY DE LA IGLESIAS'S

THE CANNIBAL MAN

starring VINCENTE PARRA as Marcos
with EMMA COHEN · EUSEBIO PONCELA · LOLA HERRERA
Produced by JOSE TRUCHADO Directed by ELOY DE LA IGLESIA

Intervision MOVIES ON VIDEO

TERROR SUSPENSE · COLOUR
A-A 0348

COLOUR
A-A 0348

REVIEW

A gloomy, depressing Spanish movie which tells of a disturbed young man (Vincente Parra) whose senses have been brutalised by his job in a local slaughterhouse (cue lots of horrid abattoir footage). One day he cracks and kills a cab driver. Then he strangles his girlfriend (who witnessed the dirty deed), tops his brother, and cuts his brother's fiancee's throat when the latter discovers the bodies under the bed in his apartment. After killing his father with a cleaver in the face, and slaughtering a visiting prostitute, his apartment is getting a bit like the morning after at Custer's Last Stand, so he tries to dispose of the bodies in a meat grinder. At this point our harassed hero is visited by a homosexual young man who has witnessed the killings from a nearby window and offers to help bury the evidence. Burnt out, the killer decides he might as well turn himself in, instead. Opportunities existed to make this a black comedy, but it has more of the atmosphere of a bleak Spanish version of Polanski's **Repulsion**. Murky but intriguing, with some very poor effects - just freeze-frame that machete-in-the-face and you'll see it for the glued-on plastic novelty it so obviously is!

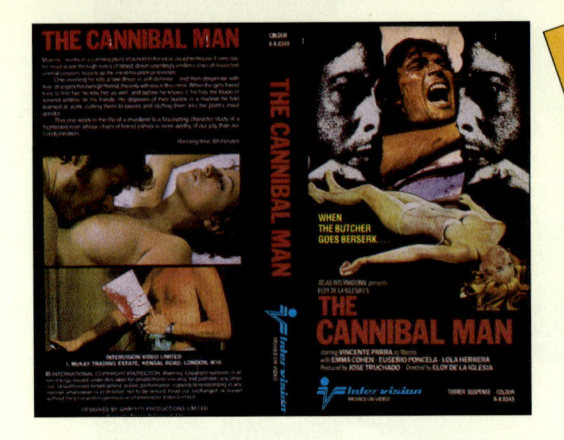

TITLE CANNIBAL MAN, THE

AKA La Semana del Asesino; The Apartment on the 13th Floor

DIRECTOR Eloy De La Iglesia

COUNTRY SP
SOURCE Intervision (UK)
YEAR 1972
TIME 94m13s

CAST Vincent Parra, Emma Cohen, Eusebio Poncela, Vicky Lagos, Lola Herrera.

PRODUCTION Atlas International presents... [prod] Joe Truchado. [assoc prod] Vincent Parra. [prod man] Louis M. Lasala. Thruchado Films. © None.

PHOTOGRAPHY DIRECTOR Raul Artigot

MUSIC Fernando G. Morcillo
EDITOR Joe Louis Matesanz

DVD Review

This Spanish-made Nasty was reissued on video by Redemption Films but in a cut version that removed some of the early slaughterhouse footage and trimmed the axe-in-the-face gore murder. The quality was good, apart from that. But it was down to Anchor Bay USA to bring us the definitive uncut **Cannibal Man** in the year 2000. As far as image quality is concerned, Anchor Bay always shines in this department and their region free disc presents the film in its original theatrical ratio of 1.85:1 (16x9 enhanced). Colours are a bit faded, but that is to be expected from a 1971 film. The transfer is very clean, with almost no blemishes appearing, and the image is sharp and clear throughout. Anchor Bay went for a standard DVD release on this one, providing just a theatrical trailer on the DVD itself. Included with the DVD is a small insert that gives some background on Spanish cinema and director Eloy De La Iglesia. To be honest, if this was resubmitted today it would almost certainly get through uncut.

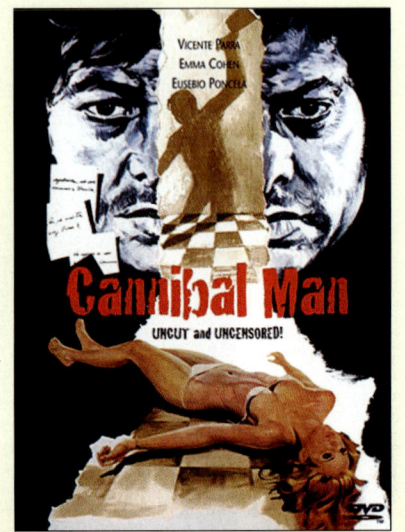

MODERN FILMS VIDEO

CANNIBAL TERROR

Starring
SILVIA SOLAR · STAN HAMILTON · BURT ALTMAN · PAMELA STANFORD
and OLIVIER MATHOT

Two small-time crooks, Mario and Roberto, kidnap Florence Danville and hide out in a friend's house, who lives by trading with the natives in a nearby jungle.

The friend's wife is raped by Mario who extracts revenge by tying him to a tree and leaving him to be eaten by the cannibals. She then informs the kidnapped girl's parents of their daughter's whereabouts, and the gangsters, when cornered, flee through the jungle only to be massacred by the cannibals in this fast-moving adventure film.

Produced by Marius Lesoeur · Directed by Allan W. Steeve

Modern Films Video Pre-recorded Video Cassettes are sold exclusively for private home viewing to non-paying audiences and are strictly for non theatrical use. Duplication of this material which is copyright renders the offender liable to prosecution by Modern Films Video and the copyright owners.

MODERN FILMS VIDEO
45 New Oxford Street, London WC1

MODERN FILMS VIDEO

CANNIBAL TERROR

WITH
SILVIA SOLAR · STAN HAMILTON
BURT ALTMAN · PAMELA STANFORD
OLIVIER MATHOT AND GERARD LEMAIRE

MD 10

93 minutes Colour

V.H.S.

REVIEW

One of the most inept cannibal movies ever made, this dull, pathetic, French-made effort concerns a bunch of small-time crooks who kidnap the daughter of a local big-wig and hightail it into the jungle, where they fall foul of a gang of flesh-eating cannibals. The usual carnage ensues. The cannibals have very odd hairstyles for jungle types, and they can hardly keep a straight face as they tuck into patently false plastic tummies stuffed with what looks like chicken and rice in barbecue sauce. Shot on the same sets as Jess Franco's **White Cannibal Queen**, the film has a few decent gore scenes but they have little impact when located in such a boring plot. The moving finale sees the tribal chief serving up a suitable epitaph for the gangsters, and indeed anybody who has been foolish enough to sit through the film: "They got all the punishment they deserved," he says, "and all the pain and suffering that was coming to them." Amen.

TITLE	CANNIBAL TERROR
AKA	NONE
DIRECTOR	Julio Tabernero (as Allan W. Steeve)
COUNTRY	FR,SP
SOURCE	MODERN UK
YEAR	1981
TIME	89m37s
CAST	Sylvia Solar, Gerard Lemaire, Pamela Stanford, Olivier Mathot, Burt Altman, Stan Hamilton, Tony Fontaine, Antony Mayans, Michel Laury, Annabelle.
PRODUCTION	Eurociné presents... [prod man] Marius Lesoeur. © None.
PHOTOGRAPHY DIRECTOR	Alain Hardy
MUSIC EDITOR	Jean Jacques Lemeztre, Roland Grillon [assistant], Dominique Petit

DVD Review

When you sit down to watch this film nowadays you may wonder what kind of magic mushrooms were growing on the roof of the BBFC building to delude them into slapping this with a banned rating! It seems likely that the use of the word 'Cannibal' in the title brought the red mist on and they chucked it out without even bothering to view it. In 2003 the UK-based Hardgore label submitted it to the BBFC and were given an 18 certificate with no cuts required. The Hardgore disc gives us an anamorphic widescreen version in its original 1.85 ratio with English audio. Extras are a gallery of video sleeves for the film and trailers for **I Spit On Your Grave**, **Demonium**, **Don't Mess With My Sister**, **Nutbag**, **Bangkok Hell** and **Reign In Darkness**. The picture quality is a bit grainy in places, but it's generally quite a nice looking transfer, with good colour and contrast levels. The problem is, this is such a godawful movie that even die-hard fans of cannibal gut crunchers will find it tough to sit through without hitting the fast-forward.

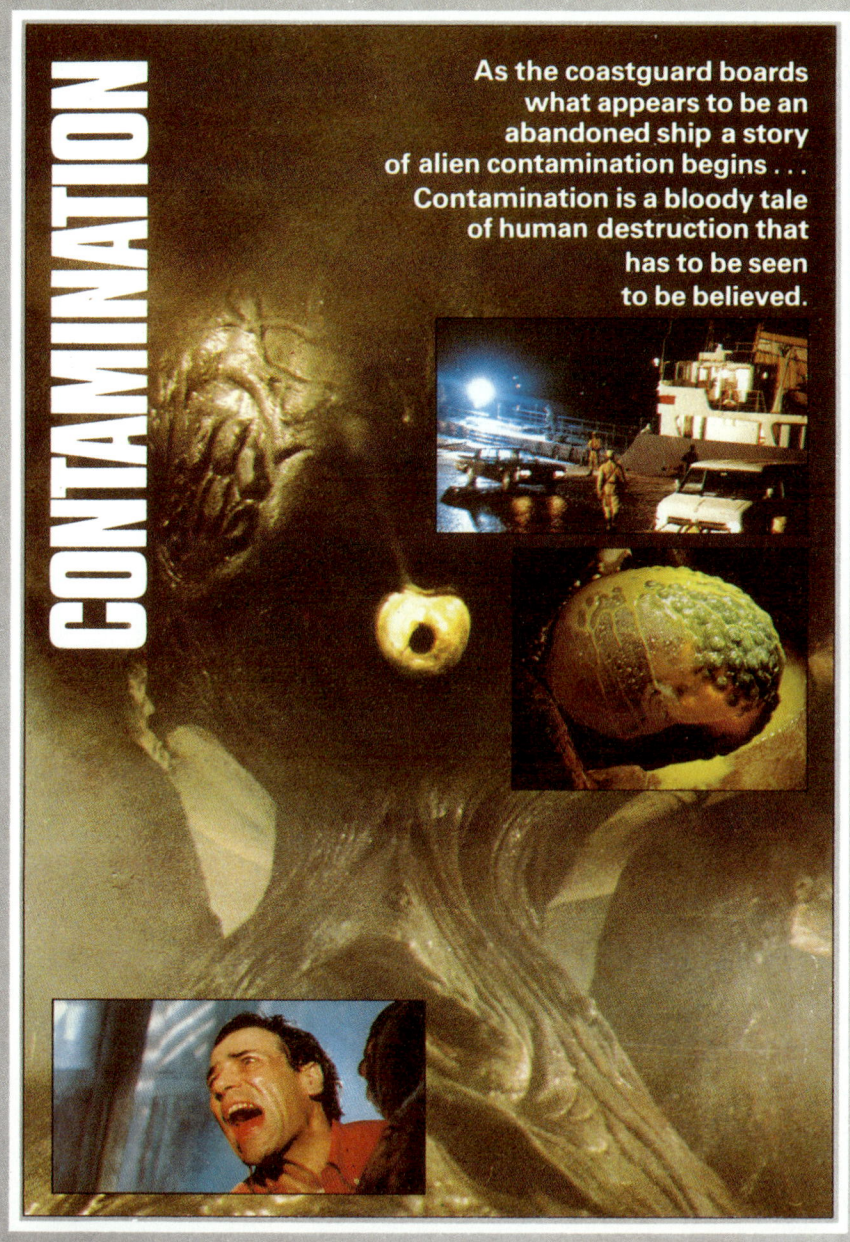

CONTAMINATION

VIP PRESENTS

CONTAMINATION

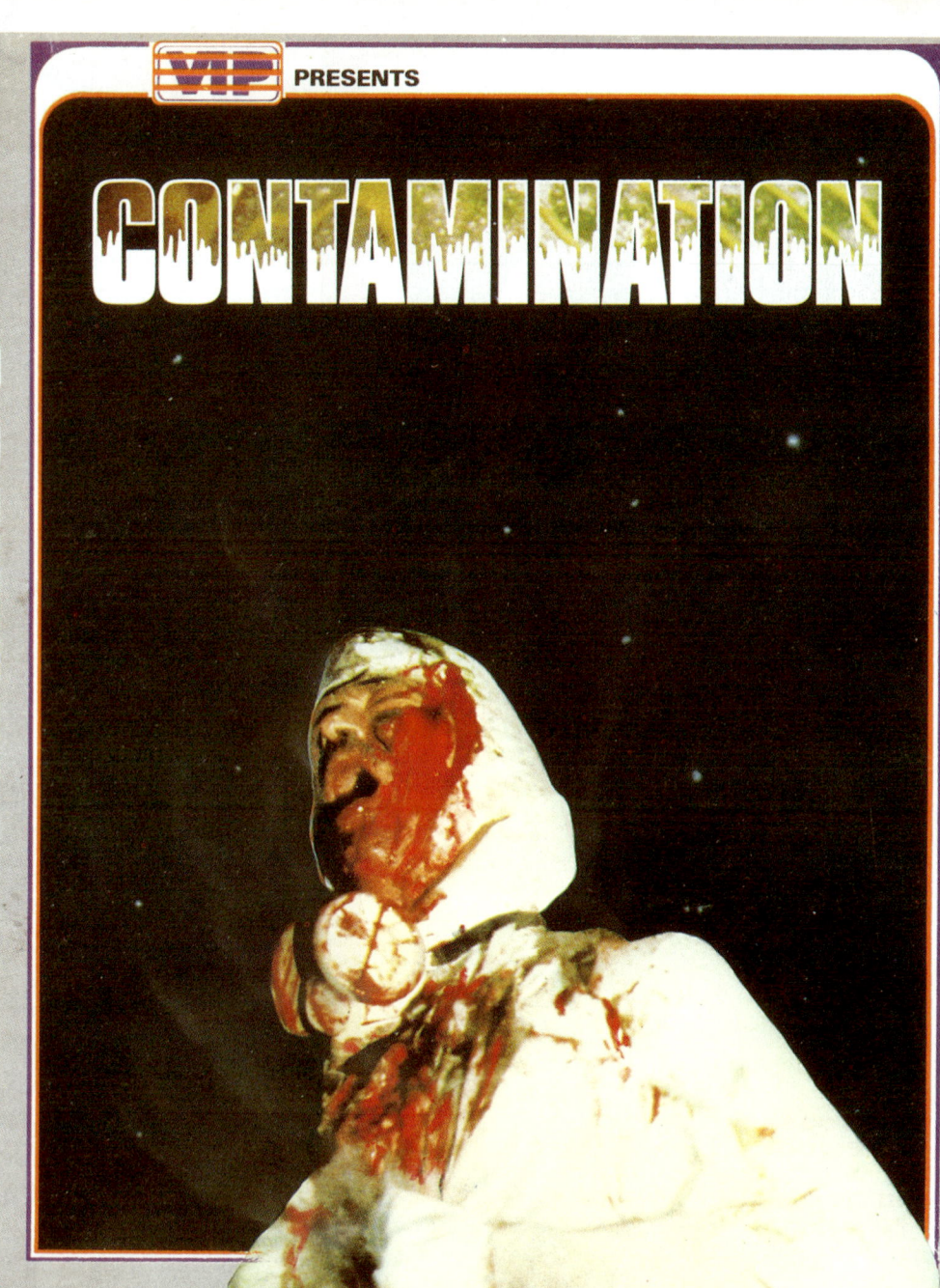

As the coastguard boards what appears to be an abandoned ship a story of alien contamination begins...
Contamination is a bloody tale of human destruction that has to be seen to be believed.

VIP001
VHS VIDEO CASSETTE

WARNING

"The copyright proprietor has licensed the film contained in this videocassette for private home use only. Any other use including making copies of the film, causing it to be seen or heard in public or broadcasting it or causing it to be transmitted to subscribers to a diffusion service, letting on hire or otherwise dealing with it in whole or in part is strictly prohibited. Any breach of the above conditions renders the offender liable to prosecution."

© Video Independent Productions Ltd.

Sleeve design by IMPRESSIONS
01 722 3939

starring IAN McCULLOCH LOUISE MARLEAU
MARINO MASE SIEGFRIED RAUCH GISELA HAHN
directed by LEWIS COATES

R RESTRICTED

REVIEW

A cheap and cheerful rip-off of **Alien** concocted by Argento-protege Cozzi, this entertaining potboiler has one decent gore effect involving people's stomachs exploding dramatically outwards in slow motion - and boy, does Cozzi get some mileage out of it! The opening scene sees a ship drifting into New York harbour containing a hold full of mysterious eggs that look like watermelons (they are actually painted balloons). When these things pop apart - as they do frequently - they shower bystanders with a sticky liquid that causes immediate inflation of the belly and - SPLAT - animal guts everywhere! It turns out the eggs are being sent down from Mars by a laughable one-eyed alien blob who has his headquarters in a Colombian coffee factory. Luckily, boozy astronaut McCulloch (of **Zombie Flesh-Eaters** fame) is on hand to join forces with sexy Louise Marleau and settle the alien's hash. The scene where an alien egg almost catches the sultry Marleau in the shower plumbs new heights of hilarity - why doesn't she just run out instead of cowering in the corner? The plot has some similarities to **Quatermass II** in the scenes where an army of brainwashed radiation-suited zombies harvest the deadly eggs. Not as bad as its reputation suggests, this one has an effective score by Goblin and is quite fun on a junk movie level.

TITLE CONTAMINATION

AKA Contaminazione; Alien 2; Alien Contamination; AstaronSrut des Schreckens; Toxic Spawn

DIRECTOR Luigi Cozzi (as Lewis Coates)

COUNTRY IT, WG
SOURCE VIP (UK)
YEAR 1980
TIME 85m30s

CAST Ian McCulloch, Louise Marleau, Marino Masé, Siegfried Rauch, Gisela Hahn, Carlo De Mejo, Carlo Monni.

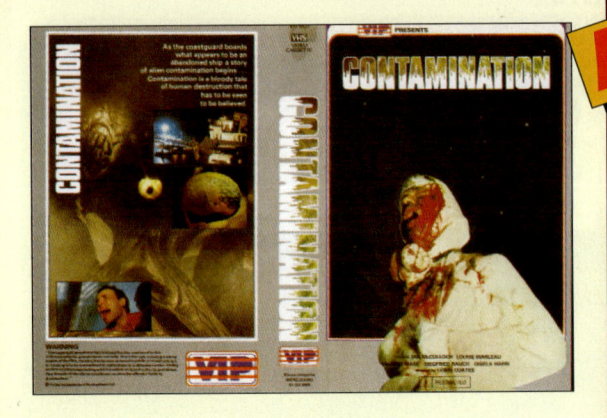

PRODUCTION Alex Cinematografica srl presents... An Italian - German co-production. Alex Cinematografica srl - Barthonia Film GmbH (Munich)- Lisa Film GmbH (Munich). [assoc prod] Ugo Valenti. [prod] Claudio Mancini. © None

PHOTOGRAPHY DIRECTOR Giuseppe Pinori

MUSIC Goblin
EDITOR Nino Baragli

DVD Review

This film is probably the most dramatic example of how the BBFC and the DPP got it all wrong back in the Nasties days. Lots of cuts were made to the film by the distributors prior to the VRA, and then the BBFC stuck their oar in and reduced the running time further, cutting it down by about 2 minutes and 40 seconds. The biggest cut was made to the opening sequence showing several men graphically exploding after tampering with alien pods. But when the complete film was re-presented to the BBFC by Anchor Bay in 2003 it was passed fully uncut - with a 15 certificate! The disc of **Contamination** was sourced in the US and Italy by Bill Lustig's Blue Underground, and it's a great-looking transfer. The new 5.1 Dolby Digital Surround audio isn't entirely bad either considering the film wasn't originally made with that specification. As for extras, Blue Underground came through with some amazing material, including a brand new 18-minute retrospective interview with co-writer/director Luigi Cozzi and a longer behind-the-scenes documentary made during the production of the film. Also included are a theatrical trailer, a poster and still gallery and the graphic novel, which can be accessed if you have a DVD-ROM drive.

DEAD & BURIED

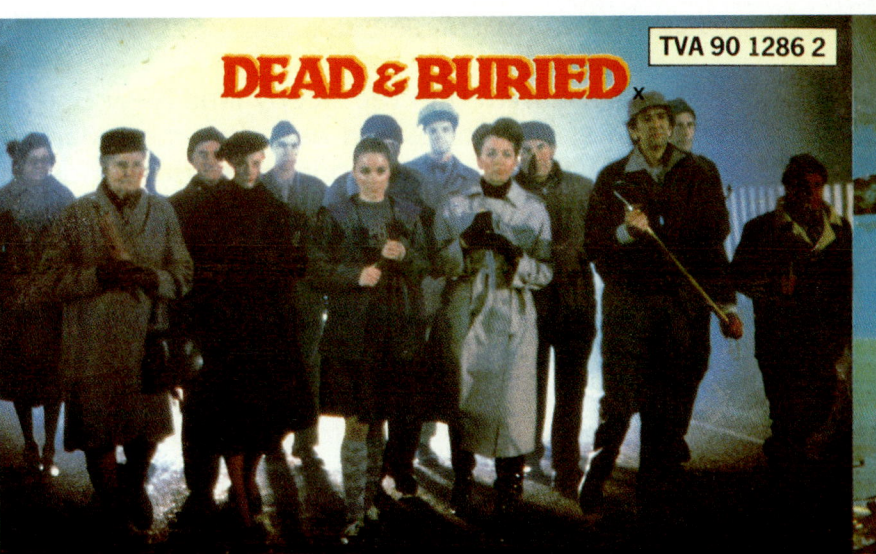

RICHARD R. ST. JOHNS presents
A RONALD SHUSETT Production "DEAD & BURIED"
Starring JAMES FARENTINO, MELODY ANDERSON
and JACK ALBERTSON
Produced by RONALD SHUSETT and ROBERT FENTRESS
Directed by GARY A. SHERMAN
Screenplay by RONALD SHUSETT and DAN O'BANNON

The natives of Potter's Bluff, a small misty seaside town in California, hide a dreadful secret in this atmospheric chiller which plays on the grisly fears of a return of the dead. With Jack Albertson as the undertaker with bizarre talents and James Farentino as the man who discovers more than is good for him, it's a roller-coaster ride through the violent and gruesome world of voodoo and the occult.

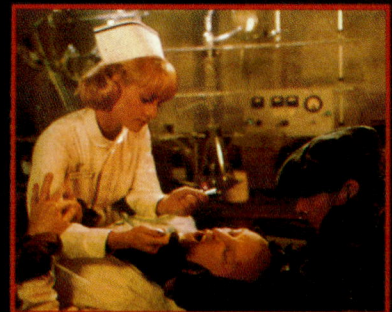

TVA 90 1286 2

VHS
90 MINS
PAL COLOUR

WARNING: FOR PRIVATE DOMESTIC USE ONLY. ANY UNAUTHORISED COPYING, HIRING, LENDING OR PUBLIC PERFORMANCE OF THIS VIDEOGRAM IS PROHIBITED.

THORN EMI VIDEO

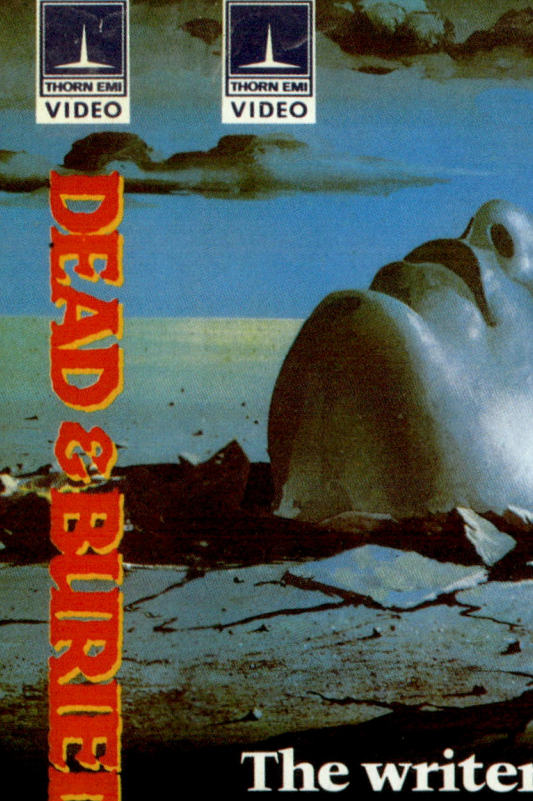

The writers of 'Alien' bring a new terror to Earth.

DEAD & BURIED

A new dimension in horror!

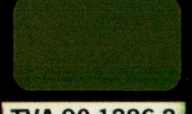

REVIEW

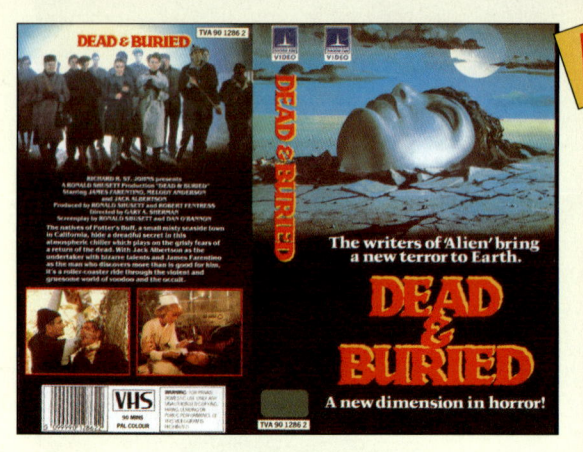

A series of gruesome murders committed in the sleepy little New England town of Potter's Bluff baffle sheriff James Farentino, and he's even more flabbergasted when the victims return as zombies! This imaginative chiller has an unusual and effective script by Ron Shusett and Dan O'Bannon (most famous for scripting **Alien**) and some quirky touches in the characterisation. Jack Albertson steals the show in his last role as a jovial mortician with a liking for 1940s swing music. It seems that jolly Jack has discovered a way to revive the dead, and the walking corpses are so grateful for this that they are going around killing anyone who passes through the town! Some of the plot twists are confusing, but splatter fans get their money's worth with future makeup and effects superstar Stan Winston serving up graphic burnings, batterings, acid injections and a show-stopping sequence in which a nurse shoves a hypodermic right through some poor schmuck's eye! Good atmospherics, and neat direction by Gary (**Death Line**) Sherman make this underrated movie well worth seeking out.

DVD Review

Shown at cinemas across the UK before it was released on video and promptly attracted the DPP's attention, **Dead And Buried** was always a borderline nasty. It was re-released in 1999 with all cuts restored, including the graphic Lucio Fulci-style shot of a needle being thrust into an eyeball! In 2003 the US distributor Blue Underground issued a Special Edition DVD featuring a brand new transfer in 1.85:1 anamorphic widescreen, plus a remastered soundtrack in 2.0 Dolby Surround, 5.1 Dolby Digital EX, and 6.1 Dolby Digital EX. Special features on the double disc set include a commentary with director Gary A. Sherman, commentary with co-writer/co-producer Ronald Shusett and actress Linda Turley, plus a commentary with cinematographer Steve Poster. Other goodies include theatrical trailers, a poster and still gallery, Stan Winston's Dead And Buried FX, plus Robert Englund on the movie, and a feature entitled Dan O'Bannon: Crafting Fear. It's difficult to think of any other disc release topping this one.

TITLE	DEAD & BURIED
AKA	NONE
DIRECTOR	Gary A. Sherman
COUNTRY	US
SOURCE	Thorn EMI (UK)
YEAR	1981
TIME	90m18s
CAST	James Farentino, Melody Anderson, Jack Albertson, Dennis Redfield, Nancy Locke Hauser, Lisa Blount, Robert Englund, Bill Quinn, Michael Currie, Christopher Allport, Joe Medalis, Macon McCalman, Lisa Marie, Estelle Omens, Barry Corbin, Linda Turley, Ed Bakey, Glenn Morshower, Robert Boler, Michael Pataki, Jill Fosse, Mark Courtney, Michael Courtney, Renee McDonell, Dottie Catching, Colby Smith, Judy Ashton.
PRODUCTION	Richard R. St. Johns presents... A Ronald Shusett Production. [prod] Ronald Shusett & Robert Fentress. [assoc prod] Michael I. Rachmil. [exec prod] Richard R. St. Johns.© 1981 Barclays Mercantile Industrial Finance Limited.
PHOTOGRAPHY DIRECTOR	Steve Poster
MUSIC	Joe Renzetti
EDITOR	Alan Balsam

DEATH TRAP

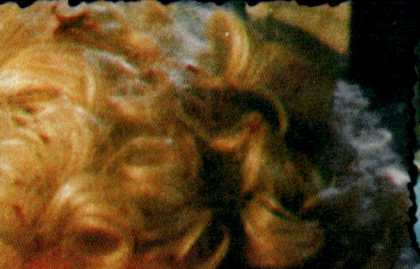

A sexually perverted homicidal maniac uses his run-down hotel to attract victims who will not be missed. The bodies – sometimes still alive – are thrown to a huge crocodile.
"Texas Chainsaw Massacre" director Tobe Hooper gives you another orgy of blood and terror!!

WARNING
"The copyright proprietor has licensed the film contained in this videocassette for private home use only. Any other use including making copies of the film, causing it to be seen or heard in public or broadcasting it or causing to be transmitted to subscribers to a diffusion service, letting on hire or otherwise dealing with it in part or any kind of exchange scheme is strictly prohibited. Any breach of the above conditions render the offender liable to prosecution by Video Instant Picture Company Limited"

VIPCO

VHS VIDEO CASSETTE

DEATH TRAP

VIP 035

VIPCO

DEATH TRAP

"Texas Chainsaw Massacre" director Tobe Hooper gives you another orgy of blood and terror!!

DEATH TRAP

Starring
Neville Brand, Mel Ferrer, Marilyn Burns, William Finley, Carolyn Jones & Stuart Whitman
Directed by Tobe Hooper Produced by Mardi Rustam

VIPCO

SEE WARNING ON REVERSE
RUNNING TIME 90 MINS. APPROX

REVIEW

Tobe Hooper followed up **The Texas Chainsaw Massacre** with this compellingly sick exercise based on a true-life story of a redneck motel owner (actually named Joe Ball) who used to feed his patrons to his pet crocodile. Neville Brand is in fine, scenery-chewing form as the proprietor of a rundown hotel in the Louisiana bayou who uses a monster scythe to lop the heads off his guests before he feeds them to the monster croc out back. Robert (Freddy) Englund makes a potent early appearance as a would-be stud ("My name is Chuck and I'm ready to fuck!") who meets a sticky end. Marilyn Burns (who survived **Texas Chainsaw**) is the lady in distress here, and guess what? - she gets tied up and tormented! The film is much more of a black comedy than its predecessor, and the sets are straight out of an old EC comic. But it definitely lacks the pounding ferocity of **TCM**, which is a shame. Though screened at the London Film Festival, it was deemed a nasty by a panel of experts at Willesden Magistrates Court after Mary Whitehouse took out a private prosecution against it! Oh dear…

TITLE DEATH TRAP

AKA Eaten Alive; Starlight Slaughter; Horror Hotel Massacre; Horror Hotel

DIRECTOR Tobe Hooper

COUNTRY US
SOURCE Vipco (UK)
YEAR 1976
TIME 86m06s

CAST Neville Brand, Mel Ferrer, Carolyn Jones, Marilyn Burns, William Finley, Stuart Whitman, Roberta Collins, Kyle Richards, Robert Englund, Crystin Sinclaire, Janus Blyth, Betty Cole, Sig Sakowicz, Ronald W. Davis, Christine Schneider, David Hayward, David 'Goat' Carson, Lincoln Kibbee, James Galanis, Tarja Leena Halinen, Caren White, Valerie Lukeart, Jeanne Reichert.

PRODUCTION Mardi Rustam presents... [prod] Mardi Rustam. [co-prod] Alvin L. Fast. [assoc prod] Samir Rustam, Larry Huly & Robert Kantor. [exec prod] Mohammed Rustam. © 1976 Mars production Corporation.

PHOTOGRAPHY DIRECTOR Robert Caramico

MUSIC Tobe Hooper & Wayne Bell
EDITOR Michael Brown

DVD Review

Tobe Hooper's controversial movie was screened at the 1976 London Film Festival, but that was the only time it saw the light of a projector bulb in the UK. After it was placed on the DPP list it languished there for quite a while before being resubmitted to the BBFC and passed with 25 seconds of cuts. Then in the year 2000 the folks at VIPCO gave it another try and got it through completely uncut. VIPCO's region 2 disc is one of their better efforts, presenting the film in a fairly colourful full screen transfer. If you prefer to have the movie in its original 1.85:1 widescreen ratio then you need to check out Elite's region free NTSC release, which gives the film its American title of **Eaten Alive**. Both the UK and US releases have trailers and small poster galleries, but no other extras worth mentioning. Somebody should do a remastering job on this and drag Tobe in to do a commentary.

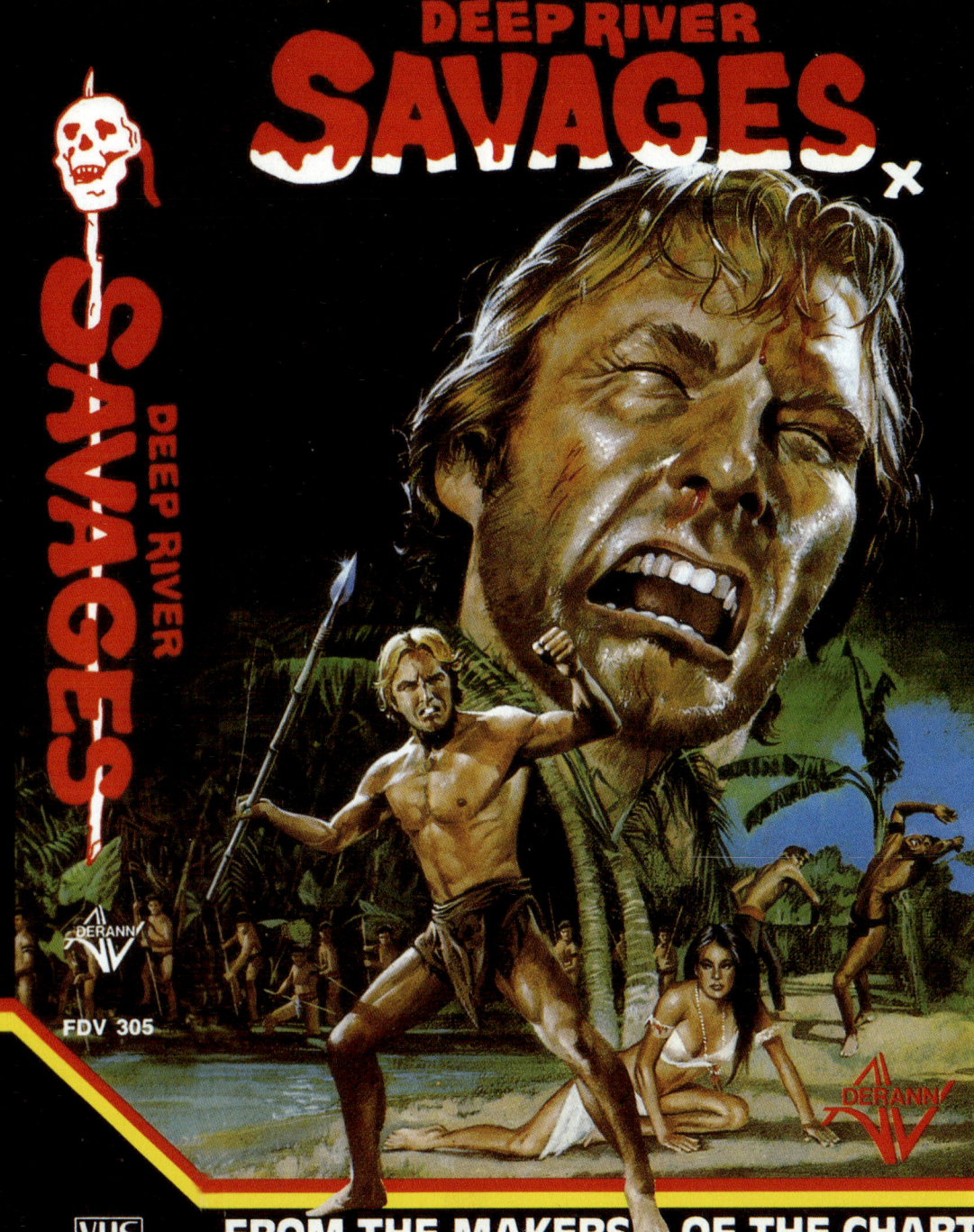

DEEP RIVER SAVAGES X

ME ME LAY   **IVAN RASSIMOV**

From the makers of the chart topping film 'CANNIBAL', comes 'DEEP RIVER SAVAGES', a story of raw savagery, tribal torture and one man's courageous fight for survival, respect and the delicate and tragic love of a beautiful native girl.
A compelling film in which character relationships are brilliantly developed and a richness of human emotions are played out against the bizarre and torturous rituals of the primitive world.

Colour   88mins   'X'

WARNING
All rights of the producer and the owner of the work reproduced reserved. Unauthorized copying, hiring, lending, public performance, radio or T.V. broadcasting of this video recording prohibited.
© 1982 Derann Film Services Ltd.

Derann Audio Visual
99 High Street, Dudley
West Midlands, DY1 1QP
England

VHS

DEEP RIVER SAVAGES X

FDV 305

FROM THE MAKERS OF THE CHART TOPPING FILM 'CANNIBAL'

REVIEW

An earlier cannibal movie from the director of the brutal **Cannibal Ferox**, this exploitative effort once again does few favours for the south-east Asian tourist board. Rassimov is a photographer who kills a guy in a bar brawl in South America and then escapes into the jungle, where he falls into the hands of the cheerful flesh-chompers of the title. In a racist twist to the tale, the cannibals adopt this white fellow as their divine leader. But before joining the club he has to partake of the same munchies as them. Former TV presenter Me Me Lay is sexy as the chief's daughter who becomes Rassimov's bride. The film may have sympathetic characters, but that doesn't stand in the way of the gore. We get to see the top of a monkey's head whacked off with a sword, and far too much animal butchery. In a scene borrowed from **A Man Called Horse**, poor old Ivan is strung up and used as a human dart board for native blowpipes. A gruelling viewing experience.

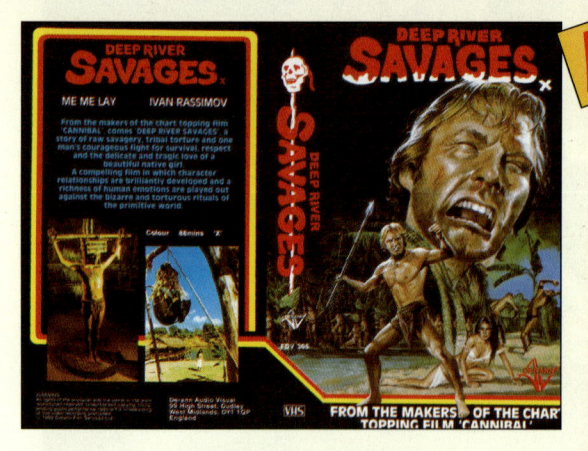

TITLE DEEP RIVER SAVAGES

AKA Il paese del sesso selvaggio; Au pays de l'exorcisme; Mondo Cannibale; Man from Deep River

DIRECTOR Umberto Lenzi

COUNTRY IT, THAI
SOURCE Derann (UK)
YEAR 1972
TIME 89m25s

CAST Ivan Rassimov, Me Me Lay, Prasitsak Singhara, Sulallewan Suxantat, Ong Ard, Prapas Chindang, Pipop Pupinyo, Tuan Tevan, Chit, Choi, Song Suanhud, Pairach Thaipradt.

PRODUCTION A Roas - Medusa Distribution Production. [prod] Ovidio Assonitis & Giorgio C. Rossi. [assoc prod] Stenio Fiorentini & Marcello Soffiantini. [exec prod] Giorgio C. Rossi. Roas produzione (Rome) - Medusa Distribuzione (Rome) - U.I.D. (Bangkok). © None.

PHOTOGRAPHY
DIRECTOR Riccardo Pallottini

MUSIC Daniele Patucchi
EDITOR Eugenio Alabiso

DVD Review

This movie was originally rejected for a UK cinema release in 1975. It was re-submitted for DVD release in the UK in 2003 by Screen Entertainment. Their disc is quite a nice-looking one, with trailer, photo gallery, an Umberto Lenzi filmography, extracts from the **Cannibal** movie book 'Eaten Alive' including production notes and 2 contemporary reviews. It's in 2.35:1 anamorphic. Trouble is, this version also has 3m 45s of cuts, removing the sight of some real animal cruelty (in this case setting a mongoose on a snake; locking a monkey into a vice and slicing off the top of its head; a cock fight; cutting a snake and bleeding it alive; and stabbing a crocodile in its neck with a small knife). There's a German release in 2.35:1 non-anamorphic PAL that is completely uncut, and the picture quality is very good, so this would seem to be the preferred version, even though it has less extras.

VTC
VideoTapeCenter

VIOLENT THRILLER

DELIRIUM

Starring:
TURK CEKOVSKY
DEBI SHANLEY
TERRY TEN BROCK
BARRON WINCHESTER

Director:
PETER MARIS

In a midwestern city Susan Narcross returns home one night to discover the body of her flatmate impaled on a spear. The only clue she can give detective is a man named Charlie whom Susan's boss had interviewed earlier in the day. The police are baffled by the murder as well as a series of suicides by known criminals. Charlie, an ex-Vietnam war veteran has escaped from a mental institution. He continually flashes back on the war as well as his own sexual impotence. He is hired as an assassin by a group of law and order businessmen headed by ex-Army officer Stern, to kill criminals who've escaped from justice. Unfortunately Charlie is out of control, killing where ever he finds a victim. Included are drowning a hitch hiker, running a pitch fork through the neck of a young farm girl and hacking to death a delivery man with a meat cleaver.

VTC
VideoTapeCenter

VTC Plc
14 Suffolk Street, Pall Mall, London SW1.

WARNING
ALL RIGHTS OF THE PRODUCER AND OF THE OWNER OF THE WORK REPRODUCED ARE RESERVED. UNAUTHORISED COPYING, HIRING, LENDING, PUBLIC PERFORMANCE, RADIO OR TV BROADCASTING OF THIS VIDEO RECORDING PROHIBITED BY LAW.

Colour 85 minutes
VTC 1022

DELIRIUM

VTC
VideoTapeCenter

VHS

VTC 1022

Colour 85 minutes
VTC 1022

REVIEW

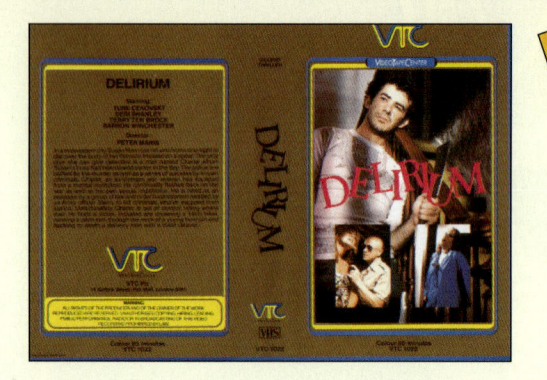

A low-budget shot-on-16mm independent film, blown up to 35mm for theatrical release. This is one of those movies that fosters the legends about Vietnam vets being killer time bombs waiting to explode and massacre large numbers of people. The story concerns members of a large underground organisation led by successful businessman (and Vietnam vet) Barron Winchester, who travel around executing criminals who have evaded justice. Things are going fine until one of their members snaps and goes on a killing spree, polishing off mainly pretty women. In the end the roommate of one of the victims helps two detectives trap the psycho killer. Poorly shot and edited, the movie uses flashbacks to explain why the killers were motivated to do what they did - it's something to do with an unpleasant experience with a Vietnamese hooker… The gore scenes are very tame, with unconvincing blood squibs. The film's unpleasantly misogynist point of view doesn't help. Everybody gets shot in the really confusing ending.

TITLE DELIRIUM

AKA Psycho Puppet (UK video re-title)

DIRECTOR Peter Maris

COUNTRY US
SOURCE VTC (UK)
YEAR 1980
TIME 84m29s

CAST Debi Chaney, Turk Cekovsky, Terry Ten Broek, Barron Winchester, Nick Pamouzis, Bob Winters, Garrett Bergfeld, Harry Gorsuch, Chris Chronopolis, Lloyd Schattyn, Jack Garvey, Mike Kalist, Myron Kosman, Rick Miller, Julie Hauck Vest, Joe Pollack, James Barry Simmerman, Dr. George Cantner Jr, Chief Eugene Camp, Police Officer Walleman, Bill Thomas, Gary Mandrell, Carol Emory, Melissa Higgins, Pat Knapko, Letty Garris, Jennifer C. Voges, Sherri Stevens, Richard Jones, Jon Frankel, Richard Yalem, David Basch, Mike Tierney, Decatur Agnew, Stephanie Maris, Todd Vest, Allen Maris, Charlotte Littrell, Randy Schulman, Glen Gelber, Dana Smith.

PRODUCTION Worlwide Productions presents… [prod] Sunny Vest & Peter Maris. [exec prod] Mark Cusumano. © 1980 Worlwide Productions, Inc.

PHOTOGRAPHY
DIRECTOR John Hudson & Bill Mensch

MUSIC David Williams
EDITOR Dan Perry

DVD Review

There is a US DVD of **Delirium**, but don't get confused because this Image release is actually a weird sex drama by Renato Polselli, starring former muscleman Mickey Hargitay. It's nothing to do with this down and dirty Viet vet thriller that remains one of the more obscure titles on the list. It's such a grimy little low budget movie and so grim and depressing in tone that it's hardly surprising nobody seems in the slightest bit interested in releasing it, though you can find it on tape in the US under the title of **Psycho Puppet**. The movie was never granted a certificate for UK cinema release, but it did get reissued on VHS here briefly with 16 seconds of violence trimmed. It seems likely that if it was reissued today it would get through uncut, but frankly nobody seems to care.

THE DEVIL HUNTER

The lovely Laura, on a modelling job in South America, is kidnapped by a gang who carry her off into the jungle from where they demand a huge ransom. Two men set off in a helicopter to rescue her, little knowing what horrors Laura is enduring in the meantime in the savage clutches of a primitive and bloodthirsty world. Laura's rescuers not only have to face the cruel violence of her captors — but also the horrifying lust for blood of a primitive and cruel god.

Al Cliver, Gisela Hahn, Robert Foster.
Running Time: 94 minutes

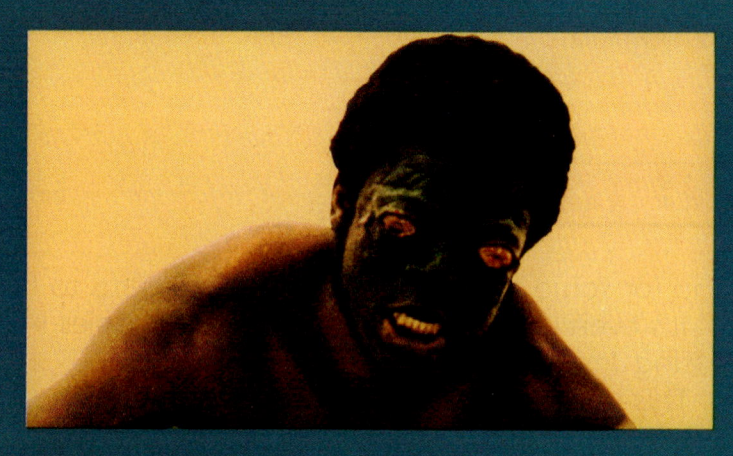

Enjoy the best films from the greatest film makers.

Exciting new titles are added monthly to our catalogue. To be placed on our mailing list and kept informed about our new releases, simply write to:

CINEHOLLYWOOD - Via Bellerio 30 - 20161 Milano - Italy.

© I.E. International Cinehollywood 1981.
This videotape is sold for private home use only. Not to be rented, leased or re-sold without the written permission of I.E. International Cinehollywood s.a.s. All other rights, privileges and licences including television, theatrical and commercial rights expressly reserved. The duplication of this videotape and/or this box is strictly prohibited. The price of this videocassette does not include the rental rights. Abuse in rental or loan of this videocassette will infringe the copyright laws and will result in prosecution.

V 1590

cinehollywood

THE DEVIL HUNTER

Al Cliver, Gisela Hahn, Robert Foster

pal vhs

colour videocassette pal vhs

REVIEW

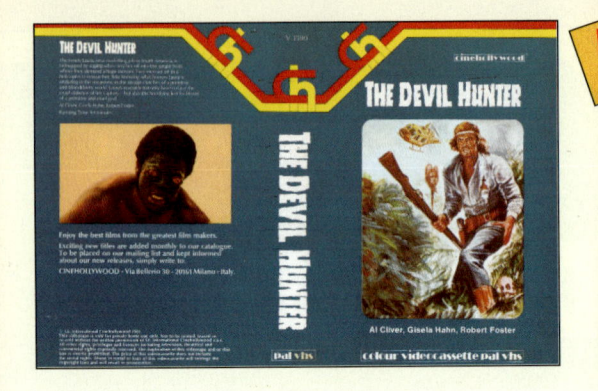

More Third World terrors, this time brought to us by our old favourite Jess Franco, hiding under yet another of his many pseudonyms. Starlet Ursula Fellner is on a modelling job in South America when she is abducted by a gang who carry her off into the jungle to model a fetching grass skirt. Held captive in a jungle village by a big black guy with eyes like ping pong balls (who calls himself The Devil) our terrified heroine must undergo various native rituals and take her clothes off frequently while her kidnappers make ransom demands. Heroic Al Cliver is the Indiana Jones clone dispatched to rescue Ursula, and he seems to take forever to do it. At one point he scales a mountain in much the same silly manner as Batman used to climb tall buildings in the 60s TV show - the camera is laid on its side and Cliver is filmed crawling across the floor! Thoroughly inept in every department, why this remains banned in the UK to this day is pretty much a mystery - but it's also a mercy.

TITLE DEVIL HUNTER

AKA Sexo Canibal; Il Cacciatore Di Uomini; Jungfrau unterKannibalen; Man Hunter

DIRECTOR Jesús Franco (as Clifford Brown)

COUNTRY SP, FR, WG
SOURCE Cinehollywood (UK)
YEAR 1980
TIME 85m23s

CAST Ursula Fellner (Ursula Buchfellner), Al Cliver (Pier Luigi Conti), Robert Foster (Antonio Mayans), Antonio De Cabo, Gisella Hahn. [and uncredited] Burt Altman, Victoria Adams, Leonardo da Costa, Lynn Mess (Aline Mess), Claude Boisson, Tibi Costa, Oscar Cortina, Ana Paula.

PRODUCTION I.E. Films Productions. [dir of prod] Joaquin Dominguez. A co-production of J.E. Films (Madrid) - Eurocine (Paris) - Lisa Film (Munich). © 1980 I.E. Films.

PHOTOGRAPHY DIRECTOR Juan Soler Cozar

MUSIC Jesús Franco & Pablo Villa (Daniel White)

EDITOR Federico Vich Iglesias & Gise Neuman

DVD Review

This movie remains banned in the UK, and for some strange reason nobody seems to have picked it up to re-present it to the BBFC. It's even odder that none of the companies in Germany or France who have been releasing Jess Franco flicks have added this to their list. This was censored for sexual imagery as well as cannibal violence, so maybe that explains it. If you want to see this nowadays the only option is to go the bootleg DVD-R route. There are a couple of discs available from French and Dutch sources that look like they were taken from the old VHS tapes! Presented full frame with no extras at all, the cheap laser copy covers make it obvious that you're getting a bog s tandard effort. Strictly for Franco completists – and if you're out there, accept my condolences!

DON'T GO IN THE HOUSE

You have been warned

Donny Kohler is sick. Very sick. He was cruelly abused as a child by his mother.

He is 27 years old now and his mother is dead.

Her death changes him – a long-dormant psychosis is brought to life. He methodically prepares his revenge. His first victim is a beautiful young girl. He burns her alive in a metal room he has built for vengeance. He cannot stop killing once he's committed this first gruesome murder. He keeps the horribly charred corpses in the house with him, dressed in mother's finest gowns. He shares his feelings and thoughts with them in a way he never could with living people, but suddenly a form of conscience begins causing him nightmares and hallucinations.

Donny Kohler is lost in the terror of his own life... and the final revenge comes from his victims.

Running time: 81 mins   Uncensored
A GTO film release

Copyright restricts the videocassette recording to private use by individuals. All other uses including other performances whether or not public and whether or not for gain including broadcasting are prohibited without the previous written consent of the copyright owner which may be applied for through VideoSpace Ltd.

Arcade Video distributing through VideoSpace

VIDEOSPACE
always more selective

272, London Road, Wallington, Surrey SM6 7DJ. Telephone: 01-773 0921/0922. Telex: 943 763.

Arcade video HiQu

High Quality Performance

In a steel room built for revenge they die burning... in chains.

DON'T GO IN THE HOUSE

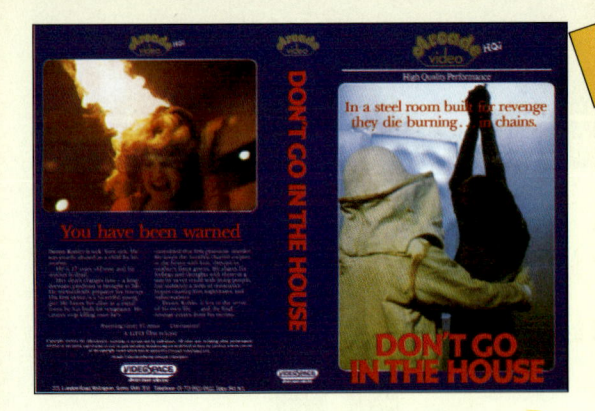

REVIEW

Nerdy Dan Grimaldi has a poor start in life being tortured by his mad mum, who liked to hold his arms above naked flames. Now he's all grown up, and has murdered mom and roasted her, keeping her crispy corpse around for company. In his spare time he kidnaps women (after cruising discos in his Travolta gear) and locks them in the fireproof basement of his house, where he burns them to death. This is a gloatingly repulsive movie in which all the female characters are bimbos or bitches (or both) and the hero is a macho jerk. Strangely enough, it was co-written by a woman! There are some good, almost too realistic make-up effects (by Tom Brumberger), but this film is just too sleazy and shoddily assembled to appeal as engrossing entertainment. The climax bears a suspicious similarity to the ending of **Maniac**. It was originally to have been called **The Burning**, but another movie beat them to it. Unlike the killer's victims, this one is not well done.

TITLE	DON'T GO IN THE HOUSE
AKA	The Burning
DIRECTOR	Joseph Ellison
COUNTRY	US
SOURCE	Videospace/Arcade (UK)
YEAR	1979
TIME	79m01s

CAST Dan Grimaldi, Charlie Bonet, Bill Ricci, Robert Osth, Dennis M. Hunter, John Hedberg, Ruth Dardick, Johanna Brushay, Darcy Sheen, Mary Ann Chin, Lois Verk, Susan Smith, Jim Donnegan, Claudia Folts, Denise Woods, Pat Williams, Colin McInnes, Ralph D. Bowman, Joey Peschi, Connie Oaks, David McComb, Jean Manning, Ken Kelsch, Tom Brumberger, Nikki Kollins, Kim Roberts, Louise Grimaldi, Commander Johhny G, Gloria Srymkovicz, David Brody, O'Mara Leary, Gail Turner, Christian ?, Eileen Dunn. [not listed on end credits] Jane Kurson, Richard Einhorn, Joseph R. Masefield.

PRODUCTION Film Ventures International. Turbine Films Presents... [prod] Ellen Hammill. [assoc prod] Mathew Mallinson & Dennis Stephenson. © 1979 Turbine Films, Inc.

PHOTOGRAPHY DIRECTOR

MUSIC Ted Daryll & Bill Heller
EDITOR Jane Kurson

DVD Review

Don't Go In The House was submitted to the BBFC in 2001 and passed with cuts of three minutes and seven seconds. Our old friends at VIPCO were behind this one, and served up a disc and tape that had plainly been sourced from an old VHS tape master. The most sensible advice, therefore, was Don't Go In The Video Shop to buy this. The only uncut DVD available is a cheap region free version that was released in 1999 by a company called Digital Versatile Disc. This presents the film in full frame with a very poor quality transfer that again looks like it may have been sourced from a VHS master of a very scratchy print with tons of grain. The flame sequences often white out the image. There are no extras on the disc and the audio is similarly lousy. I can't imagine that this film ever looked great, but a decent home video version of it remains elusive.

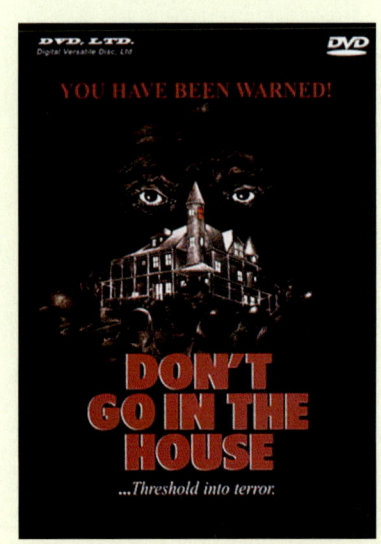

HOME VIDEO MOVIE

V.R.O.

Running time approx. 88 minutes

Don't Go in The Woods ...alone!

Four young campers, Craig, Peter, Ingrid and Joannie, back-pack through the mountains for a relaxing weekend in the wilderness.

They enter a forest which becomes denser and darker as they progress. Peter (*Nick McClelland*) and Ingrid (*Mary Galeartz*) fear they are lost. The brush moves and something is there. Suddenly a large form rushes forward. A wide machete gleaming in the light falls fast. Craig, (*James P. Hayden*) slips dead to the ground.

Peter and the others flee screaming into the forest. The rest of the day and terrifying night is spent running and hiding from the maniac murderer (*Tom Drury*) who is constantly in pursuit.

video network
DISTRIBUTORS OF VIDEO MOVIES
TEL: 01 553 2860

COPYRIGHT NOTICE

The Copyright proprietor has licensed these films contained in these video cassettes for private home use only and other use including making copies of the films, causing them to be seen or heard in public or broadcasting them or causing them to be transmitted to subscribers to a diffusion service or selling, letting on hire or otherwise dealing with them in whole or in part is strictly prohibited.

Don't Go in The Woods ...alone!

VHS

VN0012

Everyone has nightmares about the ugliest way to die.

Don't Go in The Woods ...alone!

R WARNING
CONTAINS SCENES OF GRAPHIC VIOLENCE

Starring NICK McCLELLAND
JAMES P. HAYDEN · KEN CARTER & TOM DRURY as The Monster

MANSON INTERNATIONAL
Copyright © 1981 Double S Productions (Astral) Ltd. all rights reserved

VIDEO RELEASING ORGANIZATION

REVIEW

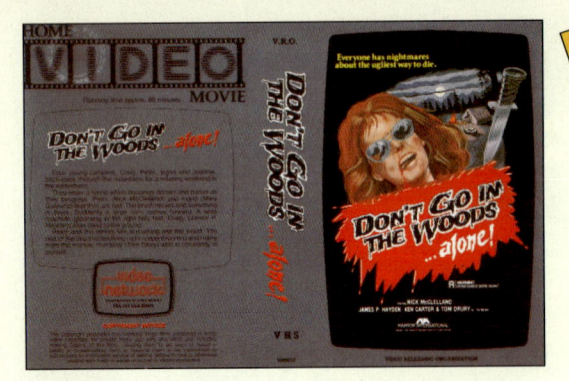

TITLE	DON'T GO IN THE WOODS
AKA	Don't go in the Woods... Alone! (UK video cover title)
DIRECTOR	James Bryan
COUNTRY	US
SOURCE	Video Network (UK)
YEAR	1980
TIME	78m15s

CAST Jack McClelland, Mary Gail Artz, James P. Hayden, Angie Brown, Ken Carter, David Barth, Larry Roupe, Amy Martell, Tom Drury, Laura Trefts, Alma Ramos, Carolyn Braza, Frank Clitus Muller, McCormick Dalten, Cecilia Fannon, Dale Angell, Ruth Grose, Hank Zinman, Leon Brown Jr, Linda Brown, Gerry Klein, Tom Ruff, Valetta Saunders, John Williams, Jeff Wood, Randy Kleffer, Jarne Harbrecht, Ann St.Michael, Bonnie Harris, Matt Noone, Matt Muller, Garth Eliassen, Susan Farris, T. Ruff, Bill Stockdale, Ebin Whiting, Brad Carter, Randy Kleffer, Eben Whitney, David Wiggins, John Warren, Paul Thorpe, Joan Forrester, Pam Srubaugh-Littig, Tawnya Crespin, Pat J. Winn, Franky Crespin, Amy Oliphant, Patrick Satterwaithe, Anne Marie Nagenga, Suzy Folsom, Eric Jenkins.

PRODUCTION JBF presents... [prod] Roberto Gomez & Suzette Gomez. [assoc prod] William Stockdale. © None.

PHOTOGRAPHY DIRECTOR Hank Zinman

MUSIC EDITOR H. Kingsley Thurber
Not credited

Don't Waste Your Money might be a more appropriate title. It's unbelievable that this stupid film managed to make the video nasty list - it's so badly made and has such crappy special effects that even the least discriminating of horror fans will have a tough time sitting through it. A bunch of unlucky teenage campers ignore the title warning and head off into the woods of Utah for a dreary confrontation with a limb-ripping "Wild Man". There's no script to speak of, just endless shots of people wandering through the woods accompanied by what must be one of the worst musical scores ever written. The photography is abysmal, and most of the time you can't even see what's going on. Squint hard and you might catch two men having plastic arms lopped off, a chap getting his face crushed in a bear trap, and several girls being butchered in their sleeping bags. In the end the murderer is hunted down by the sheriff, a fat cat who looks like he has more lunches than hunches. But it's up to two vengeful victims to give the maniac the treatment he deserves. If you can sit through this one then you can sit through anything.

DVD Review

Still banned in the UK for reasons that remain unfathomable to sensible folk, this one's only going to come into your possession if you spot an old tape copy at a car boot, film fair or Cash Converters. Or alternately you could order a bootleg DVD-R on the net – but be warned these are well nigh unwatchable full screen transfers that make the original VHS versions look like remastered Special Editions! It's worth making the effort though, if only to experience the immortal words of one of the best end title songs ever committed to celluloid:

"Don't go into the woods tonight, you probably will be thrilled.
Don't go into the woods tonight, you probably will be killed.
There's a friendly beast that lurks about,
And likes to feast, you won't get out,
Without being killed and chopped up in little pieces."

Don't Go Near the Park

12,000 YEARS AGO a brother and sister are condemned to perpetual dying but never death by their evil mother Petronella.

To stave off their premature ageing they have to rejuvinate their bodies by consuming human flesh. Their only salvation is to wait until the planets have completed a revolution of the Zodiac and the moon is flanked by the twin stars of the wolf. On this night they have to find a young virgin and sacrifice her soul in exchange for their own. If they succeed they will achieve eternal life, if they fail damnation for all eternity.

**THAT NIGHT IS TONIGHT...
DON'T GO NEAR THE PARK...!**

INTERVISION VIDEO LIMITED
1, McKAY TRADING ESTATE, KENSAL ROAD, LONDON, W10

© INTERNATIONAL COPYRIGHT PROTECTION. Warning: Copyright subsists in all recordings issued under this label for private home use only and prohibits any other use. Unauthorised broadcasting, public performance, copying or re-recording in any manner whatsoever is prohibited, not to be re-sold, hired out, exchanged, or leased without the prior written permission of Intervision Video Limited.

DESIGNED BY MORRIS ASSOCIATES

HORROR COLOUR
A-AE 0429

Home VIDEO Productions

Don't Go Near the Park

VHS

intervision
THE FIRST NAME IN VIDEO
THE LAST WORD IN ENTERTAINMENT

Produced & Directed by
LAWRENCE D FOLDES

starring
ALDO RAY

DISTRIBUTED BY
intervision
THE FIRST NAME IN VIDEO
THE LAST WORD IN ENTERTAINMENT

HORROR - COLOUR
A-AE 0429

REVIEW

A really obscure and generally unmemorable vampire flick which kicks off with the bizarre statement that: "This film is fiction, though it is based on actual occurrences which happened over the centuries." Fair enough. After a prologue in which a curse of eternal damnation is placed on some kids, we move forward 12,000 years or so to the present day, where the kids are still around. It seems they've been surviving on a diet of ripped-open stomachs, but the centuries haven't sharpened up their acting skills. The disembowelling scenes are obviously what attracted the DPP's attention, since the rest of the movie is so damn pathetic, with some of the most abysmal effects ever committed to celluloid. Linnea Quigley turns up in one of her first film performances and promptly gets her togs off as usual. She plays a supernatural brat named Bondy, who is given a glowing amulet that makes rapists explode. You probably need to be on some kind of medication to enjoy this. The director went on to make the trashy Linda Blair vehicle, **Night Force**.

TITLE DON'T GO NEAR THE PARK

AKA Nightstalker; Curse of the Living Dead

DIRECTOR Lawrence D. Foldes

COUNTRY US
SOURCE Intervision (UK)
YEAR 1979
TIME 80m00s

CAST Aldo Ray, Meeno Peluce, Tamara Taylor, Barbara Monker, Crackers Phinn, Linnea Quigley, Chris Riley, Lara Morann, Earl Statler, Cambra Foldes, K. L. Garber, David Ariniello, Steven Lovy, Janet Giglio, Doug White, Steven Leider, Rich Buendia, Stephan Hun, Nicholas J. Vincent, Mark Meadows, Lawrence D. Foldes, Linwood Chase, Shane O'Brien, Beverly Bruce, Marlene Warner, Gabor Lovy, Inez M. Dugan, Audrey Bruce, Barry Friedman, John Racine, Andrew Rowe, John Raisin, Peter Carpenter, Marcus Carpenter, David Cole, Walter C. Snyder, Kirstin Fife, Leigh Ash, Stephanie Fuller, Sherrie McRae, Stephanie R. Perkins, Michele Chamber.

PRODUCTION A Star Cinema Production. [prod] Lawrence D. Foldes.[exec prod] George Foldes. © 1979 Star Cinema Productions.

PHOTOGRAPHY DIRECTOR William DeDiago

MUSIC Chris Ledesma
EDITOR Dan Perry

DVD Review

This was one of the first films to be officially 'pardoned' and released from the list. It went to live a quiet life in the suburbs as a decent law-abiding citizen and was never heard of again. That's about true, actually, since this ultra-cheap effort quickly disappeared off the radar and rarely resurfaces, even at car boot sales. The original VHS tapes were of such dreadful quality that nobody even bothered to bootleg this as a DVD-R. However, I did hear as we were going to press on this book that Salvation UK were planning a restored special edition DVD for 2004. I'll believe it when I see it, but it hardly seems something to get excited about .

From the makers of: THE LAST HOUSE ON THE LEFT.

Don't Look in the Basement

**WILLIAM BILL McGHEE   JESSIE LEE FULTON
ROBERT DRACUP   HARRYETTE WARREN**

Brilliantly convincing performances heightened by thoughtfully moody photography combine to make this a tension filled terror picture with heart stopping shocks and an ingeniously unexpected twist in the tail.

The story is set in a private sanatorium where the unusual methods involve total integration between staff and patients. A new nurse arrives to take up the post she has been offered by Dr Stephens who is fatally attacked by a patient just before the girl's arrival. Dr Masters takes over, and with the nurses' help intends to restore calm.

The girl confronted by some of the bizarre patients, finds it difficult to adjust to their strange, unnerving ways. A feeling of unease creeps over her. All is not as it should be, and a series of frightening outbursts from the patients and horrifying attacks herald the terrible conclusion.

1hr 35mins 'R'

CRYSTAL VIDEO

WARNING
All rights of the producer and the owner of the work reproduced reserved. Unauthorized copying, hiring, lending, public performance, radio or T.V. broadcasting of this video recording prohibited.
© 1983 Deranri Film Services Ltd.

Derann Audio Visual
99 High Street, Dudley
West Midlands, DY1 1QP
England

FCV 604

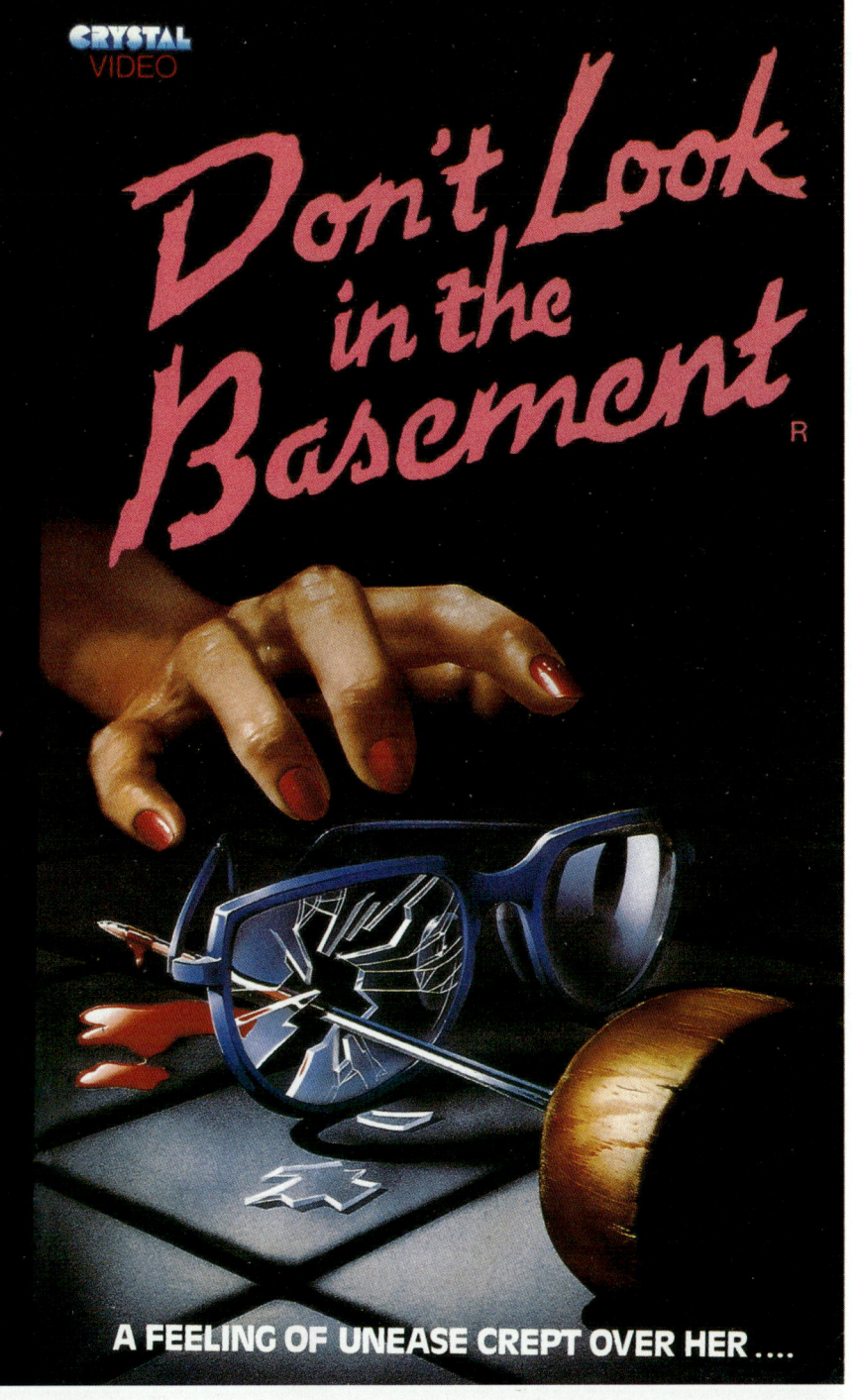

VHS

Don't Look in the Basement

CRYSTAL VIDEO

R

A FEELING OF UNEASE CREPT OVER HER....

REVIEW

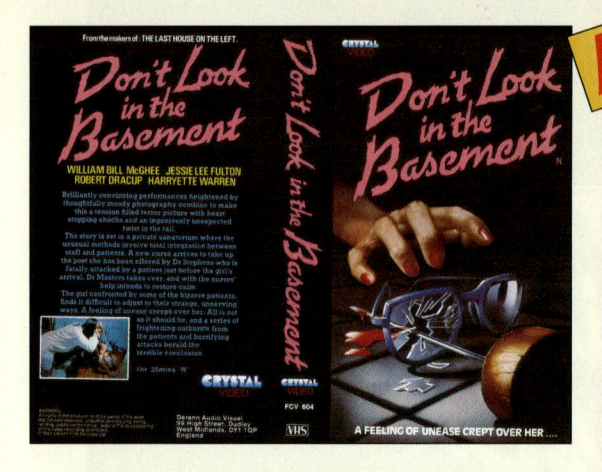

Care In The Community reaches its logical conclusion and the inmates take over the asylum in this celebrated sleaze horror yarn from Texas filmmaker Brownrigg. Rosie Holotik is the psycho patient who assumes control of a loony bin when the director of the place is butchered. People then begin to meet violent and gory deaths until only one person remains. It's difficult to imagine an odder bunch of characters. There's a girl who thinks a doll is her baby, a big black guy with the brain of an infant, and an axe-wielding judge - and that's just the staff! Gore scenes include the Director of the asylum having his bonce removed with an axe and a receptionist getting her tongue ripped out. The funniest sequence has a couple of frisky old ladies stabbing some telephone repairmen to death for rejecting their sexual advances! Quite well done of its kind, this was a massive hit at American drive-ins and was originally advertised with that hoary old slogan: "Just keep telling yourself it's only a movie!"

TITLE DON'T LOOK IN THE BASEMENT

AKA NONE

DIRECTOR S. F. Brownrigg

COUNTRY US
SOURCE Derann (UK)
YEAR 1973
TIME 78m43s

CAST William Bill McGhee, Jessie Lee Fulton, Robert Dracup, Harryette Warren, Michael Feagin, Betty Chandler, Camilla Carr, Gene Ross, Anne MacAdams, Rosie Holotik, Rhea MacAdams.

PRODUCTION Camera 2 Productions in association with Century Studios presents... [prod] S. F. Brownrigg. [exec prod] Walter L. Krusz. © None.

PHOTOGRAPHY DIRECTOR Robert Alcott

MUSIC Robert Farrar
EDITOR Jerry Caraway

DVD Review

Passed with cuts for an X-certificate UK cinema release, this movie was eventually removed from the DPP Nasties list, but it has never been put out on video or DVD in an uncut form. I can't imagine it doing great business if it was. There is, however, an uncut region free US disc on the VCI label. The quality of the fullscreen transfer is not great. It has a lot of grain and the print used is pretty scratchy in places, but it's a step above a DVD-R and we get a decent selection of trailers and text-based extras. As of time of writing it has been reported that there is a special edition of the movie in the works which has been sanctioned by the director, who will also supply a commentary, but this may just be internet gossip. Just keep saying to yourself, 'It's only a movie…'

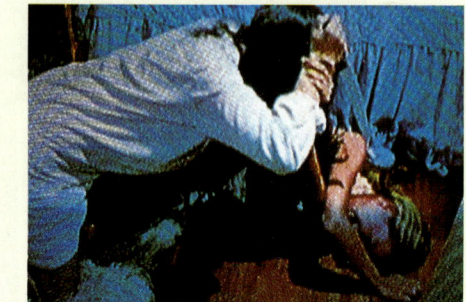

THE DRILLER KILLER

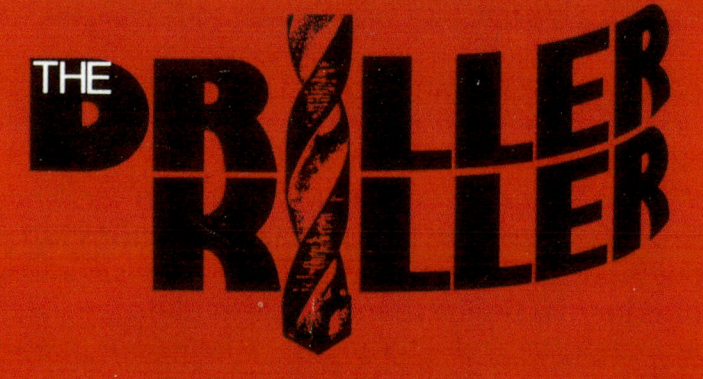

THE BLOOD RUNS IN RIVERS...

As the screaming drill closes on its victim you don't really believe what you are seeing . . . until blood starts pouring and another tearing scream joins the drill.
A steel stomach is required to watch the final scenes of mayhem.

WARNING
"The copyright proprietor has licensed the film contained in this videocassette for private home use only. Any other use including making copies of the film, causing it to be seen or heard in public or broadcasting it or causing to be transmitted to subscribers to a diffusion service, letting on hire or otherwise dealing with it in part or any kind of exchange scheme is strictly prohibited. Any breach of the above conditions render the offender liable to prosecution by Video Instant Picture Company Limited".

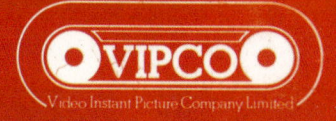

VIPCO
Video Instant Picture Company Limited

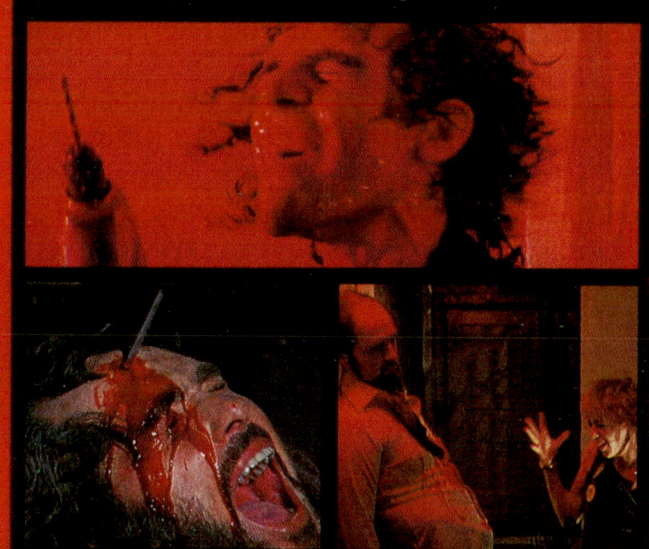

VHS VIDEO CASSETTE

THE BLOOD RUNS IN RIVERS...

...AND THE DRILL KEEPS TEARING THROUGH FLESH AND BONE

THE DRILLER KILLER

VIPCO

SEE WARNING ON REVERSE

Starring: Carolyn Marz, Jimmy Laine & Bavbi Day
Music by: Joseph Felia.
Directed by: Abel Ferrara. Produced by: Mavaron Films.
Running Time 84 Minutes

REVIEW

This odd punk horror fable from maverick (and now mainstream) director Ferrara is unlikely ever to be seen in the UK because it was successfully prosecuted as a video nasty back in the bad old days before the Video Recordings Act. The director himself stars (using the acting *nom-de-plume* of Jimmy Laine) as a druggy loony who sets about clearing the winos from the streets of New York by select use of a portable power drill. The film has no money for gory special effects but is shot in a documentary style that is convincing. The problem is that it doesn't make it as entertainment, having no interesting characters to empathise with and no real beginning or end - it just sort of fades out in an unsatisfactory fashion. Considering its reputation, this is surprisingly unexploitative. Writer Nicholas St John is a regular collaborator with Ferrara, and the two went on to make the far superior **MS 45**. Along with **I Spit On Your Grave**, this notorious movie is most often cited as having kicked off the video nasties furore in the UK. In fact it was VIPCO's lurid advertising for the film - full page colour ads showing a drill going into a guy's bonce - that made it an obvious main attraction for the private viewing cinema in the basement of Scotland Yard!

TITLE	DRILLER KILLER, THE
AKA	NONE
DIRECTOR	Abel Ferrara
COUNTRY	US
SOURCE	Vipco (UK)
YEAR	1979
TIME	85m10s

CAST Jimmy Laine (Abel Ferrara), Carolyn Marz, Baybi Day, Harry Schultz, Alan Wynroth, Maria Helhoski, James O'Hara, Richard Howorth, Louis Mascolo, Tommy Santora, Rita Gooding, Chuck Saaf, Janet Dailey, Joyce Finney, Dutch Morris, Paul Fitze, John Fitze, Karl Metner, Chris Amato, Rich Bokun, Michael Canosa, Greg Schirrira, Thomas Baeza, Frank Hazard, Jack MacIntyre, John Coulakis, Lanny Taylor, Peter Yellen, Steve Cox, Stephen Singer, Tom Constantine, Anthony Picciano, Bob De Frank, Rhodney Montreal, Dicky Bittner, Steve Brown, Laurie Y. Taylor, Trixie Sly, Andrea Childs, Hallie Coletta, Victoria Keiler, Claire Mailer, Paula Nichols.

PRODUCTION A Rochelle Films release. Navaron Films presents... [prod] Navaron Films. [exec prod] Rochelle Weisberg. [assoc prod] Douglas Anthony Metro. © 1979 Rochelle Films.

PHOTOGRAPHY DIRECTOR Ken Kelsch

MUSIC EDITOR Joseph Delia, The Roosters Orlando Gallini, Bonnie Constant, Michael Constant & Jimmy Laine (Abel Ferrara)

DVD Review

Driller Killer was banned in the UK until 1999, then passed with 54 seconds of cuts. The main cuts were to the head drilling scene but two earlier drill killings also suffered. 46 seconds of footage was added to smooth over some of the gaps. It was eventually passed uncut in 2002. Visual's Region 2 disc (cut) has an introductory commentary by cult film academic of the University of Nottingham, Xavier Mendik, plus bonus trailers for **Atolladero**, **The Holy Mountain**, **Possession**, and **The Washing Machine**. There's also a filmography for director Abel Ferrara. The film is presented in 4:3 non anamorphic PAL. The version to buy is the later ILC Prime R2 disc which is uncut and features an audio commentary with director Abel Ferrara, a theatrical trailer, a filmography for Abel Ferrara and is in 1.85:1 non anamorphic PAL. The best-looking version is a R2 French edition which has an English track and is anamorphic.

'THE ULTIMATE EXPERIENCE IN GRUELLING TERROR'
'PURE HORROR' CITY LIMITS

SAM RAIMI'S
THE EVIL DEAD

PRODUCED BY ROBERT TAPERT· SAM RAIMI· BRUCE CAMPBELL·
DIRECTED BY SAM RAIMI· STARRING BRUCE CAMPBELL· ELLEN SANDWEISS· BETSY BAKER· HAL DELRICH· SARAH YORK·
MUSIC BY JOE LODUCA· SPECIAL EFFECTS BY BART PIERCE· RENAISSANCE PICTURES LTD·

'SUPREMELY WELL DONE. THE HORROR'S UNRELENTING AND SUPERBLY SUSTAINED; THE SPECIAL EFFECTS ARE MARVELLOUS; AND THE GUT'N'GORE ARE LADLED OUT WITH SUCH CECIL B.DeMILLE EXCESS THAT YOU'D HAVE TO BE UTTERLY WITHOUT HUMOUR NOT TO FIND THE FILM OFTEN FUNNY' VIDEO TIMES

'SET TO TAKE OVER WHERE CRONENBERG AND ROMERO LEAVE OFF. THE KIND OF CAPTIVATING, ROLLERCOASTER ENERGY THAT TYPIFIED HOLLYWOOD AT ITS GREATEST. NO HORROR FAN SHOULD MISS IT' SID LANGLEY (NORTHAMPTONSHIRE) EVENING TELEGRAPH

'A BLACK RAINBOW OF HORROR' STEPHEN KING

'SHOT WITH A DEVASTATING POWERFUL FLAIR... SEE THE EVIL DEAD AND GASP' ALAN JONES-CINEMA

'I LOVED EVERY DISGUSTING MINUTE' NME

— IN THE LITERARY TRADITION OF STEPHEN KING (THE WORLD'S TOP-SELLING HORROR AUTHOR — CARRIE, THE SHINING, SALEM'S LOT) AND IN THE CINEMATIC MODE OF GEORGE ROMERO (NIGHT OF THE LIVING DEAD, ZOMBIES) AND WITH THE COMIC STRIP GUSTO OF E.C. COMICS (WEIRD TALES, UNCANNY TALES ETC.) 'EVIL DEAD' IS A VISUAL AND AURAL ATTACK ON THE SENSES WHICH REQUIRES A STRONG STOMACH AND A HEALTHY SENSE OF HUMOUR. WHILST HOLIDAYING IN THE TENNESSEE WOODLANDS, FIVE INNOCENT TEENAGERS UNWITTINGLY UNLEASH THE SPIRIT OF THE EVIL DEAD — WHICH POSSESSES FIRST THE TREES AND THEN THE BODIES OF THE FRIENDS THEMSELVES. THE DEMONIC MONSTERS CAN ONLY BE HALTED IN THEIR FRENZIED FLESH-EATING RAMPAGE BY THE ACT OF BODILY DISMEMBERMENT.......
TENSION MOUNTS AS ONE BY ONE THE TEENAGERS FALL VICTIM TO THE DIABOLICAL SUMERIAN SPIRIT UNTIL FINALLY, AMIDST A TOUR-DE-FORCE DISPLAY OF SPECIAL EFFECTS THE LONE SURVIVOR SOLVES THE MYSTERY WHICH HAS UNLEASHED THE NIGHTMARISH TERROR........

A PALACE PICTURES RELEASE USA 1982.

"WARNING — The copyright proprietor has licensed the film (including its soundtrack) comprised in this videocassette for home use only. All other rights are reserved. Any unauthorised copying, editing, exhibition, renting, exchanging, hiring, lending, public performances, diffusion and/or broadcast of this videocassette or any part thereof is strictly prohibited." Marketed and Distributed by PALACE VIDEO LTD, 275-277 Pentonville Rd, London N1. 01-278 0751

SAM RAIMI'S **THE EVIL DEAD**

COLOUR
APPROX 90 MINS
PVC 2018A

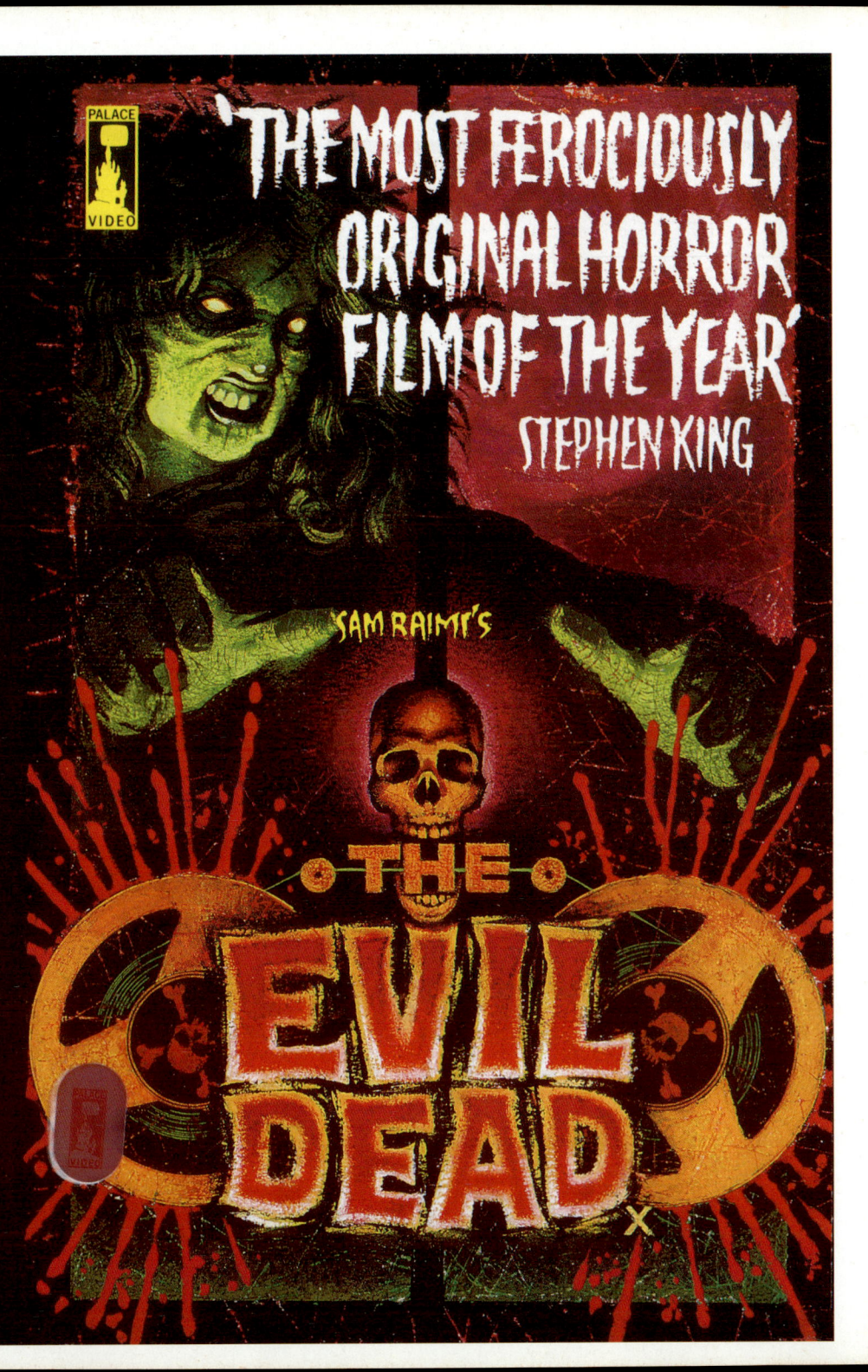

'THE MOST FEROCIOUSLY ORIGINAL HORROR FILM OF THE YEAR'
STEPHEN KING

SAM RAIMI'S
THE EVIL DEAD

REVIEW

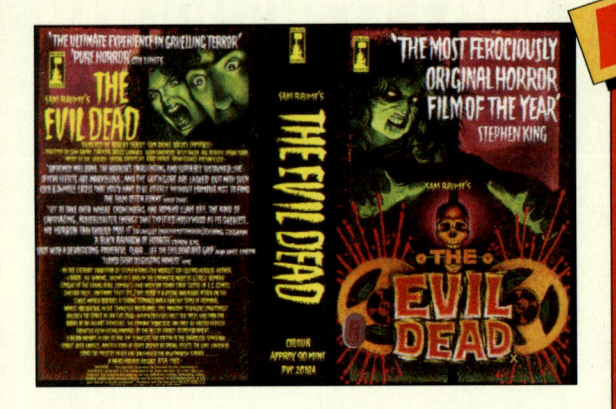

TITLE	EVIL DEAD, THE
AKA	Book of the Dead (shooting title)
DIRECTOR	Sam Raimi
COUNTRY	US
SOURCE	Palace (UK)
YEAR	1982
TIME	80m49s
CAST	Bruce Campbell, Ellen Sandweiss, Hal Delrich, Betsy Baker, Sarah York.
PRODUCTION	Renaissance Pictures presents... [prod] Robert Tapert. [exec prod] Robert Tapert, Bruce Campbell & Sam Raimi. © 1982 Renaissance Pictures Ltd.
PHOTOGRAPHY DIRECTOR	Tim Philo
MUSIC	Joe Loduca
EDITOR	Edna Ruth Paul

Sam Raimi's seminal horror classic came along at the birth of the video explosion, before the market was glutted with cheap looking shot-on-video rubbish. In fact watching it again today reveals how superior it is to its hundreds of shoddy imitators, and Sam Raimi's direction is so stylish and inventive that it is little wonder he has managed to move on to a successful Hollywood career. 22-year-old Raimi shot the picture for about $250,000, money which he raised by going door-to-door with his investment package - most of the investors were doctors, dentists and estate agents! You all know the plot: five teenagers take shelter in an abandoned cabin deep in the woods. Inside they find an audio tape and an arcane volume which turns out to be the **Sumerian Book Of The Dead**. The tape translates some of the incantations in the book and giant demons are unleashed in the woods. One by one the teenagers are taken over by the demons, who have to be chopped into little pieces before they can be completely destroyed! Well shot on 16mm, with what looks like impressive steadicam photography (but was in fact achieved by strapping a camera to a motorbike and racing through the woods with it), this is straight-ahead horror that sets out purely and simply to frighten the living daylights out of a teen audience. The effects are generally pretty poor, but they are yukky and plentiful and work brilliantly in context. The tree rape is the most unpleasant scene, and it's a bit at odds with the breezy tone of the rest of the movie. In retrospect Sam says he wishes he had taken it out. Also pretty ghastly is the card-reading sequence where a demon plunges a pencil into Ellen Sandweiss' ankle and twists it about a bit! The film is only for genuine horror devotees who want a darn good scare leavened with a sizeable dose of tongue-in-cheek black humour. A cause célèbre in the "Nasties" debate of the early 80s, **The Evil Dead** led to two sequels, neither of which was a patch on the original.

DVD Review

Nowadays this is the easiest of all the Nasties to find on DVD, and your only problem is deciding which version you would rather have in your collection. It seems strange to think that when the film was originally resubmitted to the BBFC in 1990 they demanded slight cuts. These were later rescinded and all new versions are totally uncut. The movie came out on laserdisc and then DVD from Elite a few years ago. Then Anchor Bay USA gave us a spiffy Special Edition featuring an audio commentary with director/writer Sam Raimi and producer Robert Tapert, and a second audio commentary with actor Bruce Campbell. The package also included a theatrical trailer, photo gallery, outtakes, deleted scenes, TV spots etc. This disc presents the film in an anamorphic 1.85 aspect ratio authorised by director Sam Raimi, but is a re-framed version based on the 4:3 original. Anchor Bay UK's limited Book Of The Dead packaging edition was fun, but the edition of choice has to be the 2003 Anchor Bay UK box set of all three **Evil Dead** movies. You get the entire trilogy, plus a fourth disc containing loads of great extras - including yours truly rabbiting on about the film - and you get the first **Evil Dead** in its original 1.33:1 full screen unmatted version (with Dolby Digital 5.1 and DTS-ES 6.1 audio choices). The only sad thing about all of these releases is that none of them contain Raimi's **Within The Woods** short - a film that remains tantalisingly unavailable for obscure legal reasons.

Evilspeak

Stanley Coopersmith is the bumbling misfit of the West Andover Military Academy, a buffoon on the soccer field and the parade ground, and the victim of the cruellest practical jokes.

Deep beneath the college chapel, sealed-off for centuries, he finds the hidden sanctuary of a satanic priest.

Here Stanley escapes his tormenting classmates. In this solitary and haunted vault he discovers a secret hoard of old demonic books that reveal the mysteries of the Satanic Arts. But only the college computer can unleash the terryfying wrath of satan's dark heart.

Through the computer Stanley makes contact with the powers of darkness and together this deadly combination deliver an appalling Judgement on every one of his tormentors.

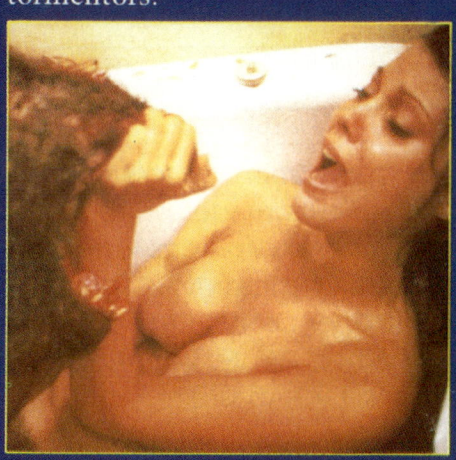

The last word in terror

HAYWOOD NELSON/DON STARK/CHARLES TYNER/Director of Photography IRV GOODNOFF
Associate Producers GERALD HOPMAN and H. HAL HARRIS/Executive Producer SYLVIO TABET
Screenplay by JOSEPH GAROFALO and ERIC WESTON Based on a Story by JOSEPH GAROFALO
Produced by SYLVIO TABET and ERIC WESTON Directed by ERIC WESTON
A LEISURE INVESTMENT COMPANY Release/Distributed by THE MORENO COMPANY, INC.

Copyright restricts the video cassette recording to private use by individuals. All other uses including other performances whether or not public and whether or not for gain including broadcasting are prohibited without the previous written consent of the copyright owner which may be applied for through VideoSpace Ltd.

Licensed from FilmTown

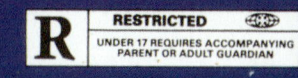

VideoSpace — always more selective

RESTRICTED — UNDER 17 REQUIRES ACCOMPANYING PARENT OR ADULT GUARDIAN

272 London Road, Wallington, Surrey SM6 7DJ. Tel: 01-773 0921/2. Telex: 8812571 VSPACE.G

Data incomplete... Human blood required
THUS SPAKE THE COMPUTER.

Evilspeak

Executive Producer	Musical Score	Special Effects
SYLVIO TABET	**ROGER KELLAWAY**	**BOB BAILEY**
Freedom Road	A Star is Born	Star Trek
Fade to Black		Superman

REVIEW

Clint Howard (brother of superstar director Ron and star of the TV series **Gentle Ben**) features here as an over-age-looking computer-obsessed nerd who is always being picked upon by his rotten classmates at a stuffy military academy. Then he discovers a book of black magic and wires it through his hard disk to summon up a programme (courtesy of Estabar, The Demon) that will enable him to get his own back - in spades! Thereafter he can command an army of wild pigs, who scoff his enemies whole in the gross final scenes. This came out around the same time as the hit computer holocaust thriller **War Games**, but plays like a madcap X-rated version of **An Officer And A Gentleman**, with stylish, energetic direction and some good special effects. The highlight is a game of football using a severed bonce as a soccer ball. There's also a stonking exploding head scene at the end. This one made the nasties list in the UK, and there are a few scenes in it that are not for the faint-hearted. The most repulsive comes when the sadistic cadets slaughter Howard's pet puppy - an unnecessary scene that makes the film dubious viewing for dog-lovers. Otherwise this fast-moving tale of a worm that turns will keep you gripped throughout.

DVD Review

This title was reclassified in May 1999, but in more or less the same cut version, which is also available in US on the CBS FOX label. The cuts made are to the scene where the pigs attack a secretary, the scene where the Captain's head explodes when hit by a sword, and part of the infamous gut-wrenching scene at the end of the movie. The UK version received even more cuts including cuts to the black magic scene. Digital Entertainment put out a cheapie disc of this in the UK but it was the heavily trimmed UK version, and from the poor look of the full screen image it appears they sourced the tape master – so much for Digital Entertainment, eh? There has been talk about this one turning up on a US DVD Special Edition with commentary by director Eric Weston, but at the moment this remains just a rumour. **Evilspeak** isn't even available on a bootleg DVD-R, and the one uncut version is the pre-VRA tape that made the Video Nasties list.

TITLE EVILSPEAK

AKA NONE

DIRECTOR Eric Weston

COUNTRY US
SOURCE Videospace/Filmtown (UK)
YEAR 1981
TIME 99m53s

CAST Clint Howard, R. G. Armstrong, Jospeh Cortese, Claude Earl Jones, Haywood Nelson, Don Stark, Charles Tyner, Hancock, Loren Lester, Kathy McCullen, Lenny Montana, Leonard O'John, Bennett Liss, Katherine Kelly Lang, Richard Moll, Robert Tafur, Sue Casey, Kristine Alskog, Thomas Hilliard, Nadine Reimers, Deborah Dawes, DeForest Covan, Jane Bartelme, Alan Harris, Kenny Ferrugiard, Sam Baldoni, Dick Drake, Victor Hunsberger Jr.

PRODUCTION Sylvio Tabet presents… A Leisure Investment Company - Coronet Film Corporation Production. [prod] Sylvio Tabet & Eric Weston. [assoc prod] Gerald Hopman & H. Hal Harris.[exec prod] Sylvio Tabet. © 1981 Leisure Investment Company N.V.

PHOTOGRAPHY
DIRECTOR Irv Goodnoff

MUSIC Roger Kellaway
EDITOR Charles Tetoni

Exposé

ADULT EROTIC DRAMA COLOUR

**NOTHING IS LEFT TO THE IMAGINATION!
IN HER FIRST SCREEN ROLE**

FIONA RICHMOND
BRITAIN's No.1 SEX SYMBOL

In a lonely farmhouse, wealthy author Paul Martin (UDO KIER) is desperately trying to finish his latest novel. His last, 'Deadly Silence', made half-a-million dollars and his publishers are hungry for another success. His agent arranges for a new secretary to live in, hoping to speed its completion.

Paul's current girl friend, Suzanne (FIONA RICHMOND) leaves for London the next morning after the author has suffered a terrifying hallucinatory attack. The arrival of his new secretary, Linda (LINDA HAYDEN), seems set to bring order back into his life.

They make impressive progress with the novel, but it soon becomes apparent that Linda is no ordinary secretary. She sends the housekeeper away on the flimsiest of excuses then makes love, before callously shooting, two village youths when she finds them spying in the wheatfields surrounding the house.

When the suspicious housekeeper, Mrs. Ashton (PATSY SMART) returns unexpectedly, someone brutally murders her with a knife. At breakfast, Paul is ignorant of these strange events. Linda seems reserved and rejects his arrogant attempts at love-making. He invites Suzanne back to the house and instructs Linda to pick her up at the station. Later, Linda seduces Suzanne watched by a furious Paul. Soon after, Suzanne is horribly murdered.

While Paul languishes, Linda finishes the novel for him. Then she tells Paul she has come to kill him. He had stolen the manuscript for 'Deadly Silence' from her husband, driving him to suicide. She has tracked Paul down for one purpose only — revenge.

In the ensuing fight in the vast wheatfields, Linda is poised ready to kill when suddenly.....!

© INTERNATIONAL COPYRIGHT PROTECTION. Warning: Copyright subsists in all recordings issued under this label for private home use only and prohibits any other use. Unauthorised broadcasting; public performance, copying or re-recording in any manner whatsoever is prohibited, not to be re-sold, hired out, exchanged, or leased without the prior written permission of Intervision Video Limited.

LINDA HAYDEN · Miss FIONA RICHMOND · UDO KIER

"Nothing, but nothing, is left to the imagination..."

Exposé

intervision
PRE RECORDED VIDEO ENTERTAINMENT

starring
FIONA RICHMOND • **LINDA HAYDEN** • **UDO KIER**
Written and Directed by JAMES KENELM CLARKE
Produced by BRIAN SMEDLEY-ASTON

intervision
PRE RECORDED VIDEO ENTERTAINMENT

ADULT - EROTIC DRAMA - COLOUR

REVIEW

A notorious British-made shocker that has psychotic secretary Linda Hayden putting the frighteners on nervous novelist Udo Kier. The setting is a small English village, where Udo has retreated to work on his latest book. Hayden is hired to help him, but she has a hidden agenda of violent revenge. She gets raped by two thugs (one of whom is Karl Howman of TV's **Brush Strokes**), and turns the tables on them in the film's nastiest scene. Later on she slaughters Udo's girlfriend (played by 70s sex superstar Fiona Richmond) in a bloodthirsty shower scene homage to **Psycho**. Some of the continuity is a bit strange: after a violent thunderstorm, suddenly everything is sunny and dry. Rumours abound that a much longer 117 minute print of this film exists but this seems to be untrue. According to the director himself, the film was cut only slightly for its original release. This version made the nasties list because of the graphic sequence where Linda Hayden is raped, and seems to be enjoying her ordeal! All in all a compelling mixture of sex and violence, with the former overwhelming the latter. **Straw Dogs** was an obvious inspiration here, and in its own way this is almost as good as Peckinpah's classic.

TITLE	EXPOSÉ (as The House on Straw Hill)
AKA	Trauma; The House on Straw Hill
DIRECTOR	James Kenelm Clarke
COUNTRY	GB
SOURCE	Intervision (UK)
YEAR	1975
TIME	80m16s
CAST	Udo Kier, Linda Hayden, Fiona Richmond, Patsy Smart, Vic Armstrong, Karl Howman.
PRODUCTION	Keith Cavele presents for Norfolk International...[prod] Brian Smedley-Aston. [prod man] Paul Cowan. © 1975 Norfolk International Pictures.
PHOTOGRAPHY DIRECTOR	Denis Lewiston
MUSIC EDITOR	Steve Gray / Jim Connock

DVD Review

It's notable that this was the only UK video that achieved Video Nasty status. **Expose** was originally released to UK cinemas with 51 seconds of cuts. The kind of thing that was removed includes a shot of Fiona Richmond's legs streaming with blood. The most contentious scene involves the rape of Linda Hayden by two country boys (one of whom is Karl Howman from **Brush Strokes** and the Flash adverts). The scene goes on for a long time and the guys are shown to be clearly enjoying it whilst the woman rubs her hand up and down the shotgun in a very suggestive manner. The fact that she manages to shoot them both didn't appease the BBFC who cut almost the entire scene. Also a scene showing Fiona Richmond getting murdered in the shower was reduced to eliminate blood on the breasts. Odyssey put out a DVD of this in 2001, but it was the same cut version that played cinemas, missing the above-mentioned footage. If you want a totally uncut version you have to seek out the Australian DVD release, under the name of **House on Straw Hill**. There's also a DVD-R version, but the picture quality is not as good as the Aussie disc.

FACES OF DEATH

PAL / Colour - 73 minutes

"Death Closes All" - so wrote Alfred Lord Tennyson over a century ago. No matter who we are, rich or poor, death is an occurrence which at some time we must all face; first of those we know and love, and finally of ourselves.

We believe this important video film will help to prepare for the enormity of the ultimate experience.

It explores the visual phenomena of death in many forms:- not only of human beings, but also of the defenceless beasts which mankind slaughters to satisfy its hungers and its greeds.

The murderous horror of seal culling is exposed with grim reality: the awful consequences of fatal motor accidents - these scenes will surely promote a more considerate attitude by those who drive cars; the atrocities of war; the even greater devastation caused by starvation, disease, and the fatal effects of lung cancer; in startlingly frank scenes the miracles of modern surgery are fearlessly exhibited, as are the perversities of mankind, its crazed need to defy death unsuccessfully with stunts such as free-fall parachuting, aeroplane acrobatics, and the more common disasters like air crashes and train derailments, its needless slaughter of dumb animals.

This video documentary will shock you: there is no doubt of that; but it will also bring you a message of hope: the possibility of life after death: the wonder of re-birth; and we believe will fundamentally change for the better the reverence and respect you will feel for the wonder of life.

Scenes in this video film are of explicit and shocking nature. They should not be viewed by young persons, or those of a nervous disposition. In the opinion of the distributors many of the scenes contained herein would not pass the British Board of Film Censors.

AN F.O.D. PRODUCTION

WARNING

© 1982 Atlantis Video Productions Ltd.

This video cassette is copyright material for domestic use only and may not be copied, sold or hired to third parties. Any infringement of this copyright will be subject to prosecution.

For details of other titles, contact:
ATLANTIS VIDEO PRODUCTIONS LTD
19 Prebend Street, London N1 8PF Telephone 01-226 6703

AVP

FACES OF DEATH

VHS
AVP
601

TRUE LIFE
HORROR

FACES OF DEATH

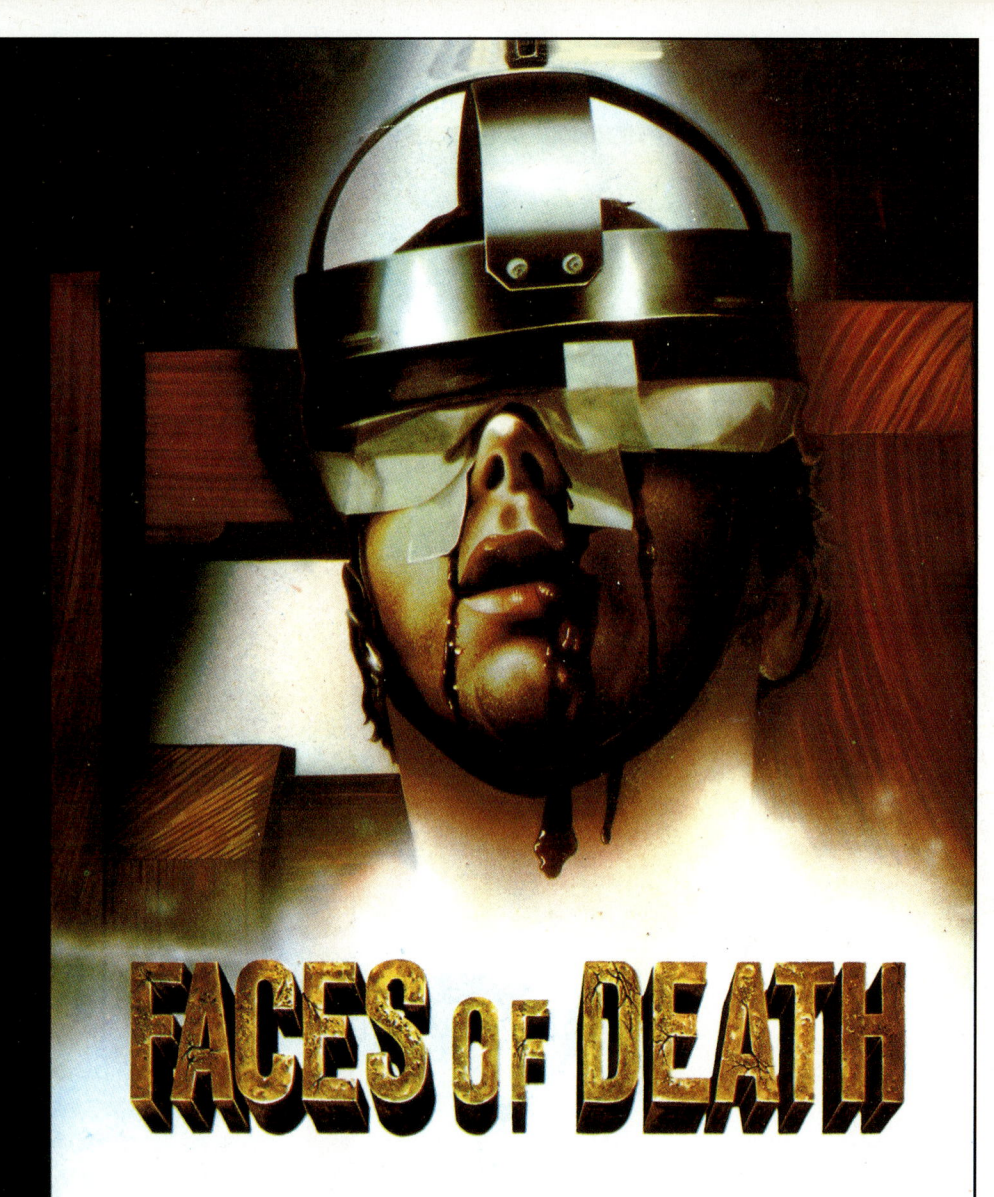

Prepare yourself for the ultimate experience.
This video cassette will change your attitude
to life.

Executive Producer: William B. James
Producer: Rosilyn T. Scott
Director: Conan Le Cilaire

TRUE LIFE HORROR
Colour - AVP 601

REVIEW

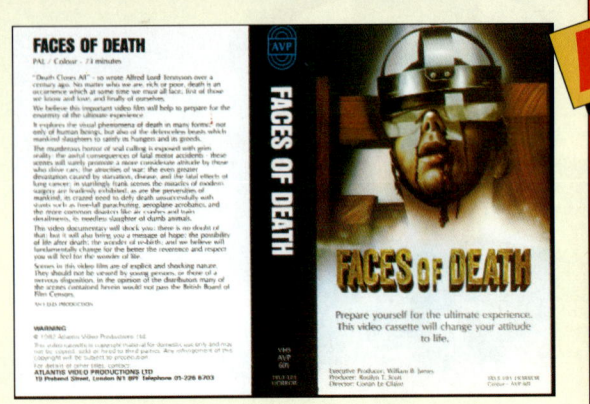

TITLE	FACES OF DEATH
AKA	NONE
DIRECTOR	Conan Le Cilaire
COUNTRY	US
SOURCE	Atlantis (UK)
YEAR	1979
TIME	77m56s
CAST	[creative consultant & narrator] Dr. Francis B. Gross (Michael Carr).
PRODUCTION	prod] Rosilyn T. Scott. [exec prod] William B. James. [assoc prod] Herbie Lee. © 1979 F.O.D. Productions.
PHOTOGRAPHY DIRECTOR	Michael Golden & Dimetri Fermo
MUSIC EDITOR	Gene Kauer

This stomach-churning nasty was made by Californians for the Japanese market and it managed to outgross *Star Wars* in Japan for 13 weeks! This was the only one of the *FOD* movies that ever got a cinema release - the other two were deservedly shunted direct to video. The first in the series is a catalogue of disasters presented by the aptly named Dr Francis Gross, a pathologist and "student of death" who talks like somebody who has been subjected to too many hours of late night *Open University* programmes (in fact his voice is supplied by actor Michael Carr). The film veers between grisly real-life footage and staged re-enactments shot with a shaky hand-held camera to make them appear real. There are obviously fake scenes of an electric chair execution, a Middle East beheading and attacks by a grizzly bear and an alligator. But while you're chuckling over these, the film suddenly hits you with gruesome scenes of autopsies and suicides, and enough slaughterhouse footage to turn you veggie on the spot. Dr Gross decides he will "never wear the skin of an animal again," but most of the cruelty here is aimed at animals, and scenes showing a live python eaten by a piranha and a pit bull battle to the death were obviously staged by the filmmakers (who use aliases). The worst scenes show chunks of charred flesh lying around after an air disaster, a body mangled under the wheels of a truck, and the mutilated victims of gang warfare. But just to cheer us all up at the end the film slides into a sappy song and close-ups of flowers, plus some photographs of ghosts, suggesting this title may be a big renter in the afterlife. If the *Faces Of Death* series had a point of view (like the excellent *Killing Of America* for example) then it might be worth watching. As it is, this hasn't and it's not.

DVD Review

UK-based Hardgore label managed to secure an 18 for the notorious **Faces Of Death** in 2003. Needless to say, this didn't go through uncut. Compulsory cuts were required to the sight of fighting dogs and a monkey being cruelly beaten to death. The BBFC also issued the following statement to clarify exactly which part of the monkey-eating scene was cut. "The part of the scene that shows the brains being eaten (out of an obviously fake rubber head) has NOT been cut. What we HAVE cut is the material leading up to that in which a clearly real and clearly terrified monkey ('goaded to fear and fury' as the Animals Act puts it) is brought to the table in a special 'monkey eating' contraption and is then bashed on the head. It seems entirely possible that the head bashing was done with rubber hammers and the monkey came to no harm. However, the monkey was clearly - at least in the short term - restricted in a cage/head clamp and terrified and law prohibits this. "The way to go with this one is obviously the region free US disc from Gorgon Video, which interestingly enough also contains a 60-minute documentary explaining which parts of the movie were faked and which were real.

FIGHT FOR YOUR LIFE

A spectacularly vicious escape releases three murderers on a trail of merciless beatings, bloody killings and multiple rape with scenes of unprintable happenings.

While holding a family under siege the captors become captives and in a terrifying climax their victim's revenge is quick, thorough and very sweet.

1977
Colour
Approx 89 min.

© INTERNATIONAL COPYRIGHT. Warning: All recordings issued under this label are licenced by the proprietor for private home use only. Any other use, including unauthorised broadcasting, public performance, copying or re-recording in any other manner whatsoever is prohibited. Not to be re-sold, hired out, or leased without the prior written consent of Vision-On Video Film Company.

vision on video film company

FIGHT FOR YOUR LIFE

VOV 016

89 minutes of sheer terror

FIGHT FOR YOUR LIFE

vision on video film company

REVIEW

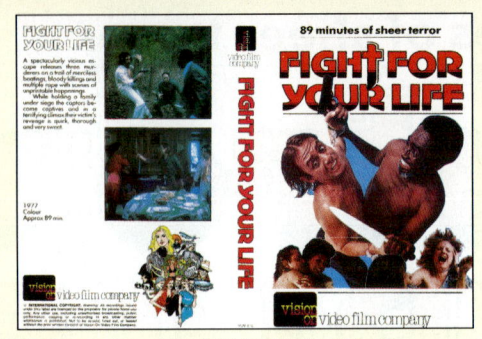

TITLE FIGHT FOR YOUR LIFE

AKA I Hate Your Guts; Bloodbath at 1313 Fury Drive; Held Hostage; Staying Alive

DIRECTOR Robert A. Endelson

COUNTRY US
SOURCE Vision On (UK)
YEAR 1977
TIME 82m11s

CAST Robert Judd, Catherine Peppers, Lela Small, Yvonne Ross, Reginald Bythewood, Ramon Saunders, Queenie Endelson, William J. Sanderson, Daniel Feraldo, Peter Yoshida, Bonni Martin, David Cargill, Richard A. Rubin, David Dewlow, Nick Mariano, Robert Whelan, Lenny Chance, Peter Charbonneau, Stephen Griffith, Maxine McCrey, David Francis, Billy Longo, William Spitz, Jane Endelson, Claudia Angelos, Steve Hasday, Cliff Balder, Joe Battaglia, Ronald Gauthier, Timothy Jones, Jeffrey Seymour, James Bertram, James Blass, Rick Endelson, Thomas Hea'd, John Laccetti, Jack Massar, Gary Mazzacano, David Balder, John Doyce, Daniel Herrick, Iivia Solomon, Mary Jane Walsh, Paul Morris, Franklyn Schaefer, Steven Rossenbloom, William Vick, Larry Walker, Bob McKinnon, Mitchell Rothman, Dick Punch.,

PRODUCTION William Mishkin Motion Pictures presents... [prod] William Mishkin & Robert A. Endelson. [assoc prod] Rick Endelson & Straw Weisman. [exec prod] William Mishkin. © 1977 Fightin Family Productions Ltd.

PHOTOGRAPHY
DIRECTOR Lloyd Freidus

MUSIC Jeff Slevin
EDITOR Robert A. Endelson

This sleazy and unpleasant low-budget exploitation pic tells the story of three escaped convicts who brutalise a black minister and his family until the inevitable **I Spit On Your Grave**-type retribution. The convicts consist of a deranged white guy who forces the minister to call him "Massa," a barbarous Oriental, and a knife-wielding Chicano. Most of the film has them terrorising the helpless family in scenes that are very nasty indeed. In fact most prints are missing a very nasty sequence where a young boy has his head bashed in with a rock. The grisly revenge bits at the end include a castration by bullet and impaling on broken glass - but at least the baddies deserve it! Some feeble attempts are made to explain the psychological motivation behind the leader of the gang's pathological hatred of blacks, but they don't fool anybody. This trashy exploitation epic is as mean and uncompromising as they come. Mind you, the ironic thing is that this was released at UK cinemas with an 'AA' certificate, meaning that at one time the BBFC thought it was suitable for 14-year-old kids…

DVD Review

It's strange that this Canadian-made rape/revenge drama made it to the list in the first place, because there isn't much in the way of contentious material here. In fact this is a very talky film and not half as exploitive as it sounds from the plot description. Even stranger is the fact that it remains banned in the UK, both as a cinema and video release. It's possibly that the extreme race hatred angle has caused the film so many problems. There has recently been talk about a major US re-release under the film's alternate title of **I Hate Your Guts**, but as of going to press the only way to get hold of a copy on disc was as a DVD-R from a company called 5 minutes To Live. Their disc is uncut and sourced from a pretty good master in full screen. There are no extras on the disc.

ANDY WARHOL'S FRANKENSTEIN

Writer-director Paul Morrissey, director of Andy Warhol's FLESH, TRASH and HEAT, brings to the screen the most outrageous version of FRANKENSTEIN ever. "Swooping bats, severed limbs, gobs of livid human entrails, a hideously efficient decapitating gadget, some well turned breasts and buttocks, plus assorted spare parts are among the treats that slither off the screen. Andy Warhol's FRANKENSTEIN is the most outrageously gruesome epic ever unleashed. Horror fans can get a kick from this one." **PLAYBOY MAGAZINE**

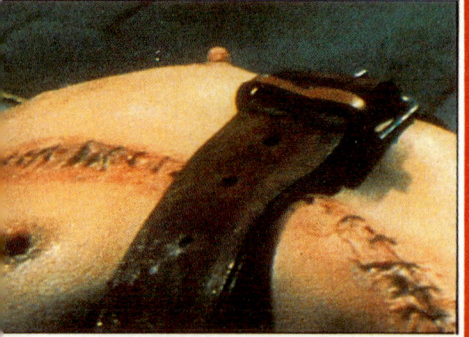

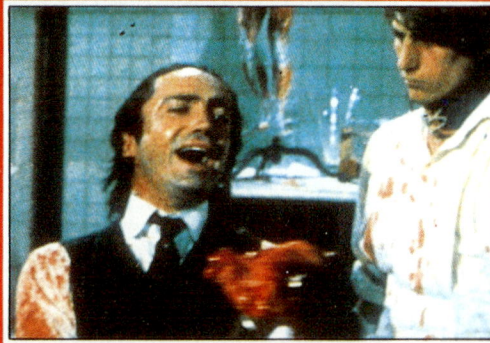

"THE MOST GRUESOME EPIC EVER UNLEASHED!"

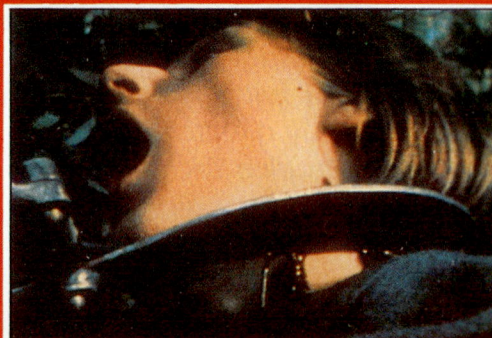

WARNING

"The copyright proprietor has licensed the film contained in this videocassette for private home use only. Any other use including making copies of the film, causing it to be seen or heard in public or broadcasting it or causing to be transmitted to subscribers to a diffusion service, letting on hire or otherwise dealing with it in part or any kind of exchange scheme is strictly prohibited. Any breach of the above conditions render the offender liable to prosecution by Video Instant Picture Company Limited"

VIPCO

VHS VIDEO CASSETTE

VIP 046

ANDY WARHOL'S FRANKENSTEIN

"The goriest and sexiest 'Frankenstein' ever filmed."

A film by PAUL MORRISSEY Starring
Joe Dallesandro — Monique Van Vooren — Udo Kier
Introducing Arno Juerging — Dalila Di Lazzaro
Srdjan Zelenovic
RUNNING TIME 95 MINS. APPROX.

VIPCO

REVIEW

Originally filmed in 3-D, this grisly Andy Warhol-produced gorefest stars Udo Kier as a degenerate Baron F. who has necrophiliac tendencies ("To know death, you must first fuck life in the gall bladder!") and is married to his own sister! His aim is to create a master race, and to this end he uses a pair of giant shears to decapitate a handsome farmer (Srdjan Zelenovic) and stick it on a stud corpse, which then becomes the perfect mate for his beautiful female creation (Dalila Di Lazzaro). Sick and silly, the film is never less than entertaining and it has a real **Monty Python** feel about it, with lots of outrageous gore and awful performances, plus some memorably amusing lines, such as: "Why did you wake me? You know I have insomnia!" The best bit of 3-D has Kier contemplating his own liver, which is dangling on a pole one inch from the audience's collective noses! It's rare to see a gore pic with these kind of half-decent production values. The movie was "supervised" by prolific Italian director Antonio Margheriti, who remains uncredited, and it was shot " back-to-back" with Warhol's **Blood For Dracula**, a movie that was actually gorier, but didn't make the nasties list for some strange reason.

TITLE FLESH FOR FRANKENSTEIN

AKA Il mostro e in tavola... barone Frankenstein; Carne per Frankenstein; Chair pour Frankenstein; Andy Warhol's Frankenstein

DIRECTOR Antonio Margheriti (uncredited) & Paul Morrissey

COUNTRY IT, FR
SOURCE Vipco (UK)
YEAR 1973
TIME 88m55s

CAST Joe Dallesandro, Monique Van Vooren, Udo Kier, Arno Juerging, Dalila Di Lazzaro, Srdjan Zelenovic, Nicoletta Elmi, Liv Bosisio, Cristina Gaioni, Carla Mancini, Marco Liofredi, Fiorella Masselli, Rosita Torosh, Imelde Marani.

PRODUCTION Andy Warhol presents... A Compagnia Cinematografica Champion (Rome) - Jean Yanne & Jean Pierre Rassam Productions (Paris) co-production. [prod] Carlo Ponti (uncredited) & Andrew Braunsberg. © None.

PHOTOGRAPHY DIRECTOR Luigi Kuveiller

MUSIC EDITOR Claudio Gizzi

DVD Review

It seems strange that the BBFC managed to get the joke with Peter Jackson's **Bad Taste** and **Braindead**, but didn't realise that Andy Warhol's 1973 movie was a Monty Python-style spoof and not to be taken seriously. The UK censors trimmed seven minutes from the movie when it was shown in London cinemas (in 3-D!) in 1975. These cuts were restored to the video, which resulted in it being banned, and it stayed that way until the 1990s when First Independent released a cut version in the UK. The definitive uncut version was released on disc as part of the prestigious Criterion collection in an impressive anamorphic 2.35:1 wide screen version - sadly not in 3-D. It featured a commentary by director Paul Morrissey, star Udo Kier and film historian Maurice Yacowar, plus production stills and publicity photos. A shame they didn't get Antonio Margheriti involved as well, because by all accounts he directed the lion's share of this picture.

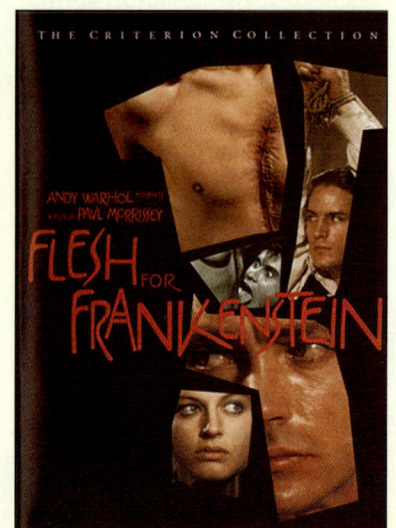

"FOREST OF FEAR"

In a remote and idyllic forest, illegal marijuana is being cultivated. Government agents locate the secret plantation. Their murder by the hippie farmers after its discovery sparks off a devastating chain of events, one of which is the indiscriminate spraying of Dromax, a yet untested toxic pesticide. The contaminated hippies embark on a bloodthirsty rampage. An innocent group of holiday makers enjoying the sport and pleasures of the once peaceful paradise are not aware that the forest now harbours frenzied ghouls bent on destruction.

The result is murder, mayhem and a stunning, spine-chilling, climax.

FOREST OF FEAR
STARRING
CHARLES AUSTIN
&
BEVERLY SHAPIRO
Written, Produced & Directed by Charles McCrann
Special Effects Director: Craig A. Harris
Approx., running time 84 minutes.

WARNING
Copyright subsists on all recordings issued under this label. Unauthorised broadcasting, public performance, copying or re-recording in any manner whatsoever is prohibited. Not to be resold, hired out or leased without the prior permission of MONTE VIDEO

FOREST OF FEAR

VHS
PAL
SECAM

FOREST OF FEAR

REVIEW

The year after they took over the Monroeville Mall, some **Dawn Of The Dead** -type zombies stalked the nearby Pennsylvania countryside in this low-budget gorefest shot on 16mm in George Romero's native Pittsburgh, zombie capital of the world! John (*Martin*) Amplas stars in the role of an incredibly youthful-looking FBI agent out to roust a bunch of hippie drug smugglers. With this in mind, the government have dumped a load of experimental herbicide (called Dromax) on the hippies' marijuana plantation, turning everyone in the vicinity into zombie-like creatures with a taste for skinning up on human flesh. From there on in it's gore galore (mainly of the "Let's rip half a butcher's shop out of his shirt" variety) as the terminally stoned zombies stumble through the woods chopping up innocent bystanders with machetes. The effects are good considering the poverty of the budget, but a boring subplot about double-dealing FBI agents detracts from the film's entertainment value.

TITLE FOREST OF FEAR

AKA BLOODEATERS; TOXIC ZOMBIES

DIRECTOR Charles McCrann

COUNTRY US
SOURCE Monte (UK)
YEAR 1979
TIME 81m05s

CAST Charles Austin, Beverly Shapiro, Dennis Helfend, Kevin Hanlon, Judy Brown, Pat Kellis, Roger Miles, Philip Garfinkel, Bob Larson, Hariet Milner, Paul Haskin, John Amplas, Claude Scales, Dennis Graber, Debra O'Leary, Bob Hanson, Gerald Cullen, Ronald Kienhuis, Kim Roff, Craig Harris, James Hart, John Kuhi, Alyssa Allyn, William Shetterly, Debbie Link, James McGonigal.

PRODUCTION CM Productions presents... [prod] Charles McCrann. © 1979 CM Productions.

PHOTOGRAPHY DIRECTOR David Sperling

MUSIC Ted Shapiro
EDITOR Charles McCrann & David Sperling

DVD Review

This one remains banned for inexplicable reasons, and it's pretty hard to find on tape or disc as well. There's a German edition under the title of **The Bloodeaters** that is presented full frame in a fairly mediocre transfer that looks very much like it was gleaned from a VHS master. The film is also available on video in the USA under the title of **Toxic Zombies**, but this version is reportedly missing some violent scenes and has also lost an epilogue that was on the banned version we saw all too briefly in this country.

Frozen Scream

A hooded figure carrying a bloody corpse approaches a mansion.

Impatiently waiting by the telephone, Tom Gerrard jumps when it rings; it is his wife, Ann, calling from the road. His anxiety is very evident and he tries to remain calm on the telephone. Immediately after hanging up with Ann he again tries to call Father O'Brien, the only person to whom he can reveal his secret. The telephone lines are cut and Tom gets ready to face his doom. He slowly approaches the door with a revolver in his hand, he knows what to expect. Minutes later when Ann arrives home she finds him dead.

Lil has assigned Catherine to be her nurse. The next day Ann goes to talk to Lil at the University where she is teaching. She overhears her lecture, it is on Immortality; she flashes back. Kevin startles her out of her thoughts, and as a friend of hers and Tom, makes himself available to help her find what actually happened to Tom over the past year and why it ended that way.

Returning home, Ann sees a vision of Tom in the mirror, turning around, only to find Catherine there. During the night there are noises in the house, frightened Ann gets up to see what they are. She sees a hooded figure, is attacked with a knife to her throat and told not to interfere with what has to take place. The attacker's hand is very cold.

At a Halloween party that same evening, given by Lil and Sven for their students, Ann manages to get away in order to inspect the house, her finding is startling. In a refrigerated room of the mansion, she finds three comatosed beings. One is Tom. Frightened she runs out of the room and finds Kevin also in the house. The secret is out. Sven instructs his zombies to kill them.

Ann is brought to the laboratory and is given the choice of joining in Lil and Svens' research in cyrogenics or becoming as Tom and their other experiments. Sven sensing the strength in Ann's character opts for the operation. Lil has confidence in Ann, but Ann has not forgotten seeing Tom as he is. There is a struggle and Sven is left dead. Ann manages to hit the power switches and the laboratory burns. That evening Ann, Lil and Father O'Brien pay a final visit to Kevin in his hospital room. It is Kevin's last visit…Thantos… Anthonatos…Death…Immortality….

INTERVISION VIDEO LIMITED
1, McKAY TRADING ESTATE, KENSAL ROAD, LONDON, W10

© INTERNATIONAL COPYRIGHT PROTECTION. Warning: Copyright subsists in all recordings issued under this label for private home use only and prohibits any other use. Unauthorised broadcasting; public performance, copying or re-recording in any manner whatsoever is prohibited, not to be re-sold, hired out, exchanged, or leased without the prior written permission of Intervision Video Limited.

DESIGNED BY MORRIS ASSOCIATES

HORROR COLOUR
AAE 0433

VHS

Frozen Scream

Directed by Frank Roach
Produced by Renee Harmon

DISTRIBUTED BY
Intervision
THE FIRST NAME IN VIDEO.
THE LAST WORD IN ENTERTAINMENT.

HORROR-COLOUR
A-AE 0433

REVIEW

Duffel-coated killers are on the loose in this anonymous chiller which found its way onto the nasties list for reasons which we mere mortals can only wonder about. The flashback-framed story concerns the search for immortality via cryogenic freezing, the only problem being that the human guinea pigs end up turning into cold-blooded zombies - the operation was a success, but the patient died! Various people are stabbed to death and there's a semi-grisly scene (not very well done) where an eyeball is punctured with a syringe. But for the most part the film is very confusing to watch and drags on forever through talky expositions of homespun philosophy, dire 70s-flavoured disco dancing scenes, and even some pointless arthouse-flavoured direction. This one deserves to remain anonymous.

DVD Review

This is perhaps the strangest addition to the list, because it's a very minor, actually pretty boring horror programmer that contains little gore. The average **Friday the 13th** movie makes this look tame, and the only scene that could remotely be considered grisly involves an injection into an eyeball. After Fulci's **Zombie Flesh-Eaters** it's obvious that the BBFC clamped down on such scenes – **Dead And Buried** committed the same transgression. Anyway, **Frozen Scream** was later removed from the official list and disappeared into obscurity. Nobody seems to have much interest in the title these days, and if you're desperate to seek it out for the sake of Nasties research then you need to check out foreign distributors. It was released on DVD as a European 'Red Edition' disc in full screen but uncut and with fairly good picture quality. It's not to be confused with another **Frozen Scream**, made in 1984 and starring Chris Mitchum.

TITLE FROZEN SCREAM

AKA NONE

DIRECTOR Frank Roach

COUNTRY US
SOURCE Intervision (UK)
YEAR 1981
TIME 77m00s

CAST Renee Harmon, Lynne Kocol, Wolf Muser, Thomas Gowen, Wayne Liebman, Lee James, Sunny Bartholomew, Bill Oliver, Bob Rochelle, Terri Argula, Art Platt, Cheryl Harmon, Julie Ann Meisels, Jennifer Flamen, Chris Hammond, Sandie Gelbard, Bill Luce, Cheryl Crandal, Chris Russell, Paul Yamanian, Ben Moase, Andy Nachtigall, Stephan Fusci, Gary Pearl.

PRODUCTION A Ciara Production. [prod] Renee Harmon. © None.

PHOTOGRAPHY DIRECTOR Roberto Quazada

MUSIC H. Kingsley Thurber III
EDITOR Mathew Muller

Starring Cooper Huckabee • Miles Chapin • Largo Woodruff • Sylvia Miles • William Finley • Introducing Elizabeth Berridge and Kevin Conway as The Barker • Also Starring Wayne Doba • Shawn Carson • Produced by Derek Power and Steven Bernhardt • Executive Producers Mace Neufeld • Mark Lester • Directed by Tobe Hooper • Written by Larry Block • A Universal Release ©1981 by Universal City Studios, Inc. All Rights Reserved.

FUNHOUSE

FUNHOUSE
CARNIVAL OF TERROR

From the director who brought you
"THE TEXAS CHAINSAW MASSACRE"
and "POLTERGEIST"

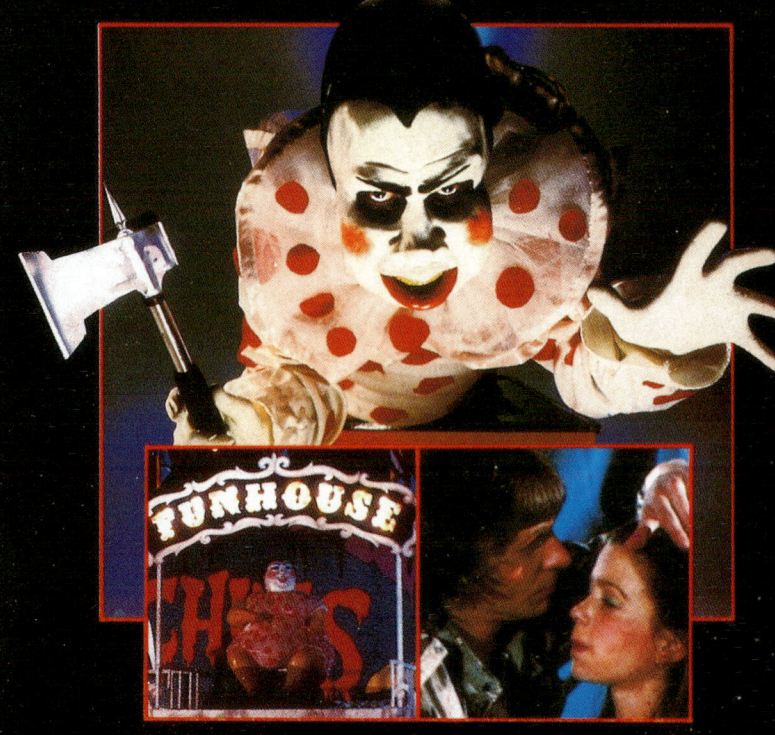

FUNHOUSE

It seemed to be a carnival funhouse just like any other: mysterious, eerie, scary, but all in good fun. Yet it wasn't just any funhouse. In this one there was murder. And the horror became real.

The story concerns four teenagers who visit a local carnival for a night of innocent amusement. They soon discover, however, that there is nothing innocent or amusing there at all. Instead, they find absolute terror when the four are trapped inside the maze of the funhouse. One by one, each victim is taken by a monster who tauntingly stalks them.

18

1981 COLOUR RUNNING TIME APPROX. 92 MINS
© 1981 UNIVERSAL CITY STUDIOS INC./All rights reserved.

WARNING The copyright proprietor has licensed the film (including its soundtrack) comprised in this videocassette for home use only. All other rights are reserved. Any unauthorised copying, editing, exhibition, renting, exchanging, hiring, lending, public performances, diffusion, and/or broadcast of this videocassette or any part thereof is strictly prohibited.
MADE IN THE U.K.

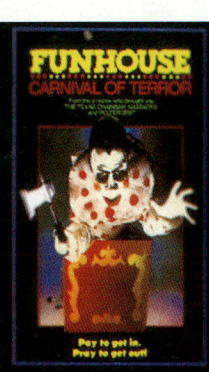

cic video

VHS PAL
VHA 1058

cic video

**Pay to get in.
Pray to get out!**

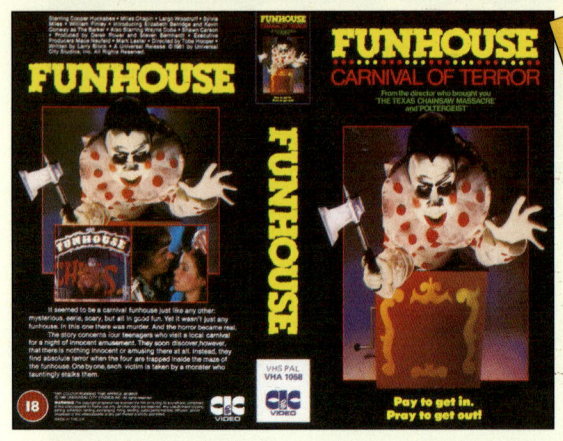

REVIEW

TITLE	FUNHOUSE, THE
AKA	The Funhouse: Carnival of Terror
DIRECTOR	Tobe Hooper
COUNTRY	US
SOURCE	CIC (UK)
YEAR	1981
TIME	88m44s
CAST	Elizabeth Berridge, Shawn Carson, Jeanne Austin, Jack McDermott, Cooper Huckabee, Largo Woodruff, Miles Chapin, David Carson, Sonia Zomina, Ralph Marino, Kevin Conway, Herb Robins, Mona Agar, Wayne Dobar, William Finley, Susie Malnick, Sylvia Miles, Sid Raymond, Larry Ross, Frank Grimes, Frank Schuller, Peter Conrad, Mildred Hughes, Glen Lawrence, Shawn McAllister, Sandy Mielke, Mike Montalvo.
PRODUCTION	A Mace Neufeld production in association with Derek Power. [prod] Derek Power & Steven Bernhardt. [assoc prod] Brad Neufeld. [exec prod] Mace Neufeld & Mark L. Lester. © 1981 Universal City Studios.
PHOTOGRAPHY DIRECTOR	Andrew Laszlo
MUSIC	John Beal
EDITOR	Jack Hofstra

Universal entrusted their first major horror movie in many years to the hands of **Texas Chainsaw** man Tobe Hooper, and what did he deliver? A video nasty! Actually Hooper did a respectable job with less than inspired material. It's obvious there isn't going to be much that's original here from the opening scenes where the comely Elizabeth Berridge is menaced **Psycho**-style in the shower - needless to say it turns out to be one of those stupid pranks that we all hate. Thereafter the story introduces us to a bunch of well-off teens (Berridge included) who decide it would be a huge laugh to spend the night in a seedy carnival funhouse. Some fun, huh? But their prank turns sour when they witness the killing of carnival fortune teller Sylvia Miles by the monstrous Wayne Doba, a cleft-headed albino who hides his deformity behind a Frankenstein mask. Of course the teens are then picked off one by one, leaving Berridge to confront the creature in the funhouse's clanking engine room. Hooper makes good use of some gorgeous widescreen colour camerawork plus a spooky Dolby soundtrack that throws scary sounds at you from all angles. But it doesn't pan out to much in the end. It is generally assumed that this title ended up on the banned list by mistake due to some confusion with Victor Janos's **Last House On Dead End Street**, which was also known as **The Funhouse**.

DVD Review

It does seem very likely that the boys in blue confused Tobe Hooper's **Funhouse** with the no-budget US movie **Last House On Dead End Street**, also known as **The Funhouse**. That particular movie was released as a Special Edition disc in 2002 by Barrel Entertainment, and is a pretty grotesque affair containing slaughterhouse footage and a snuff movie scenario. It's believable that this would have been banned. As for Tobe Hooper's movie, well it's nothing more than an old-fashioned fright flick with a creature who looks like the old Universal Frankenstein monster. The film played UK cinemas uncut before it went out on video, and when resubmitted by UIP it was given a BBFC video certificate with no cuts. **The Funhouse** is available as an uncut region 1 DVD in a good quality 2.35:1 transfer. The disc contains a trailer but no other extras.

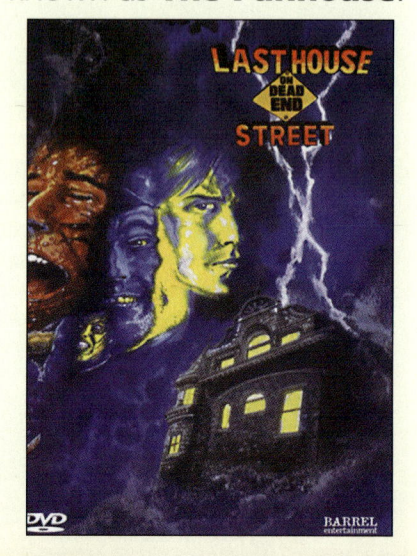

WARNING

Gestapo's
Last Orgy

... depicts scenes of such an explicit and violent nature, that any persons who are likely to take offence to such displays are advised not to view this film.

WARNING

"The copyright proprietor has licensed the film contained in this video cassette for private home use only. Any other use including making copies of the film, causing it to be seen or heard in public or broadcasting it or causing it to be transmitted to subscribers to a diffusion service, letting on hire or otherwise dealing with it in whole or in part is strictly prohibited. Any breach of the above conditions renders the offender liable to prosecution." © Video Film Promotions Ltd.

Sleeve design by
IMPRESSIONS
01-722 3939

VFP004

VHS FORMAT

Gestapo's Last Orgy

VIDEOFILM PROMOTIONS

REVIEW

One of the better concentration camp movies inspired by the success of **The Night Porter**, **TGLO** is pitched somewhere between that arty Liliana Cavani picture and the likes of Sergio Garrone's more honestly exploitative **S.S. Experiment Camp**. Whether its more polished approach makes this saga of sado-masochistic love between a camp commandant and one of his Jewish prisoners any less reprehensible than Garrone's notorious effort is open to question. Anyway, it's a slick exploitation piece which begins five years after the end of the war. The sadistic ex-commandant of a Nazi love camp has just been cleared of war crimes thanks to a sympathetic character reference from Lisa, one of the camp's inmates. In flashbacks we learn that Lisa had not been truthful. In reality she was brutally tortured by the commandant, who was out to break her spirit and make her his love slave. When the nasty Nazi gets out she invites him back to the camp to "refuel old passions," but revenge is the thing on her mind and she gets it in a suitably nasty fashion. The flashback scenes are the meat of the movie and contain gory sequences of skulls being crushed by rifle butts and people being lowered screaming into vats of acid. Of course as promised by the title we get a long and explicit orgy scene. Trivia buffs might care to note that Canevari made the first ever film adaptation of **Emmanuelle**, several years before Just Jaeckin's better-known version with Sylvia Kristel.

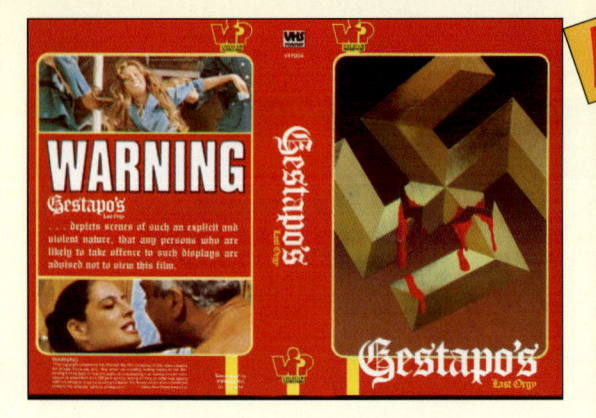

TITLE GESTAPO'S LAST ORGY, THE

AKA L'ultima orgia del III Reich; Bourreaux SS; Last Orgy of the Third Reich; Des filles pour le bourreau; Caligula Reincarnated as Hitler

DIRECTOR Cesare Canevari

COUNTRY IT
SOURCE VFP (UK)
YEAR 1976
TIME 80m56s

CAST Marc Loud, Daniela Levy (Daniella Poggi), Maristella Greco, Fulvio Ricciardi, Antineska Nemour, Caterina Barbero, Domenico Serengai, Vittorio Joderi, Pietro Bosco, Pietro Vial, Renato Paracchi, Maria Grazia Cisera, Santino Polenghi.

PRODUCTION A Cine LU. CE. Production (Milan). [prod] Cesare Canevari (uncredited). © None.

PHOTOGRAPHY DIRECTOR Claudio Catozzo

MUSIC Alberto Baldan Bembo
EDITOR Enzo Monachesi

DVD Review

Any film with the word Gestapo in the title and containing scenes in which sexy birds are dunked in quick-lime, forced to fellate pistols and sodomise the commandant of a concentration camp with the butt of a whip isn't going to be found on the shelves of your local Blockbuster store any day soon. Like many of the notorious Nazi Nasties this remains banned in the UK and many other countries as well. The only way you'll get your sticky mitts on this is to track down the DVD-R version sold by companies such as Xploited.com. It's in a non-anamorphic 1.85 ratio and uncut, with quite decent picture quality (though what's going on in the picture is often far from decent!). The problem is, this disc was sourced from a Japanese laser and has Spanish and Italian dialogue only, with Japanese subtitles. It also suffers from the usual Japanese complaint of optically blurring any pubic hair or genitalia – quite annoying here because there's so much full frontal nudity! The region 2 NTSC disc also contains a trailer.

THE HOUSE BY THE CEMETERY

The House by the Cemetery had a gruesome past for it was once the property of Dr. Freudstein — a dabbler in bizarre surgical practises.

But Norman, his wife Lucy and their young son, Bob, know nothing of this when they rent the foreboding New England residence.

Before the full dossier of facts about the Freudstein legend become known, many innocent victims fall into the hands of the demented, marauding zombie, forever seeking freshly severed limbs and organs to keep his corrupt, rotting flesh alive.

As past and present collide in a vortex of fear, each member of the terrified family find themselves, in turn, fighting for their lives in the underground, gore-soaked, charnel-house that is one of the House by the Cemetery's many secrets.

Who will survive — and what will be left of them in the House where an unspeakable — and unstoppable — evil dwells?

"Tremendously exciting. Builds to one of the best sustained climaxes of Gothique melodrama seen in recent years". STARBURST MAGAZINE

The latest film from Lucio Fulci, Italy's undisputed Crown King of Horror who has been called "one of the most influential horror directors of the past decade".

Running time: 83 minutes

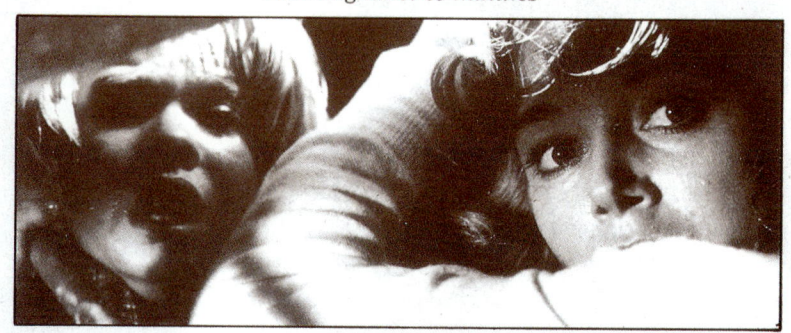

Vampix
A VIDEOMEDIA RELEASE
VIDEOMEDIA LIMITED
70 WARDOUR STREET, LONDON W1V 3HP

All rights of the producers and owners of the recorded work reserved. The film contained in this video cassette is protected by copyright and use of this recording is restricted to private home use only. Any other manner of exhibition, broadcast public performance, diffusion, copying, re-selling, hiring or editing constitutes an infringement of copyright unless the previous written consent of the copyright owner thereto has been obtained.

DESIGNED BY Graffiti PRODUCTIONS LIMITED

CAN ANYONE SURVIVE THE DEMENTED MARAUDING ZOMBIES IN...

LUCIO FULCI'S HORROR EPIC

THE HOUSE BY THE CEMETERY

KATHERINE MacCOLL in
THE HOUSE BY THE CEMETERY • A LUCIO FULCI Film
PAOLO MALCO • GIOVANNI FREZZA • SILVIA COLLATINA
and GIOVANNI DE NARI as Dr. Freudstein
Screenplay by DARDANO SACCHETTI, GEORGIO MARIUZZO,
LUCIO FULCI • Music by WALTER RIZZATI
Produced by FABRIZIO DE ANGELIS
Directed by LUCIO FULCI
COLOUR

CERT-X
COLOUR
HVM 1027
VHS PAL

Vampix A VIDEOMEDIA RELEASE

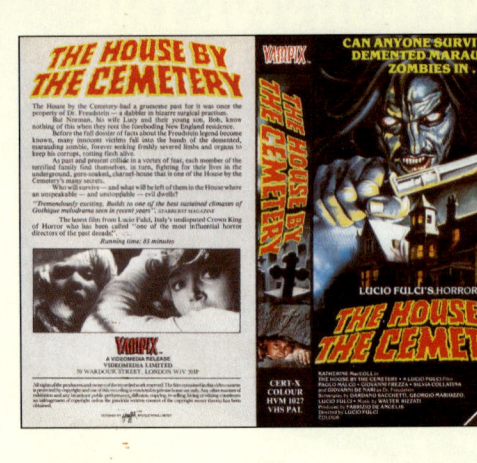

REVIEW

College professor Paolo Malco, his wife Katherine MacColl, and their young son Giovanni Frezza shouldn't have any reason to complain about the neighbours when they move into the Boston property of the title, but being as this is a Lucio Fulci film it's not long before the dead start raising hell. It turns out that the house used to belong to a certain Dr Freudstein, a deranged medic whose living dead remains are still knocking about in the cellar. One of Fulci's more complex films, this intriguing effort borrows **The Shining's** plot device of having the young boy possess the gift/curse of foreseeing dire events, and there's even a bit of **The Turn Of The Screw** in the subplot about a ghostly little girl who urges the lad to get away from the hell house while all his body parts are still intact. Gore fans certainly get their money's worth, with numerous throat-slittings, beheadings and even bat-skewerings (with a pair of scissors). The intense finale is one of the best scenes Fulci ever directed. On the whole I still prefer **The Beyond**, but this legendary "nasty" rates high on the list of Italian gore classics.

DVD Review

When released to UK cinemas in 1982 with an 'X' certificate, this film required 6 cuts totalling 34 secs. 3 cuts totalling 16 secs removed an estate agent being subjected to two stabs with a poker, including the slow motion gushing of blood from her wounds. A further 3 cuts totalling 18 secs were imposed on the scene of a nanny having her throat cut. The same version released on pre-VRA video caused it to get an entry in the Video Nasties list. Elephant Video finally released a BBFC-sanctioned video but this required a further 4 minutes and 11 secs of cuts, many of them performed by the distributor in advance. The kind of stuff that went was the girl being stabbed through the back of her head, through to her mouth, and of her body being dragged away. Also trimmed was the entire poker killing mentioned above, the killing of a vampire bat and related blood spattering, shots of decomposing bodies in the cellar and the disembowelled man on the table. Nowadays you can get an uncut Japanese laserdisc version, a Danish release from VIPCO (avoid the British one) and a Dutch release from Chainsaw Video. But the definitive version is available from Anchor Bay in the US as a region free disc, presenting the film in a terrific uncut print (2.35:1 anamorphic).

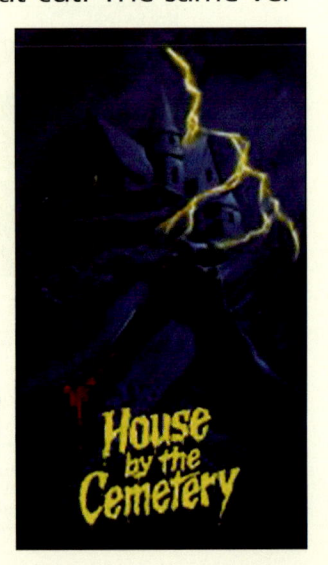

TITLE	HOUSE BY THE CEMETERY, THE
AKA	Quella villa accanto al cimitero
DIRECTOR	Lucio Fulci
COUNTRY	IT
SOURCE	Videomedia/Vampix (UK)
YEAR	1981
TIME	81m06s
CAST	Katherine MacColl (Catriona MacColl), Paolo Malco, Ania Pieroni, Giovanni Frezza, Silvia Collatina, Dagmar Lassander, Giovanni De Nava, Daniela Doria, Giampaolo Saccarola, Carlo De Mejo, John Olson, Elmer Johnson, Ranieri Ferrara, Teresa Rossi Passante.
PRODUCTION	[prod] Fabrizio De Angelis. Fulvia Film s.r.l. (Rome). © None.
PHOTOGRAPHY DIRECTOR	Sergio Salvati
MUSIC	Walter Rizzati
EDITOR	Vincenzo Tomass

HOUSE ON THE EDGE OF THE PARK

Starring David A. Hess and Annie Belle.

Directed by Ruggero Deodato.

Nice type, Alex. If you didn't know him you could even be fooled when he amuses himself by playing the "nice guy".

For some time he's been wearing one more necklace. He ripped it off a girl; Susan, whom he then raped and killed. His brain flipped. This happens often because Alex is just a dangerous vicious animal.

He's happy tonight. He's about to leave the garage he uses as a cover for recycling stolen cars. He wants to go out and have fun with Ricki. Ricki's a strange guy. He's highly strung and the slightest thing will crack him up.

They're about to leave the garage when two kids, Tom and Liza arrive. Their fabulous car has something wrong with it. Alex refuses the $50 a day they offer him to repair it. His tone changes when he hears the two are going to a party. He becomes friendly and says that if they invite him and his friend Ricki the fun is guaranteed.

Two violent hoodlums who rape and are prepared to kill. A pistol found by chance in a drawer, and no alternative but self-defence. This is the story he will give to the police.

A shot and Alex falls into the pool, which reddens with his blood. The cry of a mortally wounded beast, and then nothing more. The vendetta is accomplished, but at what price?

Running time 1 hr. 42 mins. approx. – colour

VHS CAT. NO: CLO V3

NOTICE This cassette is hired on the condition that the hirer undertakes:– (1) not to do or permit any of the following acts: copying of the recorded material or any part thereof, public performance, broadcasting or other transmission, hiring or offering for hire or distributing by way of trade without proper licence from SKYLINE VIDEO; (2) not to permit any third party to permit any of the above acts and not to alter or remove this notice or the similar notice on the cassette itself. This cassette is for hire/sale only from an authorised dealer. Copyright exists in the recorded material in this cassette.

DISTRIBUTED BY
VIDEO FORM PICTURES
Unit 4, Brunswick Industrial Park,
New Southgate, London N11.

SKYLINE VIDEO

Starring David A. Hess and Annie Belle.

NOT SUITABLE FOR PERSONS UNDER 18 YEARS OF AGE

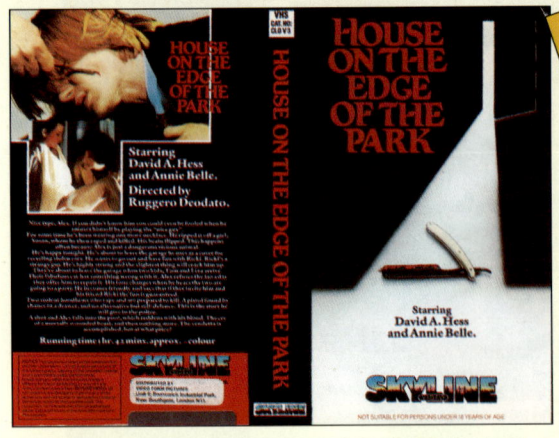

REVIEW

A sleazy shocker from the director of **Cannibal Holocaust**, starring **Last House On The Left** psycho David Hess, back in the old routine playing a crazed rapist who, along with his brain-dead mate John Morghen (a regular in nasties like **Cannibal Apocalypse** and **Cannibal Ferox**) terrorises a group of spoiled yuppies after gate-crashing a party in a posh mansion. One rich kid is thrown into the swimming pool, and when he tries to climb out Hess urinates on him. Torture, rape, lesbianism and a 9mm castration are on the menu here, plus one of the most stupid "surprise" endings you are ever likely to see. In fact the ending is *so* ridiculous that it tends to negate everything that has gone before. Europorn starlet Annie Belle provides plenty of nudity and bad acting, and it's intriguing to see Morghen reunited with his **Ferox** co-star Lorraine de Selle. Hess seems to be enjoying his portrayal of a truly vile character who calls all women "Twats" and likes slicing his name on their naked bodies with a straight razor. Mind you, he certainly suffers for his indiscretions at the end, and his death scene is filmed in such excruciating slow motion that you could grow a beard watching it! This Italian-made shocker is deeply unpleasant to watch, and that may be more than enough recommendation for some of you!

TITLE HOUSE ON THE EDGE OF THE PARK

AKA La casa sperduta del parco; La casa al confini del parco; Der Schlitzer

DIRECTOR Ruggero Deodato

COUNTRY IT
SOURCE Skyline (UK)
YEAR 1980
TIME 87m48s

CAST David A. Hess, Annie Belle, Cristian Borromeo, Giovanni Lombardo Radice, Marie Claude Joseph, Gabriele Di Giulio, Brigitte Petronio, Karoline Mardeck, Lorraine De Selle.

PRODUCTION Franco Palaggi & Franco Di Nunzio present... An F. D. Cinematografica Production. [in charge of prod] Giovanni Masini. © None.

PHOTOGRAPHY DIRECTOR Sergio D'Offizi

MUSIC Riz Ortolani
EDITOR Vincenzo Tomassi

DVD Review

When **The House On The Edge Of The Park** was first submitted to the BBFC in 1981 for a UK cinema release it shared the fate of the similarly titled (and themed) **Last House On The Left**, and was turned down point blank as being unacceptable - even with cuts. The film was therefore a natural for the Nasties list. At first it seemed like good news when it was announced there would be a UK video release last year, but the bad news was a staggering 11 mins 23 secs of cuts were required to various scenes of sex and sadism before this butchered version found its way into High Street shops. Not to worry, though, because there's a fantastic region 1 disc of this available from Media Blasters that presents us with an excellent quality, totally uncut transfer in anamorphic 1.85:1, plus theatrical trailers and interviews. It's amazing to see how well photographed this movie was, and since it's unlikely to be passed here uncut at any time in the near future then this has to be worth picking up if you can still find a copy – it was officially released at the end of 2002.

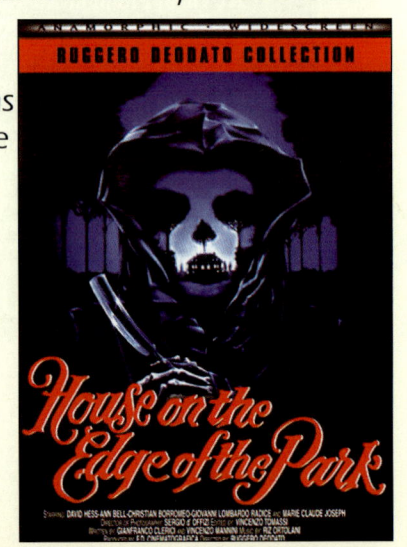

HUMAN EXPERIMENTS

Story Outline: A beautiful night club singer, Rachel Foster, witnesses a brutal murder for which she is wrongly convicted and sentenced to death.
At night bizarre animals and huge spiders appear in her prison cell. She can't sleep and deteriorates both mentally and physically. Dr. Kleine, the prison psychiatrist, has created the terror which is driving Rachel mad.
She escapes from her cell through the terror filled passages of the prison into the death cell where Kleine, dressed as the hangman, waits for her and the final degradation begins...

XF121

VHS

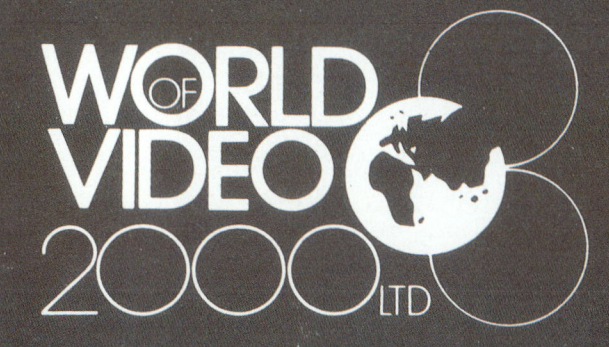

WORLD OF VIDEO 2000 LTD

SALES OFFICE
MAINE HOUSE · 15 LYON RD
LONDON SW19 2SB

Tomorrow's world of video entertainment today.

A Jaguar Video Release

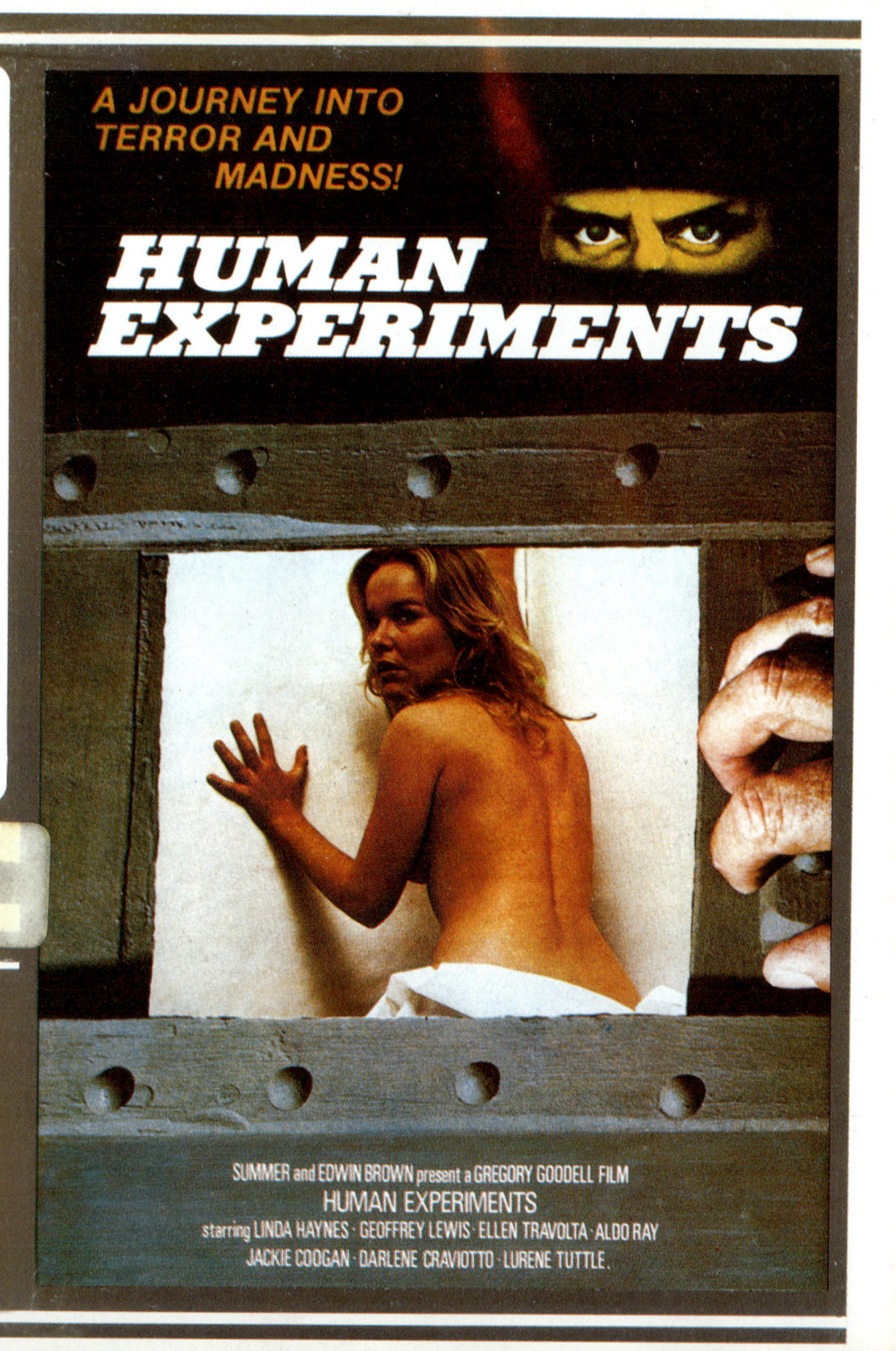

HUMAN EXPERIMENTS

A JOURNEY INTO TERROR AND MADNESS!

HUMAN EXPERIMENTS

SUMMER and EDWIN BROWN present a GREGORY GOODELL FILM
HUMAN EXPERIMENTS
starring LINDA HAYNES · GEOFFREY LEWIS · ELLEN TRAVOLTA · ALDO RAY
JACKIE COOGAN · DARLENE CRAVIOTTO · LURENE TUTTLE.

REVIEW

One of the early casualties of the "Video Nasties" crackdowns in the UK, it's difficult to see what caused such offense about this boring psychological horror tale set in a lunatic asylum where country singer Linda Haynes is imprisoned (wrongly, of course) and subjected to the usual round of WIP indignities. Doctor Geoffrey Lewis (a regular in Clint Eastwood movies) is conducting bizarre behavioural experiments there, and rape and torture are all part of the learning curve. He exposes his human guinea pigs to bugs and spiders, shocking them into a state of catatonia. But he meets his match in the resourceful Haynes, who makes the bad Doc fall victim to his own treatment. Not in the slightest bit interesting, this one wastes an unusual cast of B-movie faves like Aldo Ray, Jackie Cooper and Ellen Travolta - yes, that's John's sister!

DVD Review

There seems to be some doubt as to whether this movie was ever officially classed as a Nasty, though it did turn up on enough lists for us to have decided in its favour with this book! Aka **Beyond The Gate**, the film had 26 secs removed for an 18 cinema release, and this seems to be the same version that's being touted around by our old friends at VIPCO on VHS only. Nobody else seems to be bothered about this one – you can't even pick up a bootleg DVD at time of writing. So if you're desperate to see it then the slightly trimmed VIPCO reissue (which is taken from the same master as the original Nasties entry, by the looks of it) seems the only way to go. As a word of consolation, you're not missing much if you skip this one entirely.

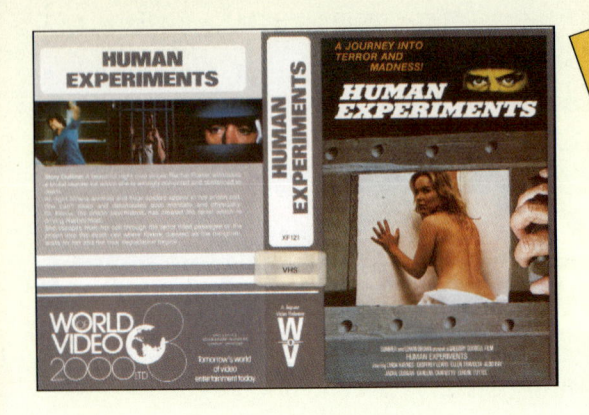

TITLE HUMAN EXPERIMENTS

AKA Beyond The Gate.

DIRECTOR Gregory Goodell

COUNTRY USA
SOURCE WOV 2000/Jaguar
YEAR 1979
TIME 81m48s

CAST Linda Haynes, Geoffrey Lewis, Ellen Travolta, Lurene Tuttle, Mercedes Shirley, Darlene Craviotto, Marie O'Henry, Wesley Marie Tackitt, Caroline Davies, Cherie Franklin, Aldo Ray, Jackie Coogan, Bobby Porter, James O'Connell, Rebecca Bohanon, Theodora Tate, Timothy Coyle, Roberta Jean Williams, Ruth Stanley, Maryanne Furman-Barrett, Millicent Crisp, Ginny Siegel, Jinaki, Joyce Davis Smith, Arthur King Williams, Mick Walker, Lou Ozonko, ::Larry Spatz, Steve Halter, Kenny Allen, Teda Bracci, Gayle Gannes, Laurie Hendricks, Debbie Pierce. [voices] Stan Bohrman, Philip Proctor, Sarah Cunningham.

PRODUCTION Summer & Edwin Brown present... [prod] Summer Brown & Gregory Goodell. [assoc prod] D. K. Miller. [exec prod] Edwin Scott Brown.© 1979 Pyramid Entertainment.

PHOTOGRAPHY DIRECTOR João Fernandes

MUSIC Marc Bucci
EDITOR Barbara Pokras & John Gregory

I miss you hugs and kisses

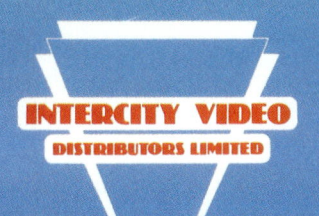

For those who like their sex with a lot of violence, 'I MISS YOU, HUGS & KISSES' is a must. Based on the sensational and notorious recent Canadian murder trial of one, Peter Demeter, it stars ELKE SOMMER, DONALD PILON, GEORGE CHUVALO and CHUCK SHAMATA.

What was the motive for the brutal slaying of Magdalene Kruschen, the voluptuous ex-model wife of Charles Kruschen, a successful Hungarian building contractor?

Why were the police determined to get Kruschen for this murder? Why did Kruschen's best friend betray him? Who was the other woman in Kruschen's life?

Through flashbacks, a bizarre story of crime, greed, lust and violence unfolds, including fantasies concerning the real murderer of this ravishingly beautiful woman.

Running Time: 84 minutes

INTERCITY VIDEO
FORD STREET COVENTRY CV1 5FN TELEPHONE (0203) 57815

COPYRIGHT WARNING: All rights of the producers and owners of the recorded work reserved. This recording may only be used in Private Homes and any other use including making copies, causing it to be seen or heard in public, hiring, re-selling, editing, TV or radio broadcasting of this tape are prohibited. © 1981 INTERCITY VIDEO

DESIGNED BY Griffith PRODUCTIONS LIMITED

ICV 111
COLOUR · X

INTERCITY VIDEO

A bizarre love, a strange death.

I MISS YOU HUGS & KISSES

STARRING: ELKE SOMMER AND DONALD PILON

With: Chuck Shamata, George Touliatos, Cec Linder. Introducing: Cindy Girling and George Chuvalo. Executive Producer – Steve Burns. Producer – Charles Markowitz, Murray Markowitz. Art Director – Carol Spier. Editor – Donald Ginsberg. Music – Howard Shore. Director of Photography – Don Wilder. Written and Directed by – Murray Markowitz. An Astral Films Release

DISTRIBUTORS LIMITED

REVIEW

TITLE	I MISS YOU, HUGS AND KISSES
AKA	Drop Dead Dearest
DIRECTOR	Murray Markowitz
COUNTRY	CAN
SOURCE	Intercity (UK)
YEAR	1978
TIME	83m24s
CAST	Elke Sommer, Donald Pilon, Chuck Shamata, George Touliatos, Cindy Girling, George Chuvalo, Cec Linder, Richard Davidson, Miguel Fernandes, Michele Fansett, Corinna Carlson, Linda Sorensen, Susan Hogan, Larry Solway, Ned Conlon, Henry Cohen, Bill Walker, Lawrence Elion, Barry Bellchamber, James Morris, James Millington, Ara Hovanessian, Don Ferguson, Melissa Gray, Kim Bailey.
PRODUCTION	The Markowitz Brothers present... A Paradise Films Limited Production. [prod] Charles Zakery Markowitz & Murray Markowitz. [exec prod] Steve Burns. © 1978 Paradise Films Limited Productions.
PHOTOGRAPHY DIRECTOR	Don Wilder
MUSIC	Howard Shore
EDITOR	Donald Ginsberg

Based on the real-life murder case of Toronto estate agent Peter Demeter, who was accused of killing his wife in 1975, this odd little movie puts forth a number of methods by which the crime could have taken place. It also concentrates on the common belief that Demeter hired an outside party to do the deed, a view which eventually guided the jurors to a guilty plea. Goodness knows why the film ended up on the nasties list, because the violence is presented in an almost abstract fashion with the screen going red as poor old Elke Sommer (a regular in low-grade Italian horrors who also starred in **Carry On Behind!**) is shown having a building block dropped on her pretty bonce and being electrocuted while swimming in a pool. The chief suspect for the role of hit man for hire is a nutty guy played by Chuck Shamata, whose hobbies include the rape and murder of hitchhikers. In the film's most amusing moment, this wild-eyed loony turns to the jury and asks: "Do I look like the kind of guy who would hurt anybody?" Well yes, actually... There's an interesting story to be told here, but it's scuttled by writer/director Markham's scattershot approach to the narrative, which is so cluttered with flashbacks that you keep getting lost as to whether you're supposed to be in the past or the present.

DVD Review

This was re-submitted a few years after the Video Recordings Act came into force. 1 min 6 secs were cut (including the gory results of a paving stone being dropped on someone's head) and the film was retitled **Drop Dead Dearest**. The distributor of the cut version was the now-defunct Heron Entertainment. Since then the film has been generally hard to find, though there was briefly a limited edition European DVD-R release that is thought to have originated in Germany. This was reportedly sourced from the same rather poor full screen master used to make up the Intercity title that was banned in the early 80s, though never having seen a copy of the disc I can't comment on the truth of this. Elke Sommer fans will have to wait until a company like Anchor Bay rescues this from obscurity – but don't hold your breath.

I SPIT ON YOUR GRAVE

A VIOLENT, SHOCKING STORY OF BLOODY REVENGE.

Jennifer Hills is a New York magazine writer on a vacation in an isolated countryside. While secluded in the house she has rented, she meets Matthew, a semi-retarded man who delivers groceries for the local store. Seeing the reverence and desire that Matthew has for her, some of the men in town, determined to make Jennifer his first sexual experience. They kidnap her, strip her, and present her to Matthew. He retreats in fear, but Johnny rapes her. She escapes.

As she tries to find her way home, the men ambush her, beat her, and rape her again. They leave her, and she makes her way home.

But inside the house, the men wait for her. When she enters, they beat her and harrass her. Matthew eventually gives in to his friends' coaxing and participates in the rape. The men leave the bloody unconscious woman on the floor of the house.

Later they return to the house to find out if Jennifer is really dead. Seeing the men awakes an animal rage within her and she turns into a creature with no emotions and only one goal . . . revenge!

She kills each man in a unique, elaborate manner. She makes love to Matthew and then hangs him. She seduces Johnny in the bathtub and castrates him. The others go out to avenge their friends' murders, only to confront Jennifer and come to violent and shocking ends.

"The copyright proprietor has licensed the film contained in this videocassette for private home use only. Any other use including making copies of the film, causing it to be seen or heard in public or broadcasting it or causing to be transmitted to subscribers to a diffusion service is strictly prohibited. Any breach of the above conditions render the offender liable to prosecution. by Astra Video Ltd.

ASTRA VIDEO

THIS WOMAN HAS JUST...
CUT, CHOPPED, BROKEN AND BURNED FOUR MEN BEYOND RECOGNITION... BUT NO JURY IN AMERICA WOULD EVER CONVICT HER!

I SPIT ON YOUR GRAVE
AN ACT OF REVENGE!

Starring **CAMILLE KEATON** **ERON TABOR** **RICHARD PACE** **ANTHONY NICHOLS**
produced by **JOSEPH ZBEDA**
written and directed by **MEIR ZARCHI**
RUNNING TIME 98 MIN

ASTRA VIDEO

REVIEW

This infamous movie features one of the most graphic and vicious gang-rape scenes ever committed to celluloid. But it's presented in a cold, dispassionate manner with no background music to cue our emotions. Camille Keaton (Buster's grand-niece) plays a writer on holiday in a backwoods community who is raped *twice* by four local thugs (one of whom is mentally retarded). They leave her for dead, but she recovers and wreaks a brutal revenge on her attackers, castrating one guy in the bath, chopping one up with an axe, and slicing another to pieces with an outboard motor. Though technically very rough, the film is nevertheless very powerful in places, and as already mentioned, the lack of background music gives it a disquieting feeling of documentary reality. It's almost as notorious as **The Last House On The Left**, and very nearly as well made. Writer/director Zarchi reportedly based his story on a real-life incident where he discovered a girl who had been gang-raped in a city park and was disgusted to see that the police were more interested in what she was doing there alone than in giving her medical help. Of course the heroine of this picture doesn't even think of going to the cops! Keaton is shown as a strong-willed character who dishes out a cold and brutal revenge for the violation of her body. The gore scenes are low budget and rely on suggestion rather than bloody effects, though the bit where our heroine relieves the main baddie of his meat and two veg will bring tears to your eyes!

TITLE	I SPIT ON YOUR GRAVE
AKA	Day of the Woman
DIRECTOR	Meir Zarchi
COUNTRY	US
SOURCE	Astra (UK)
YEAR	1978
TIME	96m47s
CAST	Camille Keaton, Eron Tabor, Richard Pace, Anthony Nichols, Gunter Kleemann, Alexis Magnotti, Tammy Zarchi, Terry Zarchi, Traci Ferrante, Bill Tasgal, Isac Agami, Ronit Haviv.
PRODUCTION	Jerry Gross presents... A Cinemagic Pictures Production.[prod] Joseph Zbeda & Meir Zarchi. © 1978 Cinemagic Pictures, Inc.
PHOTOGRAPHY DIRECTOR	Yuri Haviv
MUSIC	Giacomo Puccini
EDITOR	Meir Zarchi

DVD Review

The UK company Hardgore gave us a UK disc of this much-reviled 1981 US rape and revenge film by Meir Zarchi. They stated that 'only 41 seconds of cuts were made,' rather than the 7 minutes, which were removed from this when it was first submitted back in 2001. But that's not the whole story. Basically, the latest submission was pre-cut by the distributor in line with the BBFC's 2001 cuts list. However, this time they decided to make the cuts differently. Some of the cuts were made by reframing (rather than removing) unacceptable material. This means that certain sequences that were previously cut are now partially present, albeit in a reframed version. As for the 41 seconds of cuts, these occurred at the one point where the BBFC didn't feel that the reframing (and their other tricks, such as use of slow motion) achieved the effect required by the 2001 cuts list. Basically, they had reframed the rape over the rock so that you couldn't see the woman being raped (she was below screen) but you could still see the attackers thrusting and enjoying the attack. The BBFC asked for this to be removed. Luckily an uncut region 1 DVD is available from Elite in the USA. This looks stunning in 1.85:1 anamorphic, and also features an audio commentary by writer/director Zarchi and cult film guru Joe Bob Briggs, plus lots of other goodies.

Inferno

A young woman is murdered when she discovers that the New York apartment house in which she lives is one of three dwellings especially designed years before for the unholy trinity of the Three Mothers — Whispers, Tears and Darkness! When her brother, a student in Rome, returns to investigate the crime he finds himself involved in a series of terrifying events — a murder by black robed figures, an attack by a horde of cats, a hideous knifing and a final trip along a secret passageway that brings him face to face with the truth...

A superior horror thriller by Dario Argento, director of the much-acclaimed *Suspiria*, and one of the most frightening movies of recent years.

SALVATORE ARGENTO PRESENTS a film by DARIO ARGENTO
INFERNO
starring ELEONORA GIORGI, GABRIELE LAVIA, VERONICA LAZAR, LEOPOLDO MASTELLONI, IRENE MIRACLE, DARIO NICOLODI, SACHA PITOEFF, ALIDA VALLI with LEIGH McCLOSKEY as Mark
Director of Photography ROMANO ALBANI
Story & Screenplay by DARIO ARGENTO   Music by KEITH EMERSON
Music arranged by EMERSON & SALMON Orchestrated & Conducted by GODFFREY SALMON
Art Director GUISEPPE BASSAN   Costumes MASSIMO LENTINI
Film Editor FRANCO FRATICELLI   Production Manager ANGELO JACONO
Production Administrator SOLLY V. BIANCO
Produced by CLAUDIO ARGENTO for PRODUZIONI INTERSOUNI (ROME)
Directed by DARIO ARGENTO

colour/running time 104 minutes

COPYRIGHT © 1980 TWENTIETH CENTURY-FOX FILM CORPORATION. ALL RIGHTS RESERVED. The Copyright proprietor has licensed the picture recorded in the video cassette for private home use only and prohibits any other use, copying, reproduction or performance in public, in whole or in part.
PACKAGING COPYRIGHT © 1982 TWENTIETH CENTURY-FOX VIDEO.
Printed and manufactured in England.
Distributed by Twentieth Century-Fox Video, London.
TM designates the Trademark of TWENTIETH CENTURY-FOX FILM CORPORATION.

VHS 1140-50

Come face to face with Hell...

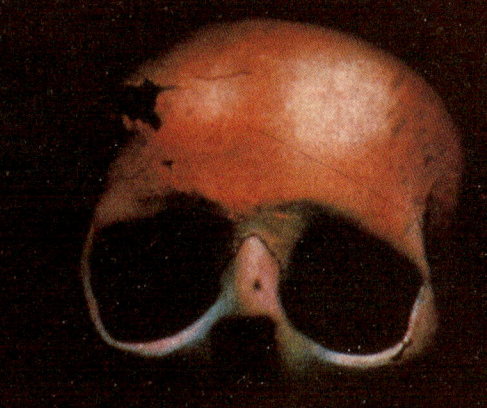

Inferno

A film by DARIO ARGENTO

TWENTIETH CENTURY-FOX VIDEO

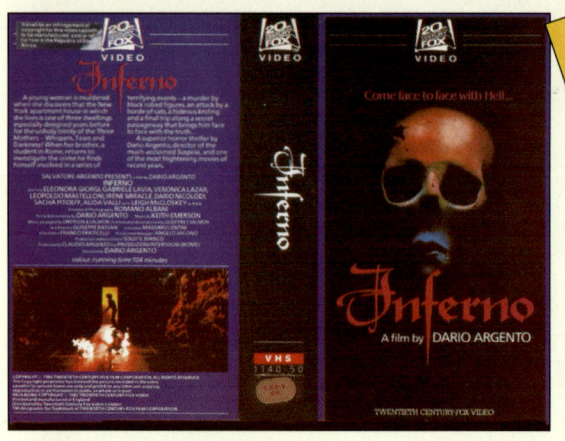

REVIEW

TITLE	INFERNO
AKA	Horror Infernal (Germany)
DIRECTOR	Dario Argento
COUNTRY	IT
SOURCE	CBS/Fox (UK)
YEAR	1980
TIME	102m08s
CAST	Leigh McCloskey, Irene Miracle, Eleonora Giorgi, Daria Nicolodi, Sacha Pitoeff, Alida Valli, Veronica Lazar, Gabrielle Lavia, Feodor Chaliapin, Leopoldo Mastelloni, Ania Pieroni, James Fleetwood, Rosario Rigutini, Ryan Hilliard, Paolo Paoloni, Fulvio Mingozzi, Luigi Lodoli, Rodolfo Lodi.
PRODUCTION	Salvatore Argento presents... A Produzioni Intersound (Rome) production. [prod] Claudio Argento. [prod man] Angelo Jacono. © 1980 Twentieth Century Fox.
PHOTOGRAPHY DIRECTOR	Romano Albani
MUSIC	Keith Emerson
EDITOR	Franco Fratcell

Though many consider this a lacklustre followup to **Suspiria**, it's actually a very good movie which contains some of the best scenes Argento has ever committed to celluloid. The opening sequence in particular, where Irene Miracle (of **Midnight Express**) has a terrifying encounter with an animated corpse in a waterlogged ballroom, is a real spine-tingler. Though the plot makes little sense from there on in, the film comes the closest in all of Argento's work to approximating the look of a waking nightmare. The thin plot follows a number of people who come into possession of a book detailing the evil secrets of "The Three Mothers," an evil trio who rule the underworld. One by one the unlucky browsers get bumped off in a gruesome fashion, being stabbed, decapitated, set on fire, having their eyes gouged out, eaten by rats etc... Imported American soap star Leigh McCloskey is the baffled-looking young hero who eventually gets to the root of the problem, and wishes he hadn't. The episodic storyline makes it less entertaining first time round than it is on subsequent viewings. Of course it doesn't exactly help you to get involved in a movie if the main character is done in every ten minutes! Keith Emerson's haunting score is a major asset, and so is Romano Albani's lurid colour camerawork. The only scene that caused controversy here involves a cat eating a mouse - doesn't that sort of thing go on in the real world?

DVD Review

This respected Dario Argento movie is another that should never have made the Nasties list in the first place, and it only took 21 secs of cuts to persuade the BBFC to allow it through with a video 18. These incorporated a 2 sec cut as Sacha Pitoeff beats a cat against the side of a chair, and the removal of 3 shots totalling 19s of a cat eating a mouse. If such sights do not easily offend you then you can head over to Amazon or some other US supplier and pick up the totally uncut region 0 American release. Available on the Anchor Bay label, this is a terrific-looking disc mastered in 1.85:1 anamorphic, with 5.1 Dolby Digital sound. Cast and crew biographies, production stills and a trailer. Special features include an exclusive Dario Argento interview.

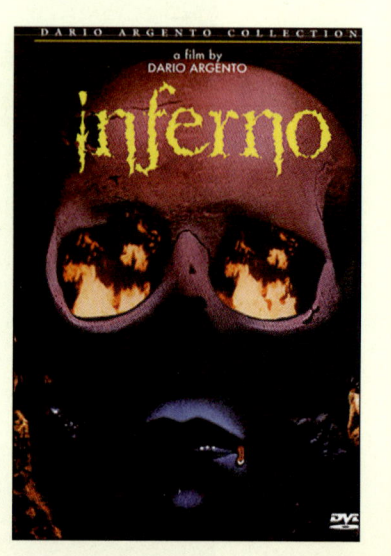

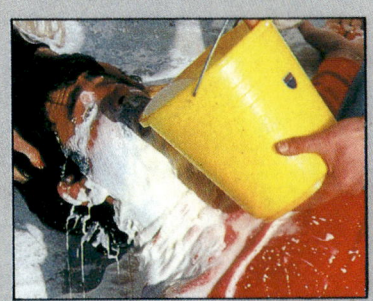

ISLAND OF DEATH

Some, they tore to pieces with a sword...
some, they decapitated with the sharp blade of a bull-dozer...
others, they burned to death with an aerosol torch...
or they brutally crucified them...
the lucky ones simply got their brains blown out.

CHRISTOPHER and CELIA arrive on the island of Myconos for a quiet winter vacation. They seem such a nice handsome couple, and they are so in love. Everyone likes them. But we are soon to discover that they are a couple of sick and perverted people, especially CHRISTOPHER who thinks that God has given him the divine right to punish perversion and so he should deliver the innocent local people purified from the evil brought to the island by the foreign tourists who flock to Myconos throughout the year. No one escaped!!

Copyright warning: The film licenced in this video-cassette is restricted to use for private home viewing only, causing it to be seen or heard in public or broadcasting it or causing it to be transmitted to subscribers to a diffusion service, copying it or otherwise dealing with it in part, is strictly prohibited without the written permission of the copyright holder and distributor.

Approved and passed by the BBFC
X CERTIFICATE

VHS
ISLAND OF DEATH
AVI 003
100 MINS APPROX

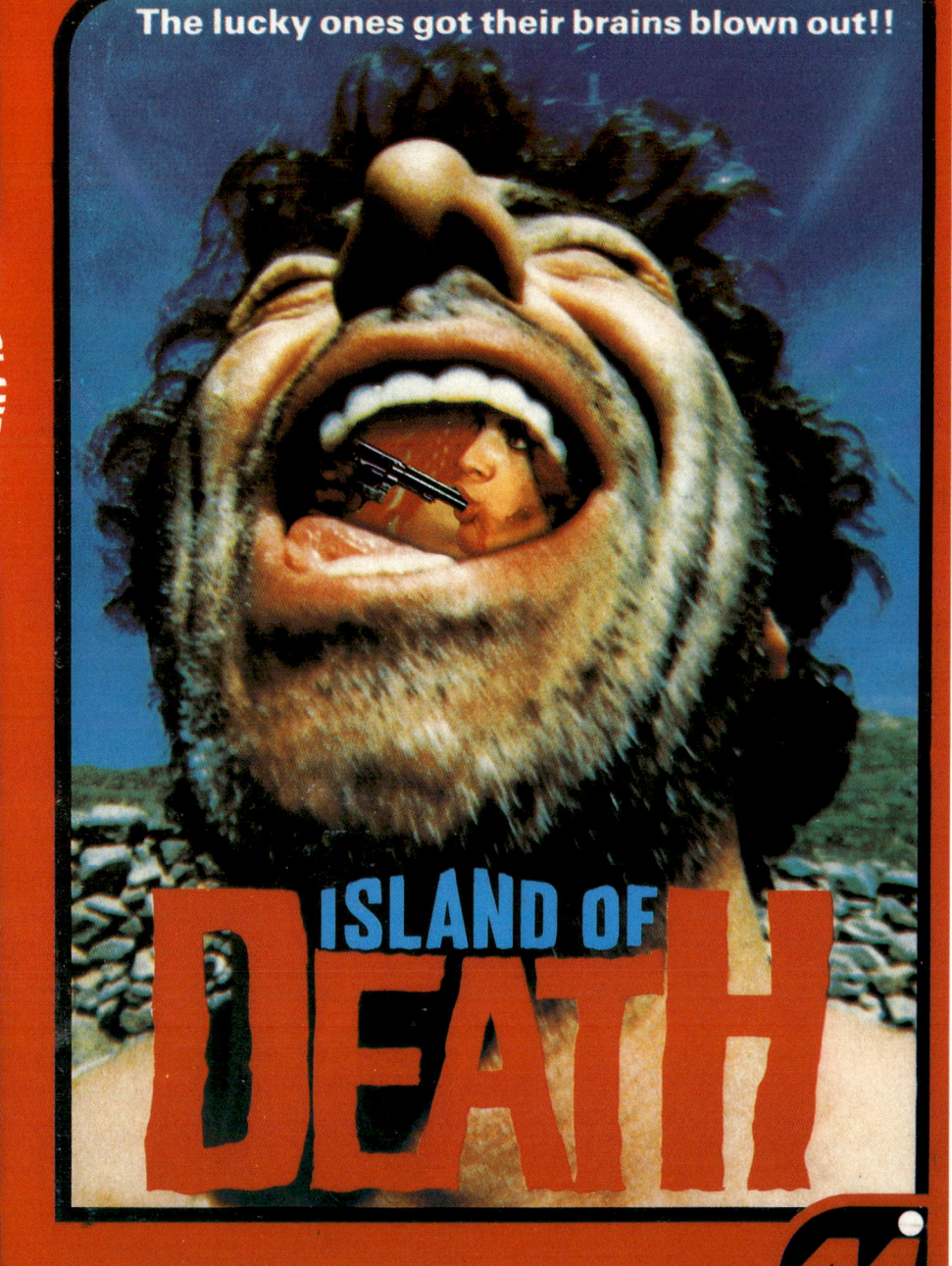

The lucky ones got their brains blown out!!

ISLAND OF DEATH

Starring BOB BELLING, JANE RYALE and NICO TSACHIRIDI
Written and Directed by NICO MASTORAKIS

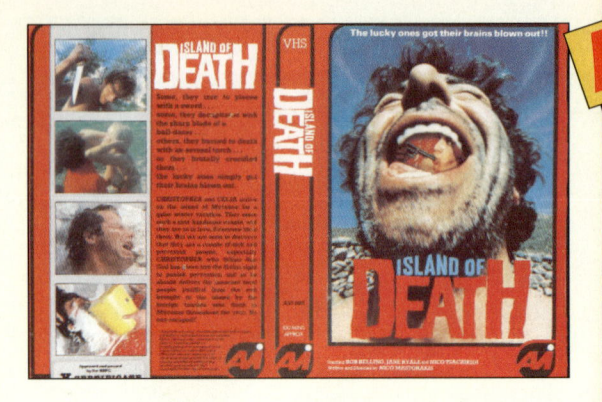

REVIEW

This is a really sick little movie, originally let loose under the more appropriate title of **Island Of Perversion**. It certainly fosters the image of Greece as a country where men are men and sheep are scared! At the beginning, a young guy named Chris is seen giving his girlfriend Celia a good seeing-to in a telephone box. What's sick about that? Well, for a start they are actually brother and sister, and secondly they have phoned their mum up in the middle so she can tune in to their orgasmic gruntings. Later on, Christopher feels he wants a bit of a change, so he goes out and fornicates with a goat, slitting its throat afterwards so that it doesn't rat on him! It seems that Celia and Chris share the same hobby: they like to watch each other having sex with strangers, and then take photographs as they murder them. These are no ordinary murders: Chris pours whitewash in the mouth of one of Celia's lovers, and on another occasion he pees on a mature American woman before burying her with a dump truck. Surprisingly puritanical when it comes to tolerating homosexuality, Chris invades a gay party with a sword, later forcing the sole survivor to fellate a gun barrel - with a predictably messy outcome. Of course in the end the couple get their comeuppance, Celia by being ravaged by a moronic shepherd and Chris by being thrown into a lime pit where he will inevitably be burned alive. Mastorakis has given us a lot of forgettable video fodder in his time, and this is by far his most memorable film.

TITLE ISLAND OF DEATH

AKA Island of Perversion; A Craving for Lust; Devils in Mykonos; Psychic Killer 2 [refused BBFC cert title]

DIRECTOR Nico Mastorakis (as Nick Mastorakis)

COUNTRY GR
SOURCE AVI (UK)
YEAR 1975
TIME 102m39s

CAST Bob Belling, Jane Ryall, Jessica Dublin, Gerald Gonalons, Janice McConnel, Clay Huff, Mike Murtagh, Jeremy Rousseau, Niko Tsachiridis.

PRODUCTION Omega Pictures. Nick Mastorakis (Nico Mastorakis) presents... A Transam Production. [prod] Nick Mastorakis (Nico Mastorakis). © None.

PHOTOGRAPHY DIRECTOR Nick Gardellis

MUSIC Nick Lavranos
EDITOR Not credited

DVD Review

Island of Death was pre-cut by 13 minutes and resubmitted to the BBFC by VIPCO as **Psychic Killer 2**. The BBFC still banned it. The film did, however, get a cinema release in cut form under the title of **A Craving For Lust**. Then in 2002 the movie was submitted again for a UK video certificate, and this time it was passed with over 4 minutes of cuts to scenes of sexual violence and 'dehumanising sexual activity' (specifically the scene where somebody gets peed on!). The film did, however, finally get an uncut release early in 2003 thanks to Image in the US. Their region free disc was taken from director Nico Mastorakis' own 35mm print, and it looks absolutely stunning. The disc includes an interview with Mastorakis himself (who has an acting role in the film) and a madcap music video, plus stills and posters.

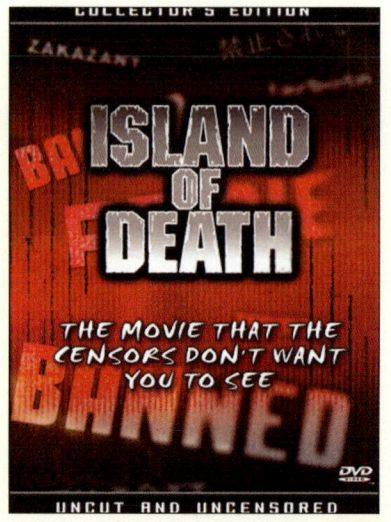

KILLER NUN

Videocassettes

V. 111

A THRILLER FULL OF SUSPENCE BASED ON A TRUE EPISODE OF CRIME THAT RECENTLY OCCURRED IN BELGIUM.

ANITA EKBERG - JOE DALLESANDRO

COLOR / 90 min.

techno film

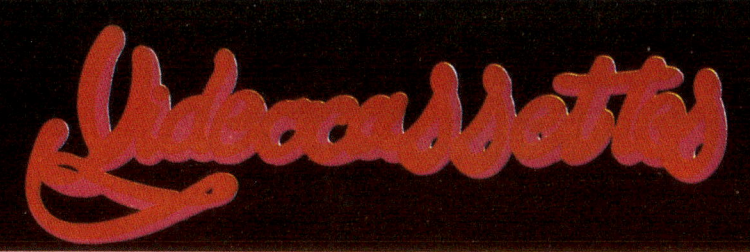

All copyrights are reserved. Partial or total reproductions, television broadcast, projection into theaters or screening before paying audiences are forbidden.

VHS PAL

Fletcher Video

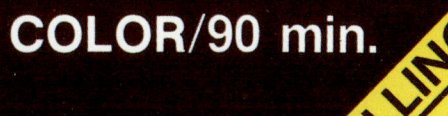

THRILLING V. 111

REVIEW

Former screen sexpot Anita Ekberg changes the habits of a lifetime in this salacious exploitation shocker supposedly drawn "From the secret archives of the Vatican." An ageing and out-of-shape Ekberg plays Sister Gertrude, a modern-day nun working in a mental asylum. Thanks to her addiction to morphine she is crazier than her patients, and though she hates men it doesn't stop her having sex with them. She bumps off some of the more troublesome inmates and diverts suspicion on to a fellow nun who also happens to be a drug addict. In the end it's up to Mother Superior Alida Valli to restore the status quo by slipping Anita a poisoned chalice. The murder scenes are the best part of the show, with patients being bashed over the head with a lamp and thrown through windows, strangled, kicked to death and perforated with pins. Though it starts out promisingly with plenty of sleazy ingredients, **Killer Nun** ends up being a rather dour and depressing sort of movie, not at all the sort of film you'd imagine from the title. Those with catholic tastes will take **Angel Of Vengeance** over this one any day!

TITLE	KILLER NUN, THE
AKA	Suor omicidi; Deadly Habit
DIRECTOR	Giulio Berruti
COUNTRY	IT
SOURCE	Techno Film/Fletcher (UK)
YEAR	1978
TIME	80m55s
CAST	Anita Ekberg, Joe Dallesandro, Alida Valli, Massimo Serato, Daniele Dublino, Laura Nucci, Alice Gherardi, Ileana Fraja, Lee De Barriault, Antonietta Patriarca, Sofia Lusy, Nerina Montagnani, Franco Caracciolo, Maria Sofia Amendolea, Chicca Thomas, Manlio Pieoretti, Brunello Chiodetti, Enzo Spitaleri, Lesly Thomas, Aldo De Franchi, Paola Morra, Lou Castel.
PRODUCTION	Enzo Gallo presents….,A Cinesud Production in collaboration with Gruppo Di Lavoro Calliope Coop s.r.l. © None.
PHOTOGRAPHY DIRECTOR	Tonino Maccoppi
MUSIC	Alessandro Alessandroni
EDITOR	Mario Giacco

DVD Review

13 seconds of cuts rescued this fairly mild nunsploitation flick from the Nasties list and allowed it to be released on the Redemption label in the late-90s. Unfortunately this cut and VHS-only release remains just about the only way to get this one at present, while many lesser nun flicks (particularly from Jess Franco) proliferate on foreign labels. At least the Redemption release is presented in 1.85:1 widescreen and drawn from a very good print. It's possible that the same company may resurrect it at some time on their Salvation label, but it was officially deleted in early 2003. There are bootleg DVD-Rs floating about if you know where to look, but these are poor quality and seem to have been drawn from a trimmed print – so purchase at your peril!

THE LAST HOUSE ON THE LEFT

MARI, SEVENTEEN, IS DYING, EVEN FOR HER THE WORST IS YET TO COME!

WARNING: The copyright proprietor has licensed the film contained in this video cassette for private home use only, and any other use including making copies of the film, causing it to be seen or heard in public or broadcasting it or causing it to be transmitted to subscribers to a diffusion service or otherwise dealing with it in part, is strictly prohibited without the prior written permission of REPLAY VIDEO.

COLOUR ● 80 MINUTES

VPD

VIDEO PROGRAMME DISTRIBUTORS LIMITED
G.E.C. ESTATE, EAST LANE, WEMBLEY,
MIDDX HA9 7FF.

R 1013

THE LAST HOUSE ON THE LEFT

TO AVOID FAINTING KEEP REPEATING, IT'S ONLY A MOVIE
..ONLY A MOVIE
..ONLY A MOVIE
..ONLY A MOVIE
..ONLY A MOVIE
..ONLY A MOVIE
..ONLY A MOVIE

WARNING! NOT RECOMMENDED FOR PERSONS UNDER 18!

DUE TO THE SPECIFIC NATURE OF THE HORRIFIC AND VIOLENT SCENES IN THIS FILM THE FRONT COVER IS NOT ILLUSTRATED TO AVOID OFFENCE.

THE DIRECTOR OF
'FRIDAY THE 13th'
IS GOING TO SCARE THE HELL OUT OF YOU...AGAIN.

VHS

REPLAY Video

REVIEW

TITLE	LAST HOUSE ON THE LEFT, THE
AKA	Krug and Company; Sex Crime of the Century; The Men's Room; Night of Vengeance (shooting title)
DIRECTOR	Wes Craven
COUNTRY	US
SOURCE	Replay (UK)
YEAR	1972
TIME	77m23s
CAST	Sandra Cassell, Lucy Grantham, David A. Hess, Fred Lincoln, Jeramie Rain, Marc Sheffler, Gaylord St. James, Cynthia Carr, Ada Washington, Marshall Anker, Martin Kove, Ray Edwards. [and uncredited] Jonathan Craven.
PRODUCTION	Sean S. Cunningham Films Ltd presents... [prod] Sean S. Cunningham. [assoc prod] Katherine D'Amato. [prod assis] Steve Miner. © 1972 The Night Co.
PHOTOGRAPHY DIRECTOR	Victor Hurwitz
MUSIC	David Alexander Hess & Steve Chapin (uncredited)
EDITOR	Wes Craven. [assis] Stephen Miner

Wes Craven's shocking drive-in reworking of Bergman's **The Virgin Spring** is one of the most reviled films in movie history. It's also famous for giving the world that infamous tagline, "Just keep repeating, It's only a movie... it's only a movie!" The film graphically details the atrocities committed by a group of escaped convicts, who kidnap, rape and murder two teenage girls on their way home from a rock concert. In a typically savage touch, one of the girls is made to pee in her pants before she is disembowelled. After hiding the bodies the gang take refuge in the home of a suburban couple who turn out to be the parents of one of the girls they have slaughtered. The parents then take equally vile revenge (a chainsaw figures prominently) in the final reel. Craven has said this film came out of his rage at the atrocities committed in the Vietnam War, but it sounds like an excuse to us. **Last House** is all the more disturbing for being well made. The acting and direction have an edge of documentary realism and, though sickening, the film does have a point to make, like who is worse, the depraved convicts who have made murder a way of life, or the girls' affluent, God-fearing parents, who allow themselves to throw away their value system to enact a bloody, tortuous revenge? If Craven had never made another movie this would still have assured his place in the Horror Hall of Fame.

DVD Review

This most contentious of Nasties was rejected for a cinema release in 1974 and again in 2000. It did achieve an arthouse circuit release in 2000, but only under private cinema club rules. In 2002 Carl Daft and David Gregory of Exploited famously picked up the film for a UK release. When the BBFC demanded fairly extensive cuts to the some of the rape and torture sequences, Carl and David fought the case via the toothless Video Appeals Committee – who then asked for even more cuts than the BBFC had! It was eventually released on DVD by Anchor Bay UK with 31 secs of cuts, but although this additional footage was not allowed to feature on the disc, it can actually be seen on the internet on a secret website. The instructions to access the site are hidden on the first disc of this double-disc set. From the Main Menu of the first disc, highlight the Play menu entry and then press Right on your remote control. This should make the windows of the house in the background turn red - pressing Enter on your remote control at this point will give you the address and password to use. Alternately, you can buy the uncut American disc, though the British one has even better extras on it. Who cares about the BBFC anyway?

VIP002

VHS
VIDEO
CASSETTE

The Living DEAD

A horror film that will make your flesh crawl. Rejuvenating themselves on the flesh of the living, the dead are revived. To walk again and torment their tormentors. A clever film with twist after twist, right up to the final horrific climax.

WARNING
"The copyright proprietor has licensed the film contained in this videocassette for private home use only. Any other use including making copies of the film, causing it to be seen or heard in public or broadcasting it or causing it to be transmitted to subscribers to a diffusion service, letting on hire or otherwise dealing with it in whole or in part is strictly prohibited. Any breach of the above conditions renders the offender liable to prosecution."

© Video Independent Productions Ltd.

VIP

Sleeve design by
IMPRESSIONS
01 722 3939

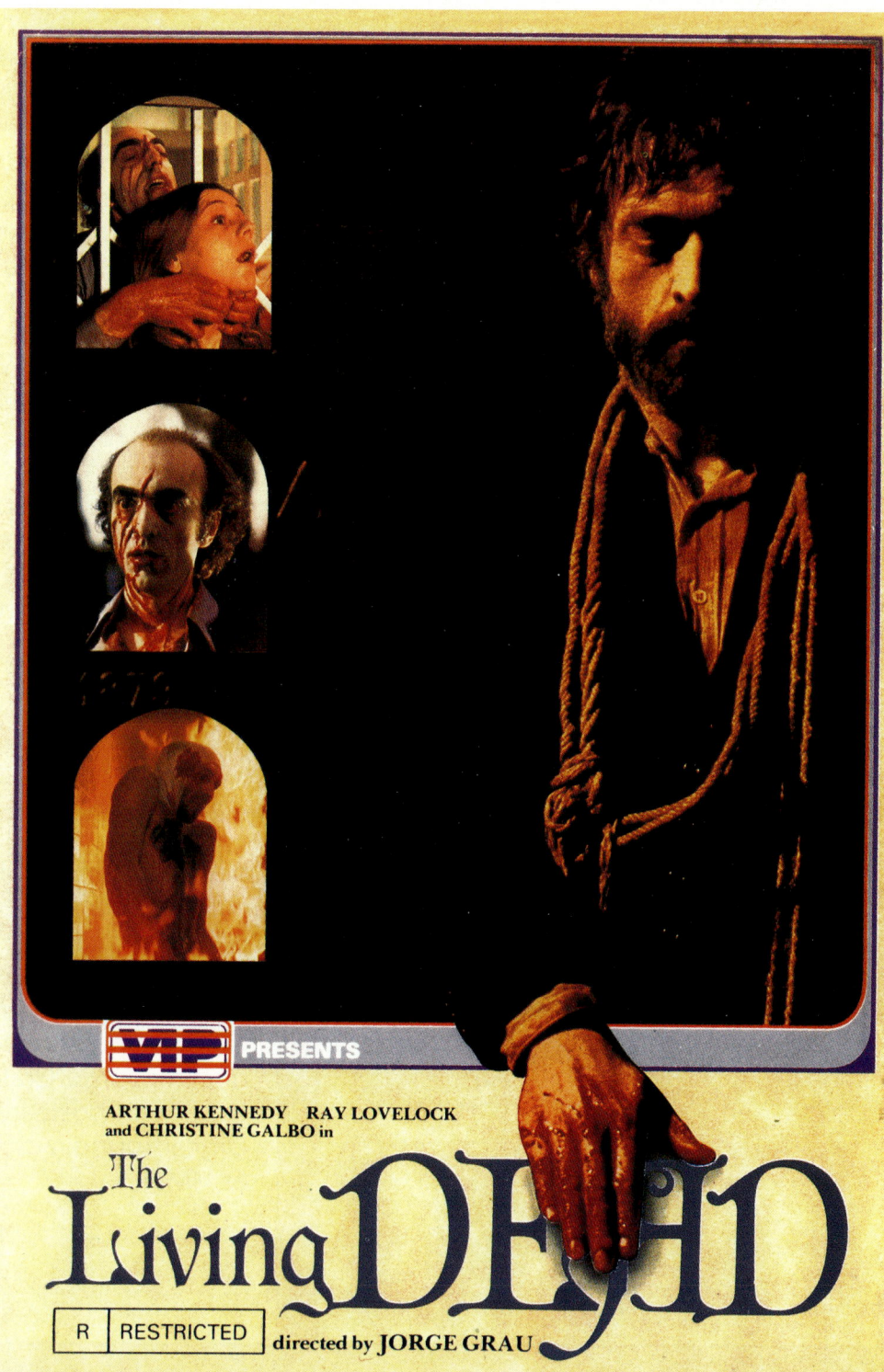

The Living DEAD

VIP PRESENTS

ARTHUR KENNEDY   RAY LOVELOCK
and CHRISTINE GALBO in

The Living DEAD

R RESTRICTED   directed by JORGE GRAU

REVIEW

Originally released to UK cinemas on a double bill with Pete Walker's excellent cannibal chiller, **Frightmare**, this early Italian zombie movie was actually shot amid the scenic splendour of our own Lake District. The hero of the film (Ray Lovelock) is a bearded art dealer whose 'hippy' looks get him the blame for a series of brutal cannibalistic murders, even though we know these were actually committed by corpses reanimated by a new government pest control device that employs sonic waves. Arthur Kennedy goes laughably over the top as a fascist cop, and the plotting is dumb to say the least. The film does have its eerie moments however, most notably in the gory climax where zombies take over a hospital and scoff most of the patients. Director Grau (a pupil of Antonioni) gets good value out of the scenery and Giannetto de Rossi's realistic gore effects. Scenes showing a nurse having her breast torn off and a policeman being graphically disembowelled were trimmed for the UK cinema release but restored for the uncut video - later branded a video nasty. He even takes a stab at some art-house pretentiousness when, in the opening scenes, he makes a comment on the dreariness of modern life by showing us rush hour crowds of zombified commuters who don't bat an eyelid when a naked woman runs through their midst. Why does this sort of thing never happen in my neck of the woods?

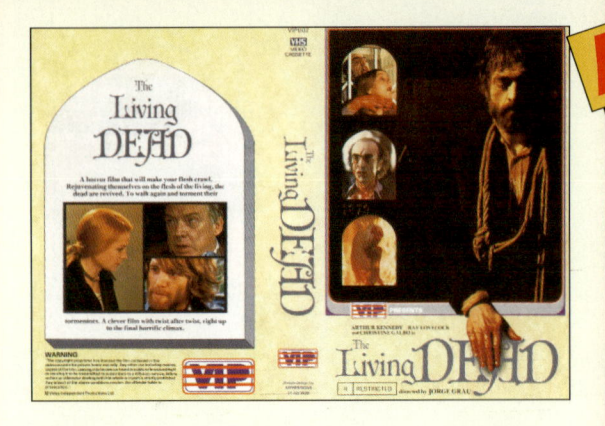

TITLE LIVING DEAD AT MANCHESTER MORGUE, THE

AKA No Profonar el Sueno de los Meurtos; Fin de Semana Paralos Muertos; Non si deve profanare il sonno dei morti; Da dove vieni?; Zombi 3; Don't Open the Window; Breakfast at the Manchester Morgue; Let Sleeping Corpses Lie

DIRECTOR Jorge Grau

COUNTRY SP, IT
SOURCE VIP (UK)
YEAR 1974
TIME 88m56s

CAST Ray Lovelock, Christine Galbo, Arthur Kennedy, Aldo Massasso, Giorgio Trestini, Roberto Posse, José Ruiz Lifante, Jeannine Mestre, Gengher Gatti, Fernando Hilbeck, Vera Drudi, Vincente Vega, Paco Sanz, Paul Benson, Anita Colby, Joaquin Hinjosa, Vito Salier, Isabel Mestrei.

PRODUCTION An Edmondo Amati production. [prod] Edmondo Amati. [prod man] Felice D'Alisera. © None.

PHOTOGRAPHY DIRECTOR Fransisco Sempere

MUSIC Giuliano Sorgini
EDITOR Vincenzo Tomass

DVD Review

1 minute 27 secs of cuts were made to this one by the distributor (European Creative Video) before it was re-submitted to the BBFC after the Video Recordings Act, and then the censors cut a further 26 seconds. But common sense prevailed in 2001 when the film was finally passed uncut for a UK DVD release on the Anchor Bay label. Anchor Bay released the same version in the States, a stunning 1.85:1 anamorphic transfer that was a hundred times better looking than either the cut cinema print or the version put out by ECT. Extras on the UK and US discs include plentiful stills and posters, a nice colour booklet, plus an interview with director Jorge Grau. Even more collectable was the Anchor Bay US limited edition in a big tin case, with postcards and further extras. All of these versions were remastered in 5.1 Dolby Digital sound. As of time of writing you can pick up cheap copies of this for around a fiver at HMV!

You will not forget in your lifetime the horrors you will witness...

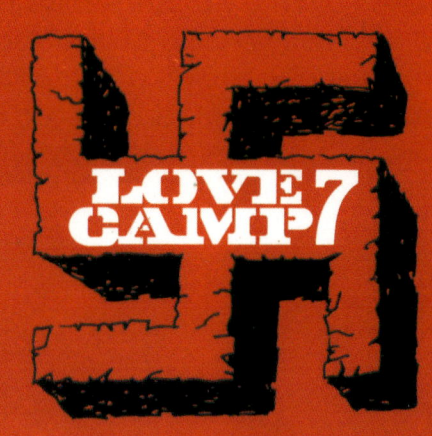

LOVE CAMP 7

The story of LOVE CAMP SEVEN is based on fact. Two young American W.A.C. Officers volunteer to throw themselves into the unspeakable indignities and horrifying humiliation of a Nazi Love Camp. These camps were used entirely to service the pleasures and perversions of the Nazi Front Line Officers. Then at 03.00 hours on the fifth day the area French Resistance was scheduled to break them free...

Filmed in Eastman Colour.
Running time 95 minutes

WARNING
This video recording and soundtrack are protected by by copyright and may only be used domestically i.e. in private homes. Any other exhibition, public performance diffusion, unauthorised copying, hiring, lending, radio or T.V. broadcasting, in whole, or part, is strictly prohibited unless expressly authorised in writing by the copyright holder and this prohibition may be enforced by legal action.

Distributed for Abbey Video by
Deegem Duplex Ltd

50 Newlay Grove, Horsforth, Leeds LS18 4LH.
Tel. Leeds (0532) 583893

LOVE CAMP 7

A Place of Total Despair
All the youthful beauty of Europe Enslaved for the pleasure of the 3rd Reich

LOVE CAMP 7

Abbey VIDEO

This is the film that goes beyond X
ADULTS ONLY

REVIEW

Though it's pretty tame stuff compared to later Nazi concentration camp exploitationers like **Ilsa, She Wolf Of The SS**, this sleazy little movie still leaves a nasty taste. The far-fetched plot has two WACs going undercover in a Nazi prison camp to get vital information from a scientist being held there. There's a lot of nudity, but not too much violence, and it's hard to take it seriously since the acting and accents are so unconvincing. The filmmakers seem more interested in sweaty softcore gropings than the hardcore torture stuff that's found in the **Ilsa** flicks. In one amusing scene a guard dog is set upon a line of female prisoners but seems more interested in playing in the jet of water they are being hosed down with! Producer R.W. Cresse plays the commandant, and famed grindhouse producer David Friedman turns up as a goose-stepping general. They have fun even if the audience doesn't.

TITLE LOVE CAMP 7

AKA Camp 7: Lager Femminile; Camp Special no. 7

DIRECTOR Robert Lee Frost (as R. L. Frost)

COUNTRY US
SOURCE Abbey (UK)
YEAR 1968
TIME 91m51s

CAST R. W. Cresse, Maria Lease, Kathy Wiliams, Bruce Kemp, John Aiderman, Rodger Steel, Rod Willmouth, Dave Friedman (David F. Friedman), John Riazzi, Louis Mazzarella, Larry Martinelli, Natasha Steel, Patricia Roddy, Carolyn Appelby, Ken Sims, Shelly Martin, Robert Baker.

PRODUCTION Olympic International presents... [prod] R. W. Cresse. [assoc prod] Wesdon Bishop. © 1968 Olympic International.

PHOTOGRAPHY DIRECTOR R. L. Frost (Robert Lee Frost)

MUSIC Not credited
EDITOR R.L.F. Enterprises (Robert Lee Frost)

DVD Review

This remains banned in the UK, and like most of the concentration camp-type Nasties there seems little point for any distributor to give them a test spin at the BBFC. Having said that, somebody did in 2002, and they were predictably given the bum's rush! It was released in Europe uncut a few years back under the Redemption Benelux label, complete with salacious stills from the movie, in a particularly lip-smacking package. This is no longer available, but a disc is available from the Netherlands-based DVD Classics label. This is completely uncut and gives us a full screen transfer in English and Italian (with subtitles). The picture quality is marginally better than the original VHS Nasties edition, but not as good as the Redemption tape. There are no extras on the disc.

MADHOUSE

A strange bond exists between Julia, and her identical twin sister, Mary, whom she has not seen for seven years.
Their Uncle, Father James, persuades Julia that she must visit Mary in hospital, but he warns her that she may not recognize her sister who has become horribly deformed.

At the hospital, Julia is startled by Mary's hideous appearance as the deformed sister suddenly grabs her wrists from the shadows and pulls her close, threatening to terrorise her again.

That night, a guard at the hospital is attacked and killed by a dog.

Julia's girlfriend, Helen, staying overnight is confronted by a vicious looking dog and a dead cat hanging in a corner. Terrified, she races down the stairs but the dog is too quick for her and attacks at her throat.

As the story develops, terror and evil become the main ingredients in this spine chilling masterpiece . . . you will never forget it!

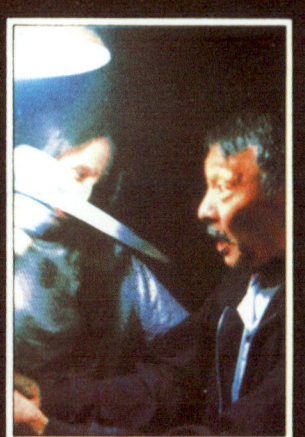

MEDUSA

WARNING: Copyright protected. All rights reserved. © Medusa Communications Ltd.

MC006
VHS

MADHOUSE

Sleeve design by
IMPRESSIONS
01-722 3939

MADHOUSE

starring TRISH EVERLY, DENNIS ROBERTSON, MICHAEL MACRAE,
MORGAN HART and RICHARD BAKER
produced and directed by OVIDIO G. ASSONITIS
Running time: 90 mins. approx. Colour.

REVIEW

Not to be confused with the thoroughly innocent Vincent Price/Peter Cushing movie of the same name, this intriguing splatter opus is a psychological thriller in the same mould as Brian de Palma's **Sisters**. The main character Julia ((Everly) is a teacher in a school for deaf children. Her mad, hideously disfigured twin escapes from an asylum with the aid of a ferocious killer dog and sets out to provide a memorable birthday "treat" for her sister, who she blames for having her banged up in the first place. Part of the surprise involves slaughtering all her friends in a gory fashion, and then setting the corpses up at the table in an imitation of party time at the Ed Gein homestead! There are plenty of cliches to be found here, but it's not bad of its kind, with some good gore to offend animal lovers (though that dog does look like a stuffed dummy) and that old DPP favourite, a harrowing drill-through-the-bonce sequence. It's also notable for being the only video nasty to quote George Bernard Shaw in the credits!

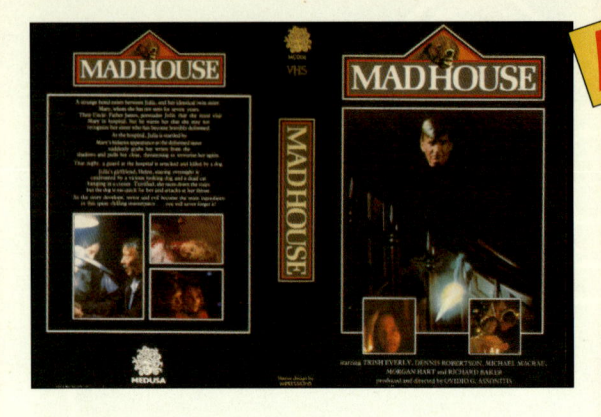

TITLE THERE WAS A LITTLE GIRL (as Madhouse)

AKA There was a Little Girl; Party des Schreckens (Germany);And when she was bad (USA)

DIRECTOR Ovidio G. Assonitis

COUNTRY US, IT
SOURCE Medusa (UK)
YEAR 1981
TIME 89m16s

CAST Trish Everly, Michael Macrae, Dennis Robertson, Morgan Hart, Allison Biggers, Edith Ivey, Richard Baker, Don Devendorf, Jerry Fujikawa, Doug Dillingham, Joe Camp, Janie Baker, Huxsie Scott.

PRODUCTION [prod] Peter Shepherd & Ovidio G. Assonitis. [exec in charge of prod] Jacques Goyard. © 1981 Chesham.

PHOTOGRAPHY DIRECTOR Roberto D'Ettorre Piazzoli

MUSIC Riz Ortolani
EDITOR Angelo Curi

DVD Review

There are a couple of other **Madhouse** movies out on video – the old Vincent Price/Peter Cushing Brit horror flick of the 70s, and a 1991 Kirstie Alley comedy. Both of these are a lot easier to get hold of than this one. **The Nasty Madhouse** remains banned in the UK, even though if it were resubmitted it would almost certainly get through uncut. The only contentious scene is the murder of a dog, but there's no way this falls foul of the BBFC's rules on animal cruelty because you can easily see the mutt is a fake one. The rights for **Madhouse** are currently being shopped around by an Italian distributor, so it seems likely it may turn up on DVD here in the near future, though at time of going to press nobody had snapped them up.

MARDI GRAS MASSACRE

Starring
CURT DAWSON GWEN ARMENT

Also starring
LAURA MISCH CATHRYN LACEY
NANCY DANCER BUTCH BENIT

Produced and directed by: J. WEIS

The colourful Mardi Gras carnival will soon be under way, but a sinister murder creates a feeling of fear amongst clubland's prostitutes, when one of them is discovered horribly mutilated. The police investigate but cannot prevent the next death, so similar to the first and they suspect a ritual killer is at work.
As the carnival takes to the streets, amongst the crowd is someone who plans his greatest sacrificial offering yet.

Colour 92mins X

DUE TO DISTURBING SCENES THIS VIDEO IS NOT SUITABLE FOR ANYONE UNDER 18.

All rights of the producer and the owner of the work reproduced reserved. Unauthorized copying, hiring, lending, public performance, radio or T.V. broadcasting of this video recording prohibited.

© 1982 Derann Film Services Ltd.

Ask your dealer for details of the fine selection of video entertainment for your leisure viewing.
Derann Audio Visual
Film House
99 High Street, Dudley
West Midlands DY1 1QP
England

FGS 900
VHS

GOLD STAR

MARDI GRAS MASSACRE

Everyone is celebrating nobody hears the screams of the victims for the sacrifice.

AMERICAN SPLATTER MOVIE

MARDI GRAS MASSACRE

DUE TO DISTURBING SCENES THIS VIDEO IS NOT SUITABLE FOR ANYONE UNDER 18.

REVIEW

Shot in New Orleans by people who **should have** been shot in New Orleans, this cheapie gore movie obviously owes a big debt of inspiration to the early films of Herschell Gordon Lewis. How the makers managed to stretch the squalid storyline out to feature length is a mystery that most sensible folk wouldn't consider worth investigating - a single photograph would have been plenty to tell the whole story. Basically, the **Blood Feast**-type plot involves the grisly activities of an Aztec priest (in a welder's mask!) who hangs around sleazy strip joints and kidnaps second-rate actresses to sacrifice to his goddess, Coatla - "God of the Four Directions and Queen of Evil in the Universe." This ineptly-made obscurity boasts one half-decent gore effect of a latex stomach being sliced open and bloody organs being removed, but it loses its impact after the makers have repeated it for the third time. Heroine Laura Misch was **Playboy's** Miss February of 1975, and her limited acting ability fits right in with the rest of the cast.

TITLE	MARDI GRAS MASSACRE
AKA	NONE
DIRECTOR	Jack Weis
COUNTRY	US
SOURCE	Derann/Goldstar (UK)
YEAR	1981
TIME	91m51s
CAST	Laura Misch, Cathryn Lacey, Nancy Dancer, Butch Benit, William Metzo, Ronald Tanet, Wayne Mack, Curt Dawson, Gwen Arment.
PRODUCTION	[prod] Jack Weis. [assoc prod] John Stimac Jr. © None.
PHOTOGRAPHY DIRECTOR	Jack Weis
MUSIC	Westbound Records
EDITOR	Not credited

DVD Review

This title remains banned in the UK and has not been resubmitted to the BBFC. The gore scenes are so phoney, and pretty much the same sliced latex torso repeated over and over again, so it's plain that the film would be passed uncut with an 18 certificate if anyone could be bothered to pick it up. However, it's such a terrible movie, padded out with interminable chat and some of the worst acting you'll ever see, that I can't see it having any commercial value whatsoever. In the States it has only ever been released on VHS and as a cut-rate DVD-R by the Florida-based Something Weird Video. The print used by SWV is a very scratchy fullscreen version with faded colours and an at-times-inaudible soundtrack. To be honest, the original VHS that made the Nasties list is probably better quality all round.

NIGHTMARE MAKER

Rejected by her lover, the only man left in Cheryl's life is the orphaned nephew she has raised as her own son. She'll stop at nothing to keep Billy with her. When her plans misfire, she is swept up into an insane frenzy that means death to anyone who comes between her and her obsession.

But the investigating detective is convinced that Billy is the real killer—and determined to prove it. Madness and fanaticism work together to drag all concerned into a terrifying vortex of blood-letting that adds a nightmarish twist to the classic Oedipus story.

BILLY LYNCH WAS TRIED FOR SECOND DEGREE MURDER AND FOUND NOT GUILTY ON GROUNDS OF TEMPORARY INSANITY

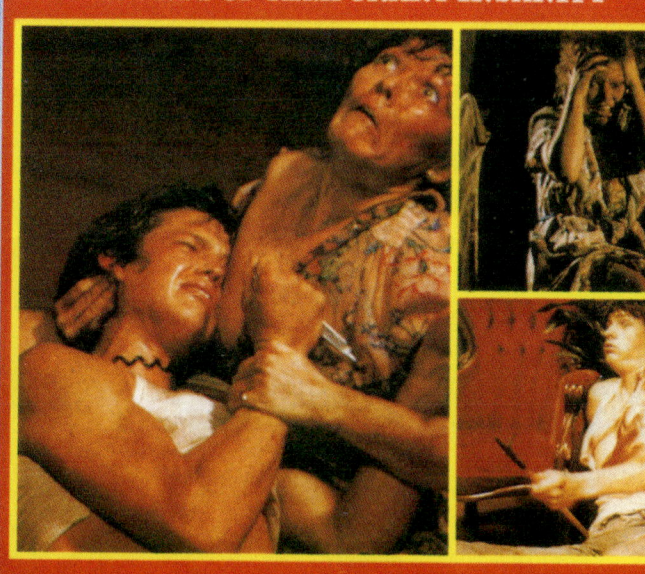

Executive Producers DENNIS D. HENNESSY and RICHARD CARROTHERS
Produced by STEPHEN BREIMER Directory of Photography ROBBIE GREENBERG
Co-Producer EUGENE MAZZOLA Screenplay by STEPHEN BRIEMER and
ALAN JAY GLUECKMAN and BOON COLLINS
Story by ALAN JAY GLUECKMAN and BOON COLLINS
Directed by WILLIAM ASHER

Designed by Len Roberts

This video cassette is copyright material for domestic use only and may not be copied, sold or hired to third parties. Any infringement of this copyright will be subject to prosecution. For details of other titles contact

---

NIGHTMARE MAKER

ATLANTIS

VHS 702

She was lonely
He was all she had
No-one would take him from her —
and live....

Named Best Horror Film of 1982 by the Academy of Science Fiction, Fantasy, and Horror.

NIGHTMARE MAKER

REVIEW

The director of many episodes of **I Love Lucy** and a lot of AIP beach movies joined the nasties list with this odd little yarn about a 17 year-old high school kid (played by McNichol - brother of Kristy) who is brought up by his aunt (Tyrrell) after his parents are killed in a superbly staged car crash. In the reverse of Norman Bates' situation in **Psycho**, she turns the boy into a surrogate husband and becomes a psychopathic killer to keep him around the house. For most of the running time, this is a superior psychological thriller in the **Whatever Happened To Baby Jane?** mould, enlivened by Tyrrell's outstanding performance. It also paints a convincingly warped picture of the xenophobia of small-town American life, and has a lot of effective black humour. There's a fair amount of graphic gore in the end scenes, but otherwise it's a good and intelligently written little movie that seems to have offended because of its overly convincing portrayal of a semi-incestuous relationship.

DVD Review

Though this has been out in the USA on tape as **Night Warning**, the film remains banned in the UK. It was resubmitted in 1987, in a version that had been pre-cut by its would-be distributor, and with the new title of **The Evil Protégé**, but this version was rejected by the BBFC. It seems likely they object to the incestuous tone of the movie as a whole rather than any gore scenes – of which there are very few, actually. As of time of writing it's rumoured that a US DVD release is in the offing through Image under the original title of **Butcher, Baker, Nightmare Maker**. Possible specs include a new 1.85:1 anamorphic transfer and maybe even a commentary by one of the stars. We'll believe it when we see it. You can get a DVD-R, but this looks suspiciously like it was mastered (not very well) from the old 80s tape!

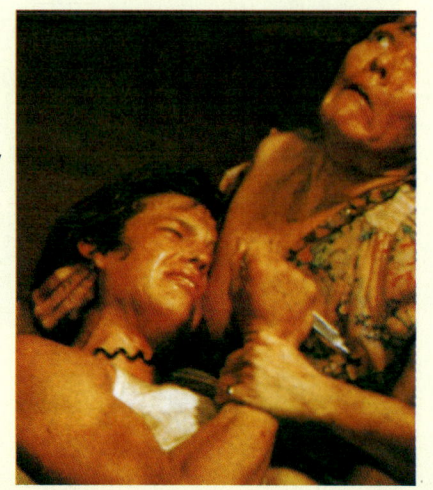

TITLE BUTCHER, BAKER, NIGHTMARE MAKER

AKA Night Warning; Thrilled to Death; Momma's Boy

DIRECTOR William Asher

COUNTRY US
SOURCE Atlantis (UK)
YEAR 1981
TIME 92m25s

CAST Jimmy McNichol, Susan Tyrrell, Bo Svenson, Marcia Lewis, Julia Duffy, Britt Leach, Steve Eastin, Caskey Swaim, Cooper Neal, William Paxton, Kay Kimler, Gary Baxley, Vickie Oleson, Clemente Anchondo, Alex Baker, Randy Norton, Kelly Kopp, Steve DeFrance, Bill Keene, Riley Morgan.

PRODUCTION A Dennis D. Hennessy - Richard Carrothers presentation. [prod] Stephen Breimer. [co-prod] Eugene Mazzola. [exec prod] Dennis D. Hennessy & Richard Carrothers. An S2D Associates Picture. Product of Royal American Pictures. © 1981 S2D Associates.

PHOTOGRAPHY DIRECTOR Robbie Greenberg

MUSIC Bruce Langhorne
EDITOR Ted Nicolaou

L.U. PRODUCTIONS Present

SCAVOLINI'S

NIGHTMARES in a....
DAMAGED BRAIN X

"A FEARFUL FILM"
Daily Star

"90 MINUTES OF TOTAL TERROR"
Variety

NIGHTMARES IN A DAMAGED BRAIN

Has been hailed as the American Cult Terror film of 1982, starring BAIRD STAFFORD and introducing C. J. COOKE. It begins with a very bloody nightmare that triggers George Tatums' journey into madness and an axe-swinging insanity that doesn't stop for 90 minutes.

DEFINITELY NOT FOR PERSONS OF A NERVOUS DISPOSITION

SCAVOLINI'S NIGHTMARES in a.... DAMAGED BRAIN X

WORLD OF VIDEO 2000 LTD
Tomorrow's world of video entertainment today

Exclusive distribution throughout the UK by World of Video 2000
15 Lyon Road
London
SW19 2SB

VHS	●
BETA	☐
PHIL 2000 GRUN	☐
CAT NO	XF 140

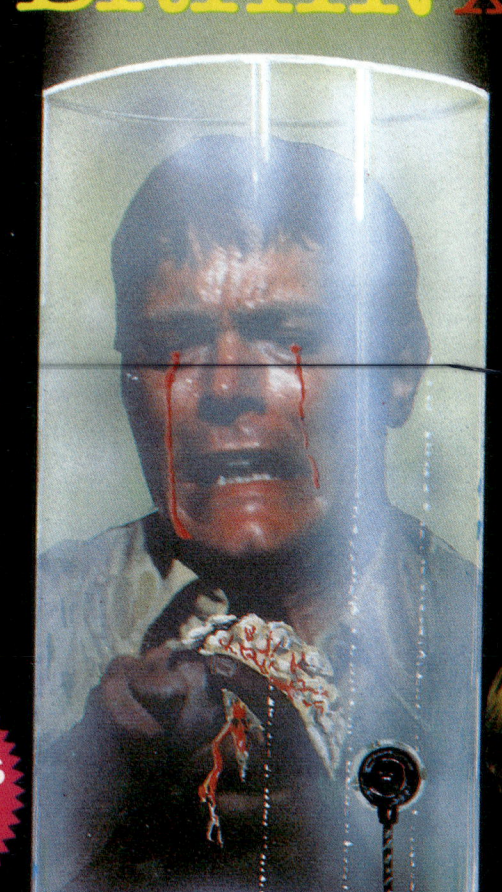

FROM THE COMPANY THAT BROUGHT YOU 'THE HILLS HAVE EYES'

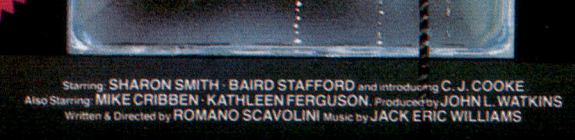

Starring: SHARON SMITH · BAIRD STAFFORD and introducing C. J. COOKE
Also Starring: MIKE CRIBBEN · KATHLEEN FERGUSON. Produced by JOHN L. WATKINS
Written & Directed by ROMANO SCAVOLINI Music by JACK ERIC WILLIAMS

WARNING NOT FOR THE SQUEAMISH OR PERSONS OF NERVOUS DISPOSITION

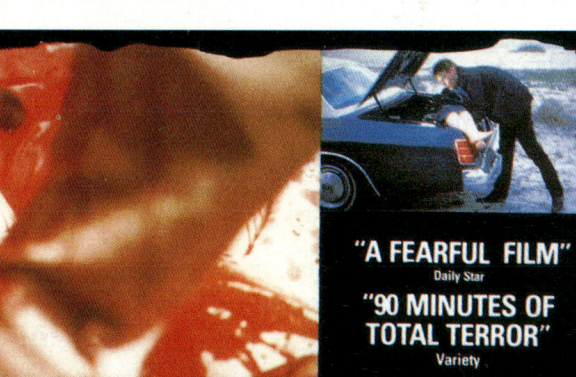

REVIEW

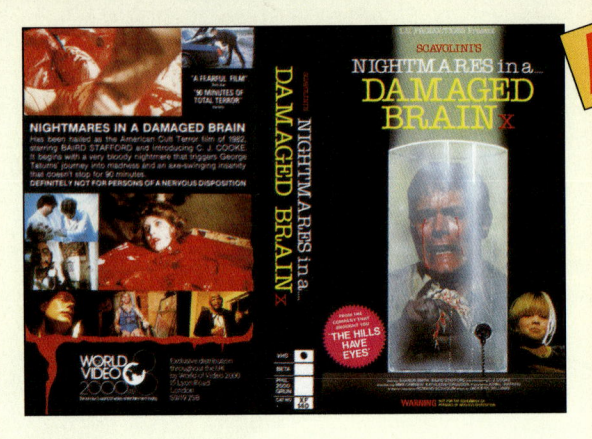

One of the most controversial of all video nasties, the distributor of this movie was actually put in prison for six months for releasing a video version that was sixty seconds longer than the BBFC-certificated version. This seems unbelievable (a fine would surely have been sufficient), but then the whole 'nasties' situation was more frighteningly absurd than the plots of most of the movies being banned. Shot in Florida by the director of **Dog Tags**, it's a lurid, extremely violent exploitation movie about a sexual psychopath under treatment for nightmares because, as a child, he axed his parents to death when he caught them having a bedroom bondage session. Supposedly cured by drug therapy, he is released. But after a visit to a New York sex shop (and a really sleazy scene where he drools at the mouth and has a fit in a peepshow booth) he sets off to terrorise single parent Sharon Smith and her three kids. The effects (Tom Savini acted as consultant) are grim indeed, with severed heads and axings galore. The oft-repeated nightmare scene is truly horrible. But what really leaves a nasty taste in the mouth is the film's misogynist tone and the way it links hardcore violence to explicit sex. The original promotion of this film involved the giving out of vomit bags and a "Guess The Weight Of The Brain" competition. Happy days, eh.

TITLE NIGHTMARE (as Nightmares in a Damaged Brain)

AKA Nightmare; Dark Games; Blood Splash

DIRECTOR Romano Scavolini

COUNTRY US
SOURCE WOV 2000 (UK)
YEAR 1981
TIME 85m51s

CAST Baird Stafford, Sharon Smith, C. J. Cooke, Mik Cribben, Danny Ronan, John Watkins, William Milling, Scott Praetorius, William S. Kirksey, Christina Keefe, Tammy Patterson, Kim Patterson, Kathleen Ferguson, William Paul, Tommy Bouvier, Candy Marchese, Geoffrey Marchese, Michael Sweney, George Kruger, Ray Baker, Lonnie Griffis, Tara Alexander, Danielle Galliana, Carl Clifford, David Massar, Mary Lee Parise, Randy Arieux, Craig Cain, Mark Davis, Ken Thomas, Robert Tenvooren, Susan Webb, Frank Rothery, Scott Trotter.

PRODUCTION A Goldmine Productions presentation. [prod] John L. Watkins. [assoc prod] Chris Cronyn & Bill Paul. [exec prod] David Jones. © 1981 Goldmine Productions, Inc.

PHOTOGRAPHY DIRECTOR Gianni Fiore

MUSIC Jack Eric Williams
EDITOR Robert T. Megginson

DVD Review

This notorious title was recently re-released in the UK as a region free disc by Screen Entertainment. Their disc included a photo gallery with posters and screen grabs. The film was presented in 4:3 fullscreen in an okay print with a fair bit of grain and lurid colours. The distributor claimed it was uncut, but that was only because they pre-cut it by 3 mins 24 secs! In Germany the movie was put out by Laser Paradise in fullscreen, but it seems likely this version was cut as well because the film was originally banned in Germany. There are many different cuts of this film. Most versions are missing most of the bloody moments, but there are also longer dialogue sequences in some cut versions than in other uncut prints. The longest version that is commonly available on VHS, runs about 99 minutes. The kind of stuff that's cut usually relates to the axe murder at the start, though the sleazy 'peep show' sequence also gets trimmed.

A Surgeon's experiment leads to a trail of terror.

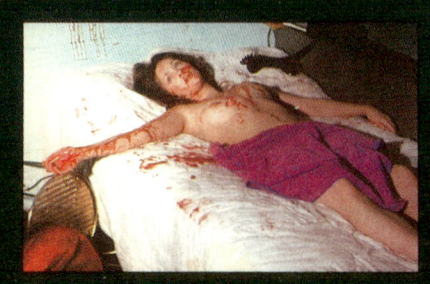

When an incurable disease threatens the life of his son, an eminent surgeon is driven to desperate measures. A secret experimental transplant is his only hope, but in this case the donor isn't human — it's an ape!

Only death lies at the end of this surgeon's knife, however. Although his son survives, he lives the life of a hideous mutant, half-man, half-ape. When the creature escapes, a small town finds itself in the fearful grip of uncontrollable carnage.

While still presenting a front of respectability, the surgeon and his assistant set out to recapture the beast, restore normality to the son, and save the area from gory destruction. Will they succeed, or will the police lieutenant get to the bottom of the bloody affair first?

This modern horror story is not for the squeamish or faint-hearted; it's an horrific catalogue of terror with no holds barred.

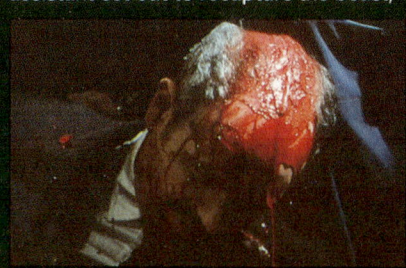

Starring
JOSE ELIAS MORENO
ARMANDO SILVESTRE
Carlos Lopez Moctezuma
Norma Lazareno   Augustin Solares

Written by Rene Cardona and Rene Cardona Jnr

Music by Antonio Diaz Conde

Directed by Rene Cardona

Uncensored, USA Rating R
Colour/Running Time 82 Minutes

Not for sale or hire to persons under the age of 18.

This high quality pre-recorded video cassette is protected by Copyright. All rights reserved. Unauthorised public performance, broadcasting and copying of this product is prohibited.

Produced on Video by
IFS VIDEO
Pinewood Studios Iver Bucks SL0 0NH

VHS
FF 30 No. 218

NIGHT OF THE BLOODY APES

NIGHT OF THE BLOODY APES

IFS VIDEO

Warning–this film contains scenes of extreme and explicit violence

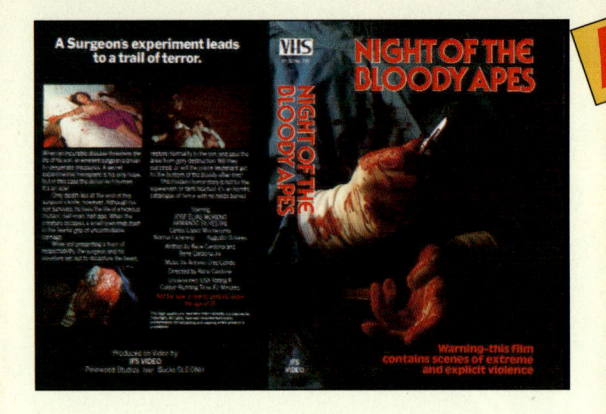

REVIEW

This madcap Mexican horror flick tells of a scientist who puts the heart of a gorilla into the body of his dying son, who is suffering from what the scientist refers to as "loose-seam-ia." The operation is a resounding success, but then the re-animated lad turns into a pug-ugly marauding killer who rapes and rips apart every living being in sight. "I was prepared for everything but this," comments the disappointed Doc. Ah well, bang goes that cover story for **The Lancet!** Anyway, old monkey-face has his lustful sights set on cat-suited heroine Norma Lazareno, but she's a professional wrestler who manages to give him a swift boot in the coconuts. There's a lot of ridiculous gore, including a scalping that is accomplished by the simple expedient of the monster pulling a wig off a bald-headed bloke! And it's funny that the monkey man's make-up doesn't go below his neck. The only people who took this daft nonsense seriously were the DPP, and the reasons for their objections seem to be centred around some graphic open-heart surgery that the makers have inserted in the "ape operation" scenes. A lot of this is unwatchable, but then so is a lot of the stuff you get on TV hospital shows, and some of that goes out at 7.00 PM in the evening!

TITLE NIGHT OF THE BLOODY APES

AKA La HORRIPLANTE BESTIA HUMANA; Horror y Sexo; Gomar, The Human Gorilla

DIRECTOR Rene Cardona

COUNTRY MEX
SOURCE Iver Film Services (UK)
YEAR 1968
TIME 79m19s

CAST Jose Elias Moreno, Carlos Lopez Moctezuma, Norma Lazareno, Agustin MTZ. Solares, Armando Silvestre, Javier Rizo, Noelia Noel, Gerardo Cepeda, Gina Morett.

PRODUCTION Jerald Intrator presents... A William Calderon Production. A Guillerno Calderon Stell production. A Jerand Films, Inc. release. A Unistar Picture. © Illegible.

PHOTOGRAPHY DIRECTOR Raul Martinez Solares

MUSIC EDITOR Antonio Diaz Conde
Jorge Bustos

DVD Review

This one's problems stem mainly from its gory footage of open-heart surgery, but since this stuff is shown on telly at times anyway, what's the problem? Something Weird Video recently released an all-region disc of this movie on a double bill with **Feast Of Flesh**. It's uncut, and among the extras are three minutes of outtakes, trailers, TV spots and a variety of ape-related short subjects. **Bloody Apes** is presented in 4:3 fullscreen and mono, and the print is quite nice, though a little grainy in places. There's also a cheapie region 1 disc from Beverly Wiltshire Filmworks, and in the UK the film was released by Film 2000/Salvation in a version that was pre-cut by the distributor to remove a minute or so. Overall, the SWV disc is the clear winner. You may also find the movie on imports under the title of **Horror Y Sexo**.

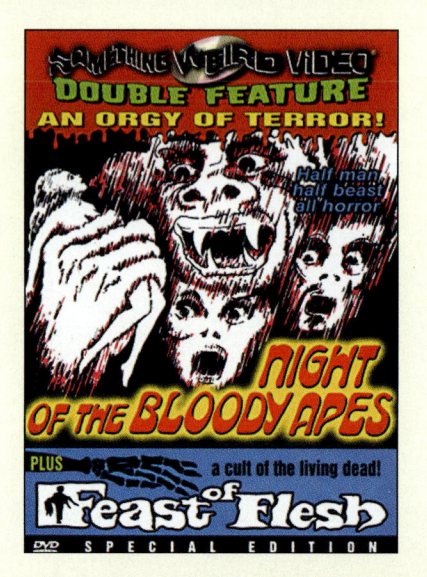

An evil mutation embarks on a wave of brutal butchery.

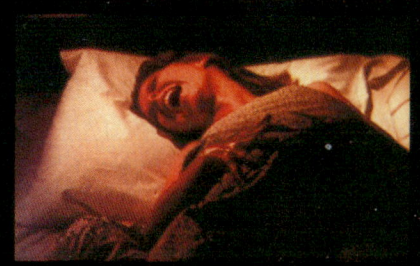

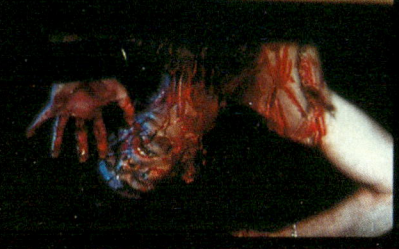

VHS
FF 30 No. 173

VIDEO GOLD

Warning - this film contains scenes of extreme and explicit violence

In shock and pain after being found in the forest with his face mutilated and most of the skin burnt away, Professor Nugent insists that the American legend of the 'Big Foot' monster is true. A number of horrific incidents are recalled in graphic flashbacks: the brutal murder of a local fisherman, the mutilation of a couple making love in their van, and the Horrendous death of a young motor cyclist. All bear the gory signs of having been butchered by the demon.

A group from the University's anthropology class, including the young daughter of the dead fisherman, set out to uncover the mystery. They disturb a Black Magic ritual, and force the truth from a hermit, Wanda. She had been raped by the monster, and gave birth to a mutation. The group are eventually trapped by the demon, only to die in the most gruesome blood bath ever filmed.

Starring:
MICHAEL J CUTT   JOY ALLEN
Bob Collins   Jodi Lazarus
Richard Fields   Michael Lang
and Melanie Graham as Wanda

Screenplay by Mike Williams
Music by Dennis McCarthy
Produced by Jim L Ball
Directed by James C Watson
Uncensored, USA Rating R
Running Time 95 Minutes

Not for Sale or Hire to Persons under the age of 18.

This high quality pre-recorded video cassette is protected by Copyright. All rights reserved. Unauthorised public performance, broadcasting and copying of this product is prohibited.

Produced on Video by
Iver Film Services Limited
Pinewood Studios Iver Bucks SL0 0NH

IFS
IVER FILM SERVICES

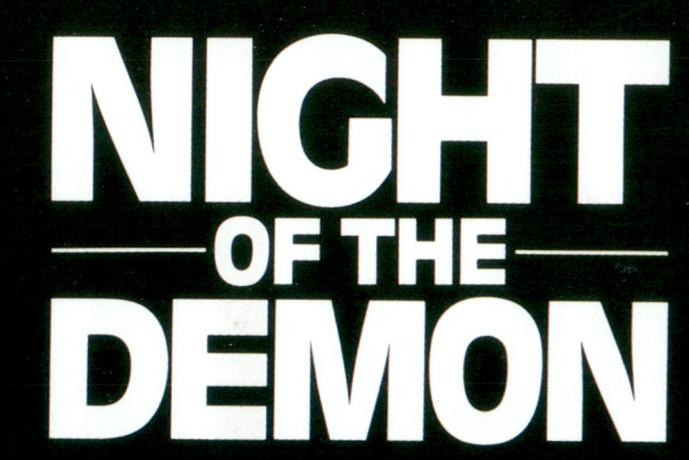

NIGHT OF THE DEMON

IFS

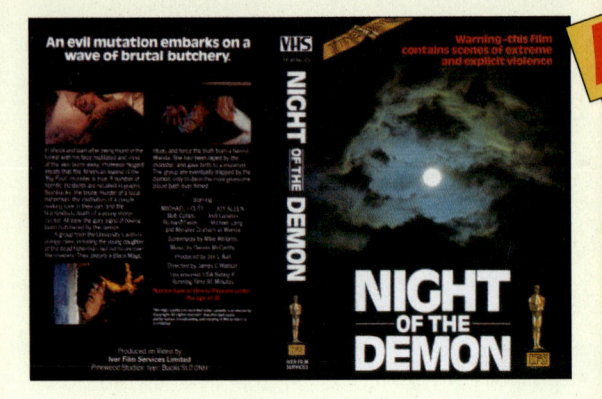

REVIEW

Not to be confused with Jacques Tourneur's classic black and white version of M.R. James' **Casting The Runes**, this is a graphic gorefest in which the legend of "Big Foot" provides the low-budget chills and spills. Murder and mayhem are the dish of the day as a big hairy monster goes on the rampage in the boonies, ripping a country bumpkin's arm out of his socket and beating him to death with the soggy end! Entrails are waved in the air, and in the most talked-about scene (well, in my household anyway) a motorist who stops for a pee by the side of the road gets his wedding tackle hoisted! The monster itself is barely shown until the end, when it turns out to be pretty daft-looking. But as graphic gorefests go, this one certainly offers value for money. The final scenes are great, with one kid getting his face fried on a hot stove and another being whipped to death with his own spilled guts - all shown in excruciating, hilarious slow-motion! Not a good movie by any means, but an understandable addition to the list.

TITLE	NIGHT OF THE DEMON
AKA	NONE
DIRECTOR	James C. Wasson
COUNTRY	US
SOURCE	Iver Film Services (UK)
YEAR	1980
TIME	91m54s

CAST Michael J. Cutt, Joy Allen, Bob Collins, Jodi Lazarus, Richard Fields, Michael Lang, Melanie Graham, Shannon Cooper, Paul Kelleher, Ray Jarris, William F. Nugent, Lynn Eastman, Dix Turner, Bunny Bernhardt, Fred Owens, Heather Eide, Virginia English, Mark Olay, Eugene Dow, Don Hurst, Terry Wilson, Kathy Stimac, Renata Lee, Philip Boyd, Mark Phalan, Sally Swift, Greg Langdon, Rob Camp, Shane Dixon.

PRODUCTION Jim L. Ball presents... An Aldan Company production. [prod] Jim L. Ball. © 1980 The Aldan Company, Inc. Hollywood.

PHOTOGRAPHY DIRECTOR John Quick

MUSIC Dennis McCarthy
EDITOR Not credited

DVD Review

Our old friends at VIPCO dusted this one off in the late 90s and ran it past the BBFC once more. The result was 1 minute 41 secs of cuts, mainly to the cabin massacre where one victim gets face-fried on a hotplate, sunny side up, and the film was re-released as an ex-Nasty. My guess is that if the film was submitted again now it would get through unscathed, since the monster is daft, the plot unbelievable, and the effects (though gloatingly lingered on) extremely unconvincing. As it is, there's no point in picking up VIPCO's hacked-about version, which is a very poor fullscreen transfer undoubtedly drawn from the same tape master as the 1980s version that made the DPP list. It has been suggested that the film is available in the UK on a limited edition DVD-R, but I have yet to hear from anyone who's seen one of these.

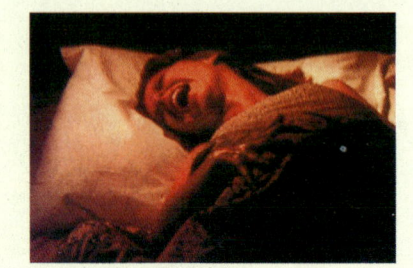

SCREAMING TERROR　　　　GF506

Don't Ride on LATE NIGHT TRAINS

Late Night Trains (AX) 89 minutes
A spine chilling thriller, but not for anybody with a weak heart. A story of rape, murder and reprisal set on the famous Trans-Europe Express. Two young girls on their way home for Christmas meet up with a couple of psychopaths and the result is - screaming terror. Voted the 'Best Late Night Horror Film' 1978. SPECIAL NOTE: *This film may contain sequences liable to cause distress to viewers with a nervous disposition.*

Late Night Trains
(AX) 89 minutes

FULL COLOUR　　　　89 MINUTES
Spine tingling thriller.
Two girls take a terror ride on the Trans European Express.

Titles available in this range

- GF501 THE BRUCE LEE STORY (AF). Kung-Fu Karate. 90 minutes. Colour.
- GF502 SOMEBODY'S STOLEN OUR RUSSIAN SPY (AF) James Bond Type Action. 84 minutes. Colour.
- GF503 DARK STAR (AF). Science Fiction. 84 minutes. Colour.
- GF504 BIM (AF). Asian/African Action Adventure. 104 minutes. Colour.
- GF505 DRAWS (AX). Side Slitting Comedy. 75 minutes. Colour.
- GF506 LATE NIGHT TRAINS (AX). Screaming Terror. 89 minutes. Colour.
- GF507 BLACK BEAUTY (AF). Children. 100 minutes. Colour.
- GF508 CREEPING FLESH (AX). Late Night Horror. 90 minutes. Colour.
- GF509 CURSE OF THE CRIMSON ALTAR (AX). Late Night Horror. 90 minutes. Colour.
- GF510 BLOOD BEAST TERROR (AX). Late Night Horror. 90 minutes. Colour.
- GF511 SUBMISSION (AX). Speciality. 85 minutes. Colour.
- GF512 STUDENT NURSES (AX). Speciality. Colour.

GF506

VIDEO WAREHOUSE INTERNATIONAL LIMITED
329 HUNSLET ROAD, LEEDS LS10 1NJ

VIDEO WAREHOUSE INTERNATIONAL LIMITED
329 HUNSLET ROAD, LEEDS LS10 1NJ
Tel: 0532 706066

Full Length Movies From The World's Leading Directors

REVIEW

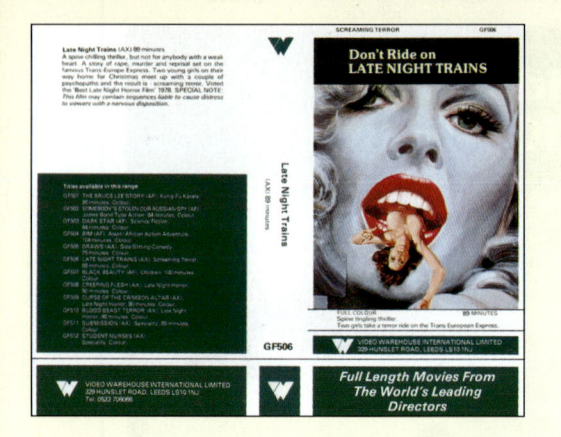

The international popularity of **Last House On The Left** inevitably led to a number of Italian rip-offs. The worst was Ferdinando Baldi's second class **Terror Express**, and the best is this efficient and compelling effort from Aldo Lado. Drug-crazed nutters Curly and Blackie (Gianfranco di Grassi and Flavio Bucci) establish their psycho credentials from the off by brutally mugging a Father Christmas. Then they terrorise two young schoolgirls on a train (one of whom is a young Irene Miracle, later to appear in **Inferno** and **Midnight Express**), eventually murdering them both with the help of a depraved woman (Macha Meril from **Deep Red**) they meet on the journey. But retribution awaits at the end of the line when they accidentally check into the home of the vengeful parents. Ennio Morricone's score adds a much-needed touch of class to the sleazy proceedings.

DVD Review

There is some doubt if this was ever actually prosecuted, and therefore it remains a borderline nasty, though it has never been passed for a UK cinema or video release by the BBFC. Also known as **Torture Train** and **The Night Train Murders**, this can now only be obtained via a bootleg DVD-R edition that appears to have been gleaned from a good quality (probably Japanese) source. The image on this is presented in 1.85 non-anamorphic widescreen and the DVD-R contains even more footage that the banned version – though there is no extra gore, violence or sex on offer, just additional dialogue scenes that flesh out the characters more. The DVD-R also contains a trailer. It is rumoured that there will be a European special edition of this title before too long, with commentary by the director, but there was no release date confirmed at time of going to press on this volume.

TITLE NIGHT TRAIN MURDERS

AKA L'ultimo treno della notte; Violenza sull'ultimo treno della notte; Night Train - Der letzte Zug in der Nacht; The New House on the Left

DIRECTOR Aldo Lado

COUNTRY FR,SP
SOURCE WOV 2000 (UK)
YEAR 1974
TIME 87m58s

CAST Flavio Bucci, Macha Meril, Gianfranco De Grassi, Enrico Maria Salerno, Marina Berti, Franco Fabrizi, Irene Miracle, Laura D'Angelo (and uncredited) Daniele Dublino, Dalila Di Lazzaro, Francesco D'Adda, Gianni Di Benedetto.

PRODUCTION A European Inc. Production. [exec prod] Pino Buricchi & Paolo Infascelli. © 1974 European Inc. Productions.

PHOTOGRAPHY DIRECTOR Gabor Pogany

MUSIC Ennio Morricone
EDITOR Alberto Gallitti

POSSESSION

VTC — 14 Suffolk Street, Pall Mall, London SW1.
VideoTapeCenter

DEMONIC HORROR

SHE CREATED A MONSTER...
AS HER SECRET LOVER!

POSSESSION

Starring
ISABELLE ADJANI, SAM NEILL
HEINZ BENNETT
Directed by
ANDREZEJ ZULAWSKI

"What started out as an overheated Berlin-set marital crisis becomes an increasingly bizarre and progressively more nauseating film that defies simple genre pigeon-holing — it's certainly horrific, as it's heroine's gradual embroilments in metaphysical notions of evil lead, via murder, adultery and corruption, to sexual congress with a hideous, slimy incarnation of the thing itself... very European, extremely impressive, undeniably gross, "Possession" is a unique, if frequently repulsive, experience. YOU CAN'T LOOK AWAY."

EVENT MAGAZINE (July 9th '82)

WARNING
ALL RIGHTS OF THE PRODUCER AND OF THE OWNER OF THE WORK RESERVED. UNAUTHORISED COPYING, HIRING, LENDING, PUBLIC PERFORMANCE, RADIO OR TV BROADCASTING OF THIS VIDEO RECORDING PROHIBITED BY LAW
© 1982 VTC Plc

VTCV 1031

VHS

Distributed by CBS   Colour 118 minutes
VTC 1031

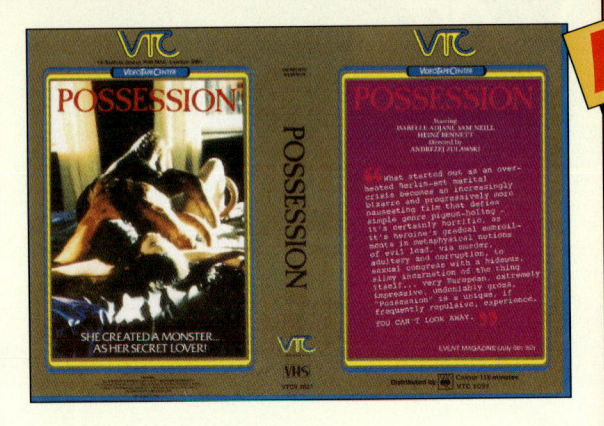

REVIEW

An enormous number of symbols, both sexual and religious, give some meaning to this bizarre story of an estranged woman (Adjani) who gives birth to a full-grown man, an exact replica of her husband, after making love to a slimy octopus-like monster. Neill has been away on special assignment for years and comes home to find his wife, Adjani, acting strangely. She admits to having a lover, ex-flower child Bennent, so Neill has detectives follow her. One detective is killed by Adjani, the other by the multi-tentacled monster. Neill thinks his wife has gone potty. But then he catches her in bed with the creature and thinks he'd better get a divorce. Good special effects help make this odd yarn believable, but the themes, camera angles and symbolism were handled much better by Roman Polanski in **Rosemary's Baby**. Among the yukky gore scenes are a bit where Adjani slices into her own neck with an electric carving knife, and of course her body-slamming, bile-spitting miscarriage on the Metro takes some beating! Do the art house crowd watch video nasties? Just ask David Lynch fans…

TITLE	POSSESSION
AKA	NONE
DIRECTOR	Andrzej Zulawski
COUNTRY	FR, WG
SOURCE	VTC (UK)
YEAR	1981
TIME	118m23s
CAST	Isabelle Adjani, Sam Neill, Margit Carstensen, Heinz Bennent, Johanna Hofer, Carl Duering, Shaun Lawton, Michael Hogben, Maximilian Ruethlein, Thomas Frey, Leslie Malton, Gerd Neubert, Kerstin Wohlfahrt, Ilse Bahrs, Karin Mumm, Herbert Chwoika, Barbara Stanek, Ilse Trautschold.
PRODUCTION	Marie-Laure Reyre presents… [prod] Marie-Laure Reyre. A co-production of Oliane Productions (Paris) - Marianne Productions (Paris) - Soma Film Produktion (Berlin). © 1981 Oliane Productions.
PHOTOGRAPHY DIRECTOR	Bruno Nuytten
MUSIC	Andrzej Korzynski
EDITOR	Marie-Sophie Dubas, Suzanne Lang-Willar, Jutta Omura & Sabine Marang

DVD Review

This was removed from the Nasties list in 1999 when it was granted a BBFC 18 uncut – surprising really, since it's more an arthouse pic than anything else. There is a rumour of a 5-minute cut to the octopus baby miscarriage on the Metro, but this appears to be false, as the old VTC version is the same as the Dutch and French video releases as well as cinema prints. The director himself has stated that the birth scene does not last 10 minutes. A fair few scenes were cut during editing one of which clarifies what happens to Anna (Isabelle Adjani). To the director's knowledge, none of these have ever made it to any release of the film. The way to go with this one is to pick up Anchor Bay's region free US disc, which gives you an absolutely stunning transfer of the film in 1.66:1 anamorphic. It's in English and runs longer than any other version, with a commentary by the director, a trailer, and extensive cast and crew biographies. Well worth picking up if you want to appreciate this very weird movie as its director intended.

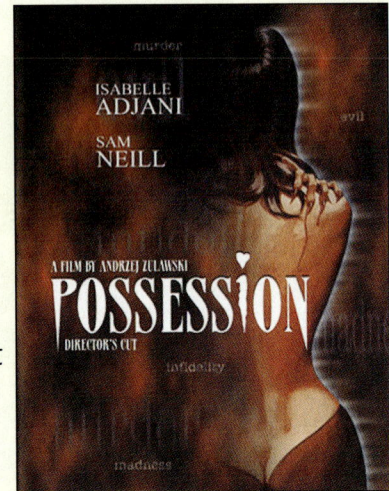

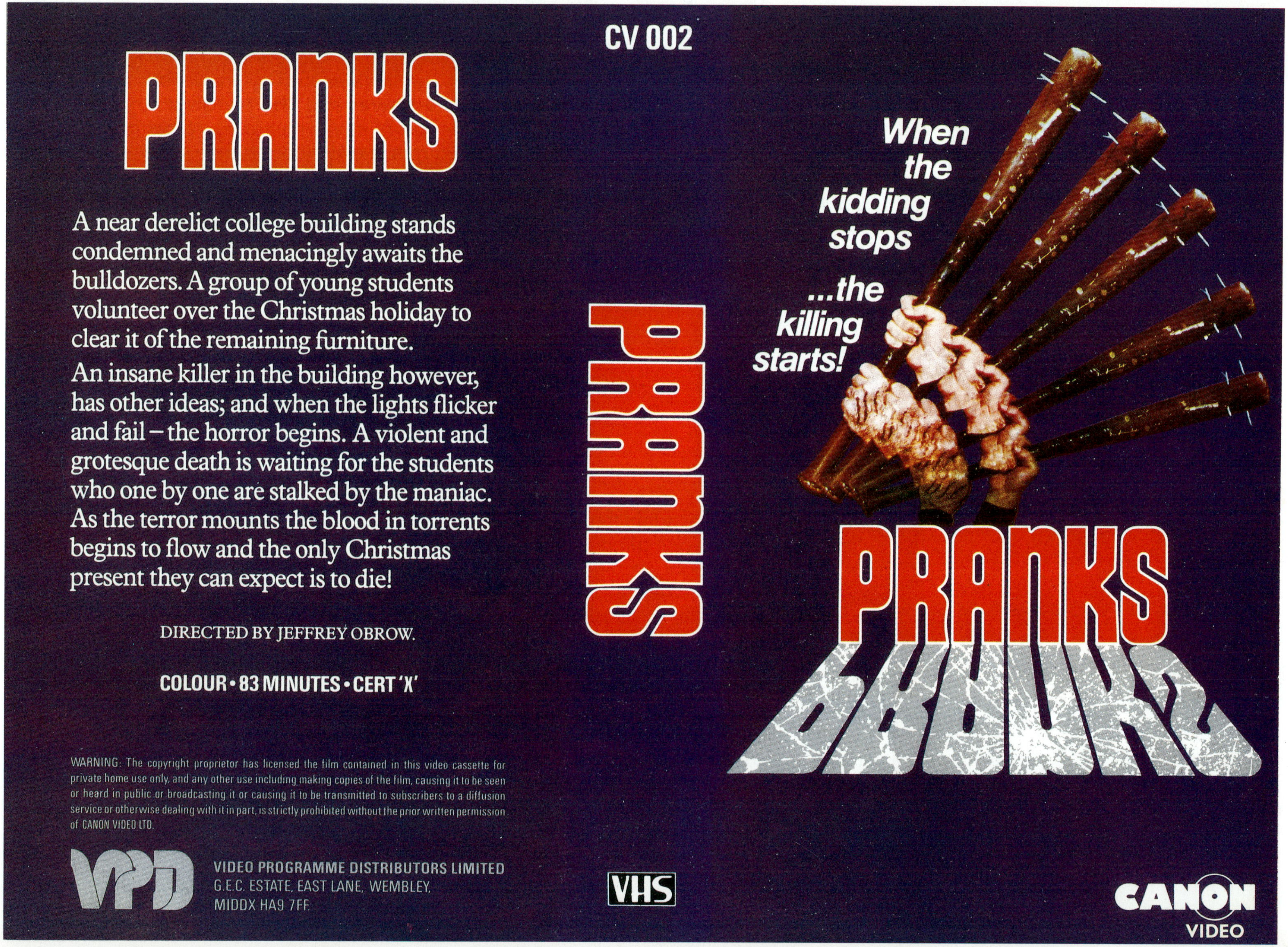

PRANKS

CV 002

When the kidding stops ...the killing starts!

A near derelict college building stands condemned and menacingly awaits the bulldozers. A group of young students volunteer over the Christmas holiday to clear it of the remaining furniture.

An insane killer in the building however, has other ideas; and when the lights flicker and fail – the horror begins. A violent and grotesque death is waiting for the students who one by one are stalked by the maniac. As the terror mounts the blood in torrents begins to flow and the only Christmas present they can expect is to die!

DIRECTED BY JEFFREY OBROW.

COLOUR • 83 MINUTES • CERT 'X'

WARNING: The copyright proprietor has licensed the film contained in this video cassette for private home use only, and any other use including making copies of the film, causing it to be seen or heard in public or broadcasting it or causing it to be transmitted to subscribers to a diffusion service or otherwise dealing with it in part, is strictly prohibited without the prior written permission of CANON VIDEO LTD.

VPD
VIDEO PROGRAMME DISTRIBUTORS LIMITED
G.E.C. ESTATE, EAST LANE, WEMBLEY,
MIDDX HA9 7FF.

VHS

CANON VIDEO

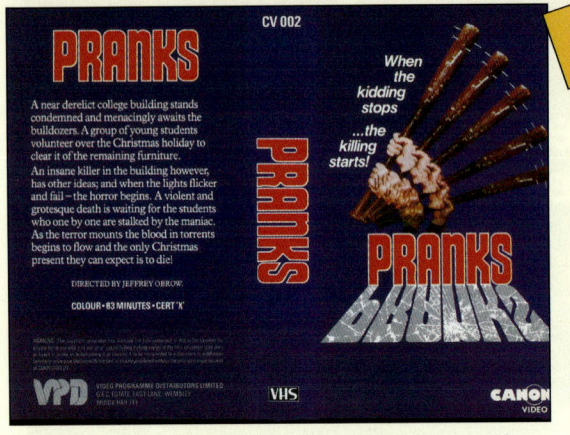

REVIEW

A group of students foolishly volunteer to spend their Christmas hols clearing a derelict building of its furniture, and are menaced by a psychotic killer in this early effort from the team who brought us **The Power** and **The Kindred** (and never had the decency to apologise). It's basically the sort of movie that gives slasher pictures a bad name. Kids wander in and out of darkened rooms even though they know that there's likely to be a guy with a straight razor waiting behind the door. Spiked clubs are driven into eyes, necks are garroted, folks are run over and reduced to limbless torsos, and human heads turn up in the Irish stew (no doubt substantially increasing the risk of BSE infection). There's plenty going on, then, but the budget is too low for the gore to be effective, and the level of characterisation is nil. On top of that, the downbeat ending really stinks! An all-round loser.

TITLE	PRANKS
AKA	The Dorm that Dripped Blood; Death Dorm
DIRECTOR	Jeffrey Obrow & Stephen Carpenter
COUNTRY	US
SOURCE	Canon (UK)
YEAR	1981
TIME	81m31s
CAST	Laurie Lapinski, Stephen Sachs, David Snow, Pamela Holland, Dennis Ely, Woody Roll, Daphne Zuniga, Jake Jones, Robert Frederick, Chris Morrill, Chandre, Billy Criswell, Richard Cowgill, Kay Beth, Jimmy Betz, Thomas Christian, Robert Richardson, Chris Schroeder.
PRODUCTION	From New Line Cinema. Jeff Obrow Productions. [prod] Jeffrey Obrow. [assoc prod] Stacey Giachino. Death Dorm © 1981 Jeff Obrow Productions.
PHOTOGRAPHY DIRECTOR	Stephen Carpenter
MUSIC	Chris Young
EDITOR	Jeffrey Obrow & Stephen Carpenter

DVD Review

This VPD release was submitted to the BBFC as soon as the new VRA laws came into effect. 10 seconds were trimmed and it was given a certificate and removed from the list. Nowadays it might even get through with a 15 if anybody could be bothered to resubmit. Instead, our old pals at VIPCO saved themselves the, er, classification fee, and just put out the original tape on disc in an atrocious-looking 4:3 transfer that you'll find kicking around bargain bins for around a fiver should you be interested. What pranksters, eh? If you're absolutely desperate to see the missing 10 secs of gore (from a scalping) then you'll have to purchase the NTSC tape from the States – where it's available under the film's alternate title of **The Dorm That Dripped Blood**.

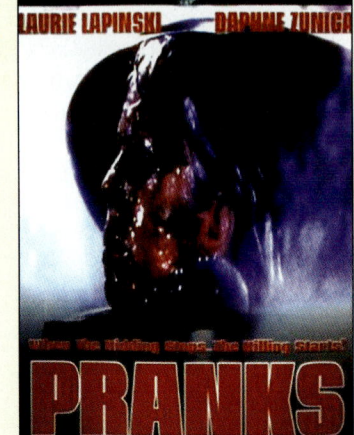

Video Movies

from Hokushin

PRISONER OF THE CANNIBAL GOD
Film Synopsis

Dr. Foster on his weekly visit to the jungle base camp of Professor Stevenson, finds the mutilated bodies of his assistants and no Professor.
When Stevensen's wife and brother learn of his disappearance and the fact that the area where he disappeared contains rich untapped uranium sources they persuade Foster to guide them to the area to search for both – Primitive tribes, cannibalistic rituals and a trail of death follow them.
English Dialogue

Video Licensee Entertainment In Video in association with Hokushin Audio Visual Ltd. 2 Ambleside Avenue, London, S.W.16 6AD.

VHS PAL SYSTEM

PRISONER OF THE CANNIBAL GOD

VM - 27

Video Movies

PRISONER OF THE CANNIBAL GOD

URSULA ANDRESS
STACY KEACH

Colour
Running Time 96 minutes

ENTERTAINMENT

from Hokushin

REVIEW

"New Guinea is perhaps the last region on earth which contains immense unexplored areas" intones the prologue of this tepid slice of jungle hokum. We find that hard to believe, what with all those Italian film crews poking around down there! One of the most mediocre cannibal films on the market, this one has Cassinelli and Andress playing a brother and sister who trek through uncharted New Guinea, ostensibly in search of Andress's missing hubby, but actually looking for valuable uranium deposits. What they find instead is a lost tribe of cannibals - called The Pooka - who worship Ursula's hubby's decomposed remains! They also meet up with Stacy Keach, a crashed pilot who has been forced to scoff human flesh and now finds it impossible to act convincingly without rolling his eyeballs around in his head. Andress fans will find the journey worthwhile because they get to see their heroine wearing some natty leather safari gear. In another scene Ursula is stripped naked by the panting natives and painted with the sludgy remains of her old man - shades of **Zombie Creeping Flesh**. There's the usual round of depressing animal cruelty, with a lizard being sliced open to the accompaniment of flaming bongos, and a turtle thrown into the jaws of a crocodile in a very one-sided "life or death struggle." The special effects are not very well done, leaving this time waster with only good camerawork to recommend it.

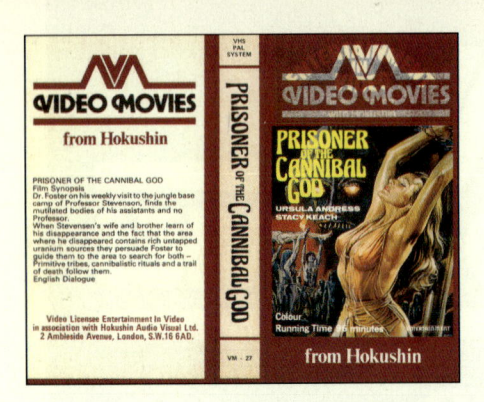

TITLE MOUNTAIN OF THE CANNIBAL GOD, THE (as Prisoner of the Cannibal God)

AKA La montagna del dio cannibale; Mountain of the Cannibal God; Prisoner of the Cannibal God; Slave of the Cannibal God; La montagne du dieu cannibale; Die Weisse Gottin der Kannibalen

DIRECTOR Sergio Martino

COUNTRY IT
SOURCE Hokushin (UK)
YEAR 1978
TIME 92m17s

CAST Ursula Andress, Stacy Keach, Claudio Cassinelli, Antonio Marsina, Franco Fantasia, Lanfranco Spinola, Carlo Longhi, Luigina Rocchi, Akushla Sellajaah, Dudley Wanaguru, T. M. Munna, M. Suki, Giovanni Masini, Franco Guccu, Gianfranco Coduti, Claudio Morabito, Alfredo Senzacqua, Angelo Pennoni, Francesco Freda, Adalgisa Favella, Rudolfo Ruzza, Giuseppe Romano, Luciana Pianella, Paolo Ricci, Matteo Giordano, Fernando Massaccesi, Mario Massaccesi.

PRODUCTION Luciano Martino presents... A Dania Film - Medusa Distribuzione production. [prod] Luciano Martino.© None.

PHOTOGRAPHY DIRECTOR Giancarlo Ferrando

MUSIC Guido & Maurizio De Angelis
EDITOR Eugenio Alabiso

DVD Review

There are plenty of DVD versions of this available, some under the alternate title of **Mountain Of The Cannibal God** - such as Anchor Bay's definitive region free release. This gives you the best-looking (fully uncut) version of the movie in 2.35:1 anamorphic NTSC and English Dolby Digital 1.0 format. It also restores the film's explicit castration sequence, not seen in many other versions. Extras include Legacy Of The Cannibal God, an interview with director Sergio Martino, plus a poster and still gallery, theatrical trailer, and cast and crew biographies. For the record, other releases include another region free US disc from Diamond in non-anamorphic 2.35:1 (no extras), a region free disc from EC in Holland that contains picture galleries and a trailer, plus bonus trailers for **Blade In The Dark** and **House On The Edge Of The Park**. This one also has a collectable booklet and Dutch and English Subtitles. It's in 2.35:1 non-anamorphic NTSC. Laser Paradise in Germany also have a pretty good disc with loads of trailers. As for the UK disc from VIPCO, would you be surprised to learn that it's missing some two and a half minutes of animal cruelty? VIPCO put this out as both a non-anamorphic 2.35:1 release and lousy-looking fullscreen. You know what to do.

VTC

No.1 Newton Street, London WC2B 5EL

VTC

HORROR

VTC

VTC 1104
Distributed by CBS

REVENGE OF THE BOGEY MAN

**SUZANNA LOVE
RON JAMES
JOHN CARRADINE**

The Bogeyman is back in Ulli Lommel's follow-up to "The Bogeyman", and this time heroine Lacey, (Suzanna Love) moves to L.A. six months after the supernatural murders in Part 1. The lethal mirror shard from Part 1 goes on the rampage again possessing the butler Joseph (Sholto Von Douglas). There's lots of blood and gore while various household objects are supernaturally levitated and used to kill some creepy guests at a Hollywood party.
There's black humour all the way to the graveyard ending which is strongly reminiscent of De Palma's "Carrie".

WARNING: ALL RIGHTS OF THE PRODUCER AND OF THE OWNER OF THE WORK REPRODUCED ARE RESERVED. UNAUTHORISED COPYING, HIRING, LENDING, PUBLIC PERFORMANCE, RADIO OR TV BROADCASTING OF THIS VIDEO RECORDING PROHIBITED BY LAW (P) 1983 VTC Plc

REVENGE OF THE BOGEY MAN
HE'S BACK

Colour
79 minutes

REVENGE OF THE BOGEY MAN

VHS
VTCV 1104

REVENGE OF THE BOGEY MAN
HE'S BACK

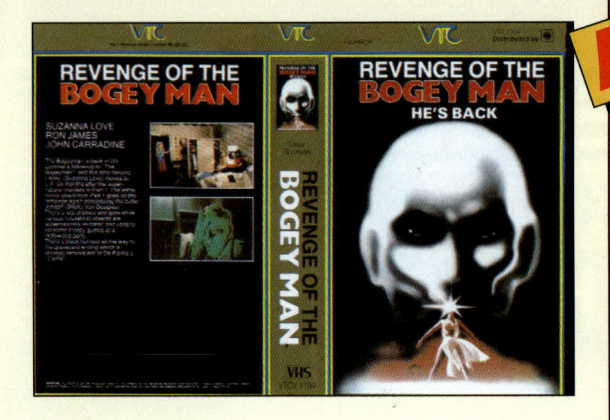

REVIEW

The man in the mirror is back in a cheeky sequel that is mainly made up of a very large amount of stock footage from the original movie (all the murder scenes, in fact, hence its similar inclusion on the DPP list). Suzanna Love (the director's wife) also returns as the woman haunted by the spirit inhabiting a broken shard of mirror. The action is set six months on, with a Hollywood director (rather appropriately played by Lommel) wanting to make a film out of Love's horrific experiences. Obviously annoyed that he's not on a percentage of the gross, the Bogey Man decides to cause carnage at a party thrown by the filmmakers, bumping off the revellers with bottle openers, barbecue tongs, electric toothbrushes and garden shears. The most impressively sick slaughter involves a gal having a car exhaust pipe rammed into her mouth and choking on its emissions in a gross parody of fellatio. It seems that art-house director Lommel (who previously worked with Fassbinder and Andy Warhol) didn't really want to make this picture, but when the backers of the original thrust half a million dollars in his hands he decided to sell out quick. It's obvious from those excessive flashbacks that he must have been able to save quite a chunk of that change for himself.

TITLE REVENGE OF THE BOGEYMAN

AKA [note:] Revenge of the Bogeyman = VTC videocover title; Boogeyman 2

DIRECTOR Bruce Starr & Ulli Lommel (uncredited)

COUNTRY FR,SP
SOURCE VTC (UK)
YEAR 1982
TIME 75m39s

CAST Suzanna Love, Shannah Hall, Sholto von Douglas, John Carradine, Ulli Lommel, Bob Rosenfarb, Rhonda Aldrich, Sarah Jean Watkins, Rock MacKenzie, Rafael Nazario, Leslie Smith, Mina Kolb, Ann Wilkinson, David D'Arnel, Ron James, Nicholas Love, Felicite Morgan, Bill Rayburn, Llewelyn Thomas, Jane Pratt, Natasha Schiano, Raymond Boyden, Jay Wright, David Swim, Cindy Zeising, Gillian Gordon, Howard Grant.

PRODUCTION assoc prod] Mark Balsam & James Dudelson. [exec prod] David Dubay & Jochen Breitenstein. © 1982 New West Films, Holywood, Ca.

PHOTOGRAPHY DIRECTOR Philippe Carr-Forster & David Sperling

MUSIC Tim Krog
EDITOR Terrell Tannen

DVD Review

Removed from the DPP list but never re-released in its original version, this was passed uncut in 2003, but it's in a re-edited version that now includes even more footage from **The Bogey Man**. The fact is, the DVD of **Boogey Man 2** released by Image is not the same as the **Revenge Of The Boogey Man** tape that made the Nasties list. It's really just the original **Boogey Man** with some scenes cut and new ones added. We also get the director babbling on between scenes in an odd fashion. There are also 'bonus clips' from never-finished **Boogey Man** sequels. The image is good quality, but frankly this so-called 'Director's Cut' is just a waste of time. Mind you, so is **Revenge Of The Boogey Man** as a whole.

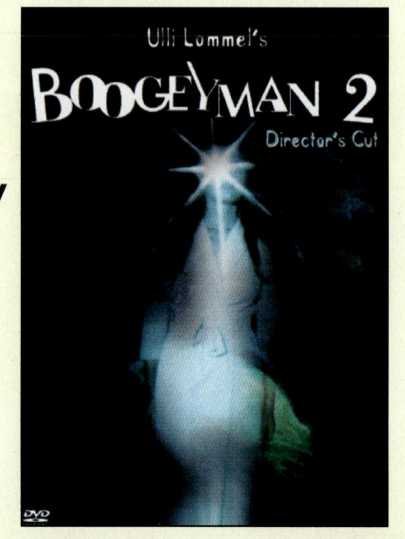

SHOGUN ASSASSIN

Sword & Sorcery...with a vengeance.

Set against the historic yet fantasmagoric backdrop of feudal Japan, SHOGUN ASSASSIN follows the legendary exploits of the undefeatable swordsman Lone Wolf, and his son Daigoro, along an endless macabre road of revenge. It is an action-packed odyssey, that is at once spectacular and terrifying, brutal and poignant.

Sword & Sorcery is the New Wave in epic screen adventure.

SHOGUN ASSASSIN is Sword & Sorcery ...with a vengeance.

VIPCO
Video Instant Picture Company Limited

WARNING
"The copyright proprietor has licensed the film contained in this videocassette for private home use only. Any other use including making copies of the film, causing it to be seen or heard in public or broadcasting it or causing to be transmitted to subscribers to a diffusion service, letting on hire or otherwise dealing with it in part or any kind of exchange scheme is strictly prohibited. Any breach of the above conditions render the offender liable to prosecution by Video Instant Picture Company Limited".

VHS VIDEO CASSETTE

SHOGUN ASSASSIN

Meet the greatest team in the history of mass slaughter

SHOGUN ASSASSIN

VIPCO present
Tomisaburo Wakayama as Lone Wolf
Music by Mark Lindsay & Michael Lewis · Edited by Lee Percy Directed by Robert Houston
SEE WARNING ON REVERSE DOLBY STEREO AT SAMUEL GOLDWYN STUDIOS **RUNNING TIME 85 MINUTES**

REVIEW

This really violent Japanese adventure is surprisingly good. It focuses on Wakayama, an "official decapitator" running around the country with his young son in tow (in a wooden pram!) seeking revenge on the men who killed his wife. The film is narrated by the man's child, making this a very weird sort of comic adventure. **Shogun Assassin** was actually edited down from two films in the popular Japanese **Lone Wolf** series: **Baby Cart At River Styx** and **Sword Of Vengeance** - both of which were based on a comic book. The American dubbing is quite good, using the minimum amount of dialogue to maximum effect. One of the voices is dubbed by comedienne Sandra Bernhard, and the music score was written by Mark Lindsay, formerly of the popular 60s rock group **Paul Revere And The Raiders**. Superbly edited from stylishly shot material, this has become a ballet of nearly continuous battles - a blood red haze of swordplay with severed body parts flying and arteries spewing, gushing and spraying the camera lens. As the samurai, Tomisaburo Wakayama is grizzled and portly, not at all your usual martial arts hero, and the constant presence of his infant son at the bloodletting adds a note of surrealism that elevates this far above the standard fare. Often quite funny and always bizarre, this is an absolutely unique martial arts movie that did not deserve to be singled out as a nasty!

DVD Review

This one originally had a mere 2 seconds of cuts for both cinema and video. The 18-cert VIPCO release is missing a short sequence early on, just before the initial decapitation. In the US version, The Shogun lowers his head to reveal the baby wearing a circular mirror like a headlamp around his head (he is carrying the baby piggy-back), the mirror blinds his enemy allowing the Shogun to whack his head off. This short sequence appears to have been cut out of the VIPCO release. Also the scene on the boat with the eye gouging is there in both versions, but is a second or so shorter in the Vipco release. VIPCO's UK version has a theatrical trailer, a photo gallery and is in 2.35:1 non anamorphic PAL and English Dolby Digital 2.0 mono. There's also a R2 Germany version from Laser Paradise. This has a pretty much the same specs, so take your choice. **Shogun Assassin** is actually a combination of two films, **Sword Of Vengeance** and **Baby Cart At The River Styx**. Robert Houston rewrote the dialogue in English, re-edited the films together, and added a new electronic score (by Mark Lindsay). The first ten minutes is the Lone Wolf and Cub origin sequences from **Sword Of Vengeance**. Then the part with the female Ninja team and the Masters of Death are lifted from **Baby Cart**.

TITLE SHOGUN ASSASSIN

AKA Kosure Ookami-Sanzu no Kawa no Ubagurama; Kozure Ohkmi n.2 [note: Shogun Assassin is actually an amalgam of two films titled 'Lightning Swords of Death' and 'Baby Cart at the River Styx']

DIRECTOR Robert Houston [US version] & Kenji Misumi (uncredited)

COUNTRY JAP
SOURCE Vipco (UK)
YEAR 1972
TIME 81m31s

CAST [US version] Tomisaburo Wakayama, Masahiro Tomikawa, Kayo Matsuo, Minoru Ohki, Shoji Kobayashi, Shin Kishida, Lamont Johnson, Marshall Efron, Sandra Bernhard, Vic Davis, Lennie Weiinrib, Lainie Cook, Sam Weisman, Mark Lindsay, Robert Houston, David Weisman, Gibran Evans [note: some of these are voice overs only].

PRODUCTION David Weisman & Peter Shanaberg present a Toho Company Katsu Production. [prod] Shintaro Katsu & Hisahuru Matsubara. [exec prod of American version] Peter Shanaberg. [assoc prod] Larry Franciose, Michael Maiello, Albert Ellis Jr & Joseph Ellis. © 1980 Baby Cart Productions.

PHOTOGRAPHY DIRECTOR Chishi Makiura

MUSIC EDITOR Michael W. Lewis & Mark Lindsay

THE SLAYER

Is it a Nightmare? or is it...
THE SLAYER

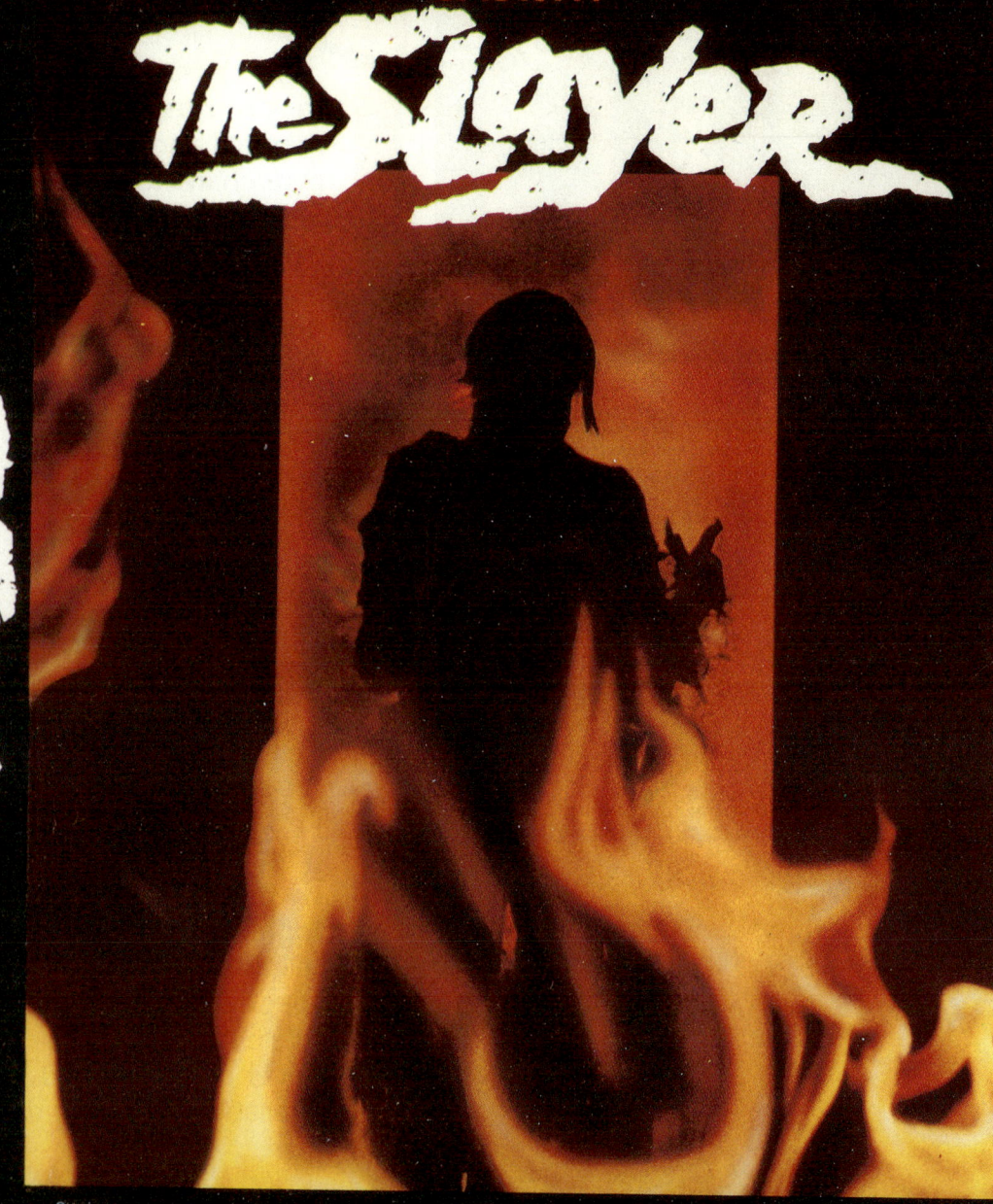

In the early morning hours of a cold and gloomy day, two young couples awoke and began preparations for a long awaited vacation. None of them anticipated the web of diabolical terror which was awaiting them on the isolated island retreat they had chosen for that vacation.

Only one of them was aware of the existence of "The Slayer" and up until that morning it lived only in the dark regions of her nightmares.

"The Slayer" is the story of what happens when imagination becomes reality and the maniacal, inanimate things which inhabit nightmares are unleashed in the real world. It is a terrifying descent into a maelstrom of horror from which those who journey rarely return.

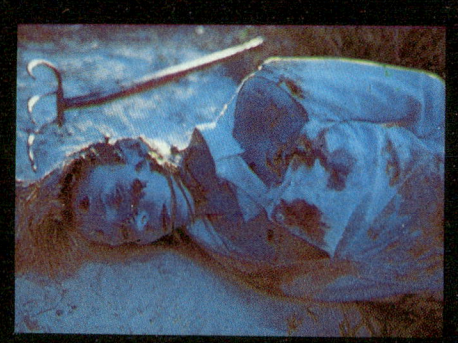

WARNING
The copyright proprietor has licensed the film contained in this videocassette for private home use only. Any other use including making copies of the film, causing it to be seen or heard in public or broadcasting it or causing to be transmitted to subscribers to a diffusion service, letting on hire or otherwise dealing with it in part or any kind of exchange scheme is strictly prohibited. Any breach of the above conditions render the offender liable to prosecution by Video Instant Picture Company Limited.

VHS VIDEO CASSETTE

VIP 036

VIPCO Video Instant Picture Company Limited

Starring
Sarah Kendall, Fredrick J. Flynn, Carol Kottenbrook, Alan McRae
Directed by: **J. S. Cardone** Produced by: **William R. Ewing**
Executive Producer: **Lloyd N. Adams**

SEE WARNING ON REVERSE   RUNNING TIME 89 MINS APPROX.

REVIEW

Four holidaymakers on a small island off the coast of Georgia run around the island looking for their companions before becoming dinner for an unseen monster. This creature seems to be summoned up from the imagination of one of the group (a bit like the Monster From The Id in **Forbidden Planet**). The deadly dreamer is played by Sarah Kendall, and she's a painter who had a recurrent childhood nightmare about being throttled by a character called "The Slayer." Whenever she goes to sleep her friends die horribly, by getting fishing hooks in the throat or having their heads slammed in doors. Thus the film gets a lot of tension out of our heroine's efforts to stay awake - think **Invasion Of The Body Snatchers**. She drinks gallons of coffee, chain-smokes and even burns herself with cigarettes, but it's all no good in the end. The gore is very effective: the monster whacks a fisherman on the head with an oar, and his torn scalp lands in his bait bucket. In another gross moment a woman has a pitchfork shoved through her back and it exits through her breasts. The make-up for the hideous monster is also quite effective until the end, when the illusion is spoiled by one close-up too many. This imaginative low-budget shocker is stylishly directed and better than most of its kind. There's even a pretty good twist in the tail.

TITLE	SLAYER, THE
AKA	NONE
DIRECTOR	J. S. Cardone
COUNTRY	US
SOURCE	Vipco (UK)
YEAR	1981
TIME	86m01s
CAST	Sarah Kendall, Frederick Flynn, Carol Kottenbrook, Alan McRae Michael Holmes, Sandy Simpson, Paul Gandolfo, Newell Alexander, Ivy Jones, Jennifer Gaffin, Richard Van Brakel, Carl Kraines.
PRODUCTION	[prod] William R. Ewing. [assoc prod] Anne Kimmel & Gerald Olson. [exec prod] Lloyd N. Adams. © 1981 The International Picture Show Company .
PHOTOGRAPHY DIRECTOR	Karen Grossman
MUSIC	Robert Folk
EDITOR	Edward Salier

DVD Review

When VIPCO first put this one in during the 1990s it was granted an 18 video certificate with just 14 seconds of cuts. It was resubmitted in 2001 and passed uncut. The R2 VIPCO disc has a theatrical trailer, a photo gallery, and is presented in 4:3 non-anamorphic PAL in a wishy-washy transfer that has obviously been taken from the same tape master VIPCO used to put together their original VHS. There is reputed to be a German release from Laser Paradise but this is elusive and therefore no specs are available. The VIPCO disc has been deleted for a while now, but copies are fairly easy to find. The film has never been released on disc in the States, but NTSC tapes are available under the title of **Nightmare Reunion**.

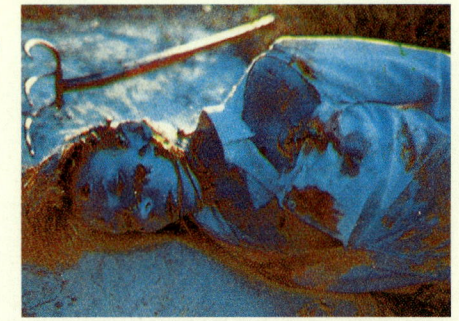

SNUFF

SNUFF — the movie they said no producer could make, no distributor would release, and no audience could stomach. This is the one and only original legendary atrocity shot by Monarch Films in South America and New York, where human life is cheap! The mystery and controversy surrounding this vicious and violent venture remains clouded to this day. Many of the actors and actresses who dedicated their lives to making this film were never seen or heard from again.

SNUFF is the film that went too far — an overwhelming assault on the senses that delves into a degree of delirium deeper than any ever achieved before.

SNUFF contains scenes of sadism, bondage, bloodshed and mutilation too real to be simulated, too shocking to be ignored!

Beautiful actresses, satanic slaves, bestial initiations, and gruesome gore beyond belief caused this picture to be banned. Are the killings in this film real? You be the judge!

RUNNING TIME 82 MINUTES

VHS

THE ORIGINAL LEGENDARY ATROCITY SHOT AND BANNED IN NEW YORK

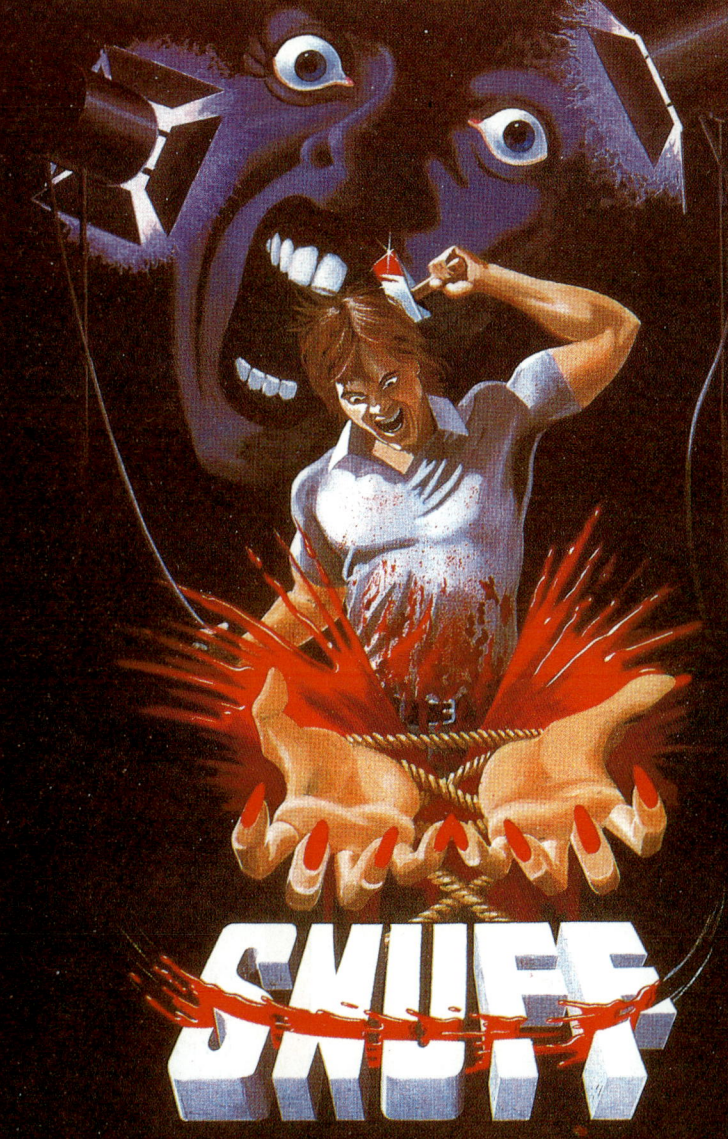

SNUFF

THE ACTORS AND ACTRESSES WHO DEDICATED THEIR LIVES TO MAKING THIS FILM WERE NEVER SEEN OR HEARD FROM AGAIN.

REVIEW

This miserable little exploitation movie about a Manson-style gang who massacre a pregnant actress and her friends was originally shot as **The Slaughter** and sat on the shelf for some time before an enterprising producer (Allen Shackerton) revived it with a fake ending. Then it became a "snuff" film, with a four minute sequence in which a woman was brutally murdered "on camera." Her fingers are cut off and then she is disembowelled, but this is all so patently phoney that the only people who swallowed it were those too squeamish to sit through the picture in the first place. Billed as a "legendary atrocity," **Snuff** does indeed live up to this description. It's quite simply one of the worst films you are ever likely to see (or not to see, considering its fate). The plot is something to do with a Manson-style gang led by a character who calls himself Sa-tan and speaks like he has a permanent echo chamber round his head. He leads an army of cycle sluts who are so ugly you need to be 18 to look at them. The plot plods along in a confused and boring fashion until the last five minutes, where we suddenly get to see the crew and cameraman lounging around the set. One of the crew suggests to an actress that they "go over to the bed and turn each other on." She looks dubious about the idea - "What, with all these people here?" But after accepting that "they'll be gone in a minute," she gets into a heavy petting session with the crew member. When she suddenly spots the camera and starts protesting about this kinky act of voyeurism, the jovial crew member lops off one of her plastic fingers and pulls a length of sheep offal from out of her jumper. "Let's get out of here!" urges one of the culprits, and most viewers will be right behind him. The ultimate joke is that this extremely pathetic little film became one of the most banned titles in the UK. Ironically, co-director Michael Findlay was killed shortly afterwards when a helicopter crashed on top of the Pan-Am building and decapitated him. Nobody was there to film it. As for the existence of real-life snuff movies, well, we all know that's a myth concocted by the sensation-hungry tabloids. After all, if you murdered someone, would you want to advertise the fact by putting the deed on celluloid?

TITLE	SNUFF
AKA	Slaughter; American Cannibale
DIRECTOR	Roberta Findlay & Michael Findlay
COUNTRY	ARG, US
SOURCE	Astra (UK)
YEAR	1976
TIME	76m39s
CAST	No credits or cast listed.
PRODUCTION	Monarch Films. [prod] Jack Bravman (uncredited). © None.
PHOTOGRAPHY DIRECTOR	Not credited
MUSIC	Not credited
EDITOR	Not credited

DVD Review

Anyone who actually sat down to watch this controversial title would quickly realise the effects are too poor for it to be convincing as a genuine Snuff flick. However, when Bill Lustig's Blue Underground released it on DVD in 2003 it's rumoured he was contacted and questioned by the FBI about it. That's his excuse for putting the movie out in a bog standard 4:3 non-anamorphic NTSC version with no extras whatsoever. Even the credits were left off the sleeve, which was like a plain brown paper bag! Limited to 10,000 copies, it seems that Blue Underground were aiming to give this release a 'bootleg' feel. The region free US release is the only one so far, but as we go to press we hear that Blue Underground have submitted **Snuff** to the BBFC and been given an 18 certificate with no cuts. How times have changed!

SS Experiment Camp

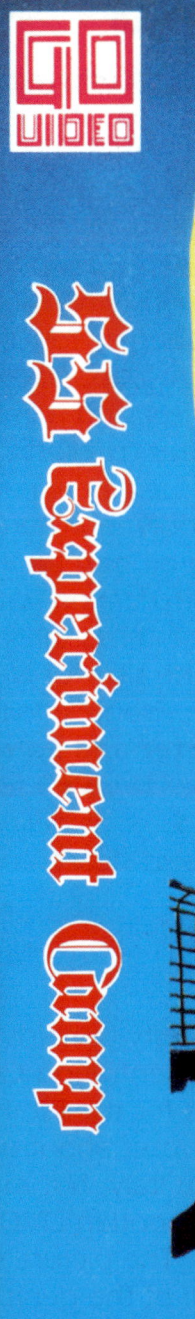

Directed by SERGIO GARRONE

A wartime German POW camp is the scene of horrifying experiments carried out on young women captives in pursuit of the fanatical Nazi objective of creating a Master Race.

Amidst the degradation and cruelty a tender affair develops between an attractive French prisoner and a handsome German officer: but he, too, is about to suffer the cruellest operation of all...

Running Time 90 minutes.

GO VIDEO LTD., P.O. BOX 4BT, 35-37 WARDOUR STREET, LONDON W1A 4BT

WARNING: All rights of the Producer and the Owner of the work reproduced reserved. Unauthorised Copying, Hiring, Lending Public Performance, Radio or T.V. Broadcasting of this Video Cassette prohibited.

CERT X

GO 118

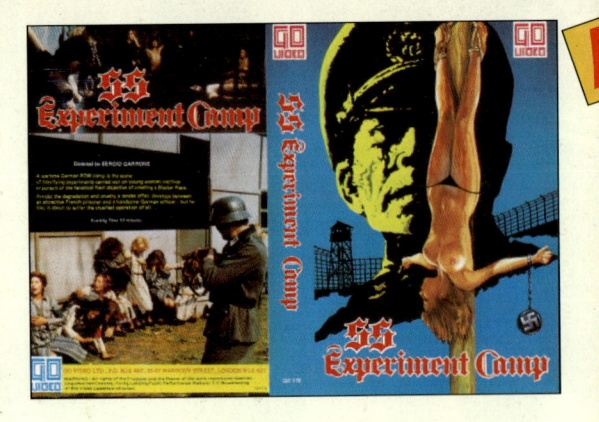

REVIEW

TITLE	SS EXPERIMENT CAMP
AKA	Lager SS adis kastrat kommandantur; SS Experiment Love Camp; Horreur Nazis; Le champs des filles perdues
DIRECTOR	Sergio Garrone
COUNTRY	IT
SOURCE	Go (UK)
YEAR	1976
TIME	89m 54s
CAST	Mircha Carven, Paola Corazzi, Giorgio Cerioni, Giovanna Mainardi, Serafino Profumo, Attilio Dottesio, Patrizia Melega, Almina De Sanzio, Matilde Dall' Aglio, Agnes Kalpagos (Szabo).
PRODUCTION	S.E.F.I. Cinematografica (Societá Europea Films Internazionali) present... Produced by S.E.F.I. Cinematografica (Rome). [dir of prod] Mario Caporali. © None.
PHOTOGRAPHY DIRECTOR	Maurizio Centini
MUSIC	Roberto Pregadio & Vassil S Kojucharov
EDITOR	Cesare Bianchini

The title might say it all, but it was the cover of **SS Experiment Camp** that first attracted PC Plod to the case. A topless girl crucified upside-down leapt out at hapless consumers from the shelves as the star of a piece of lurid artwork that was tacky even by Go Video standards (and no-one came tackier, believe me!). Some morally concerned video magazines insisted that a black bra be painted over the exposed breasts on the full page ads they ran. It made all the difference, I'm sure… The plot of the film is basic, to say the least. Nasty Nazis are rounding up the local female Jews for use in the camp of the title. They are routinely tortured, molested and raped by the doctors, guards, and just about anybody else who happens to wander along. Despite this, a 'tender affair' develops between one German officer and a French prisoner. But, to quote the sleeve once again, "He too is about to suffer the cruellest operation of all..." And how! It seems that the camp commandant is in the market for a new pair of testicles, and I'm sure you can guess who the unlucky donor is. Amazingly, our hero doesn't realise that he has been surgically emasculated (in an eye-watering bit of real-life medical footage) until he's in mid-clinch with his girl. His subsequent confrontation with the commandant offers one of the great moments in Trash Cinema, with the immortal line of dialogue: "You bastard! What have you done with my balls?" Most of the slew of Nazi camp films that appeared in the mid-70s were nothing more than women-in-prison exploiters dressed up in WW2 costumes to cash in on the success of **The Night Porter** and **Salon Kitty**, and **SS Experiment Camp** is no different. Not as slick and glossy as **Gestapo's Last Orgy** or **Salon Kitty**, or as outrageously camp as **Ilsa, She Wolf Of The SS**, or as deliriously… er…personal as **Love Camp 7**, it is merely a passable exercise in tasteless sleaze - nothing more, nothing less.

DVD Review

This notorious Nasty remains banned in the UK and the situation isn't likely to change in the near future. Concentration Camp exploitationers such as this and the **Ilsa** series (never submitted, but certs for the list if they had been) are best bought from Japan, where they don't seem remotely upset about these things. There's rumoured to be a Special Edition disc of this on the way from Italy, but meanwhile fans of this sort of thing will have to be content with seeking out the bootleg DVD-R, which contains a fullscreen transfer drawn from a Japanese laserdisc source. The picture quality is marginally better than the original VHS 'Nasty,' but unfortunately all of the genitalia is digitally 'fuzzed out' here. There's also an American VHS of the film that can be ordered online, but this also appears to be censored.

TENEBRAE
...TERROR BEYOND BELIEF

From the acclaimed director of "Suspiria" — TENEBRAE ... Terror beyond belief.

Take a bizarre voyage into the psycho-sexual as premier exponent of the horror thriller, Dario Argento, will strip your nerves raw!

'He realised every human obstacle, every humiliation could be swept aside by this simple act of annihilation: Murder.' — *from "TENEBRAE" by Peter Neal.*

American author Peter Neal is on his way to Rome for a press conference as his new detective novel, "TENEBRAE", is high on the best-seller list. On arrival he is greeted by a threatening anonymous phone call and the news that a young girl has been found with her throat slashed — her mouth stuffed with pages from his book! Suddenly Neal is plunged into the centre of a series of senseless, violent murders.

"TENEBRAE" holds the key to who the bloodthirsty homicidal maniac is. And that crucial link must be found before others pay the ultimate price for their hidden desires.

TENEBRAE, the latest masterpiece from "the New Hitchcock", has been called "Brilliant", "A tour de force", "A sublimely involving yarn" and "A shattering bloodbath", which made it a blockbuster in European cinemas.

"A stylised view of sex and violence highlighted by ingenious and bloody murders"..........*Ritz magazine*

"I doubt whether this year will bring a more compelling, more satisfying or more emotionally charged high-tech contemporary nightmare than Dario Argento's magnificent TENEBRAE"..........*Starburst magazine*

Running Time: 101 minutes

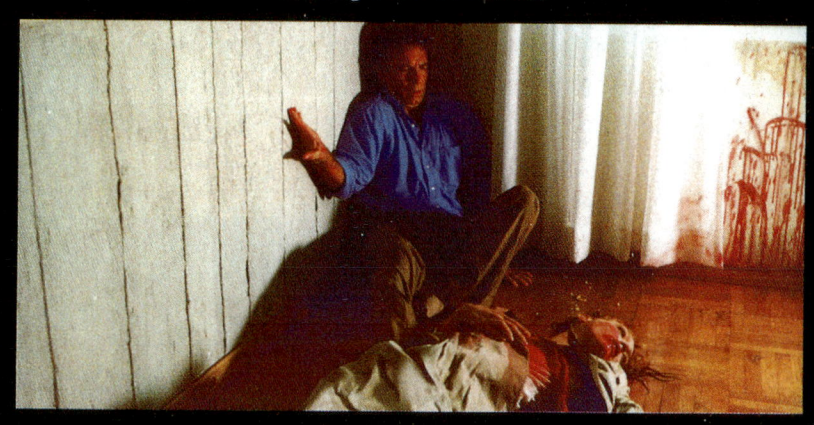

A VIDEOMEDIA RELEASE
VIDEOMEDIA LIMITED
70 WARDOUR STREET, LONDON W1V 3HP

All rights of the producers and owners of the recorded work reserved. The film contained in this video cassette is protected by copyright and use of this recording is restricted to private home use only. Any other manner of exhibition and any broadcast public performance, diffusion, copying, re-selling, hiring or editing constitutes an infringement of copyright unless the previous written consent of the copyright owner thereto has been obtained.

DESIGNED BY Graffiti PRODUCTIONS LIMITED

A VIDEOMEDIA RELEASE

TENEBRAE
...TERROR BEYOND BELIEF

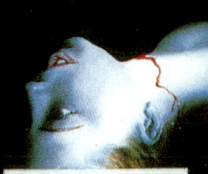

VIDEOMEDIA

18

HORROR
COLOUR
HVM 1032
VHS PAL

FROM THE UNDISPUTED MASTER OF THE MACABRE...
SALVATORE ARGENTO PRESENTS A FILM BY
DARIO ARGENTO

TENEBRAE
...TERROR BEYOND BELIEF

STARRING
ANTHONY FRANCIOSA

CHRISTIAN BORROMEO / MIRELLA D'ANGELO / VERONICA LARIO / ANIA PIERONI / CAROLA STAGNARO
WITH   ALSO STARRING   SPECIAL GUEST STAR
JOHN STEINER / LARA WENDEL / JOHN SAXON / DARIA NICOLODI / GIULIANO GEMMA
Director of Photography LUCIANO TOVOLI / Music by SIMONETTI-PIGNATELLI-MORANTE
Produced by CLAUDIO ARGENTO / Directed by DARIO ARGENTO / TECHNICOLOR

A VIDEOMEDIA RELEASE

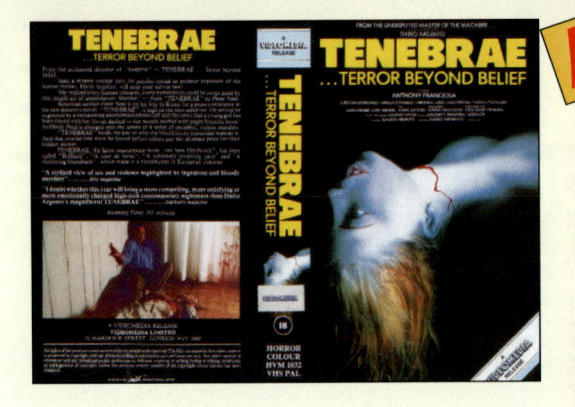

REVIEW

Though not one of Argento's best movies, this convoluted psychothriller still offers a number of stylish moments and some impressive gore sequences. Franciosa is an American writer of detective stories who visits Rome on a promotional tour and finds himself caught up in a series of murders of young women. It seems the killer is imitating the slayings in Franciosa's most recent novel. The question is, is it Franciosa himself, gone completely off his rocker from writing those penny dreadfuls? The plot is somewhat more coherent than we've come to expect of Dario (though what the heck are those kinky S&M flashbacks all about?), and there's a spectacular dismemberment-by-axe at the climax. The best sequence demonstrates Argento's technical virtuosity: the camera prowls an apartment house where a murder is about to be committed, gliding over the rooftops and into an open window like a silent accomplice. Classic stuff in comparison with most of the other movies on the nasties list.

TITLE	TENEBRAE
AKA	Tenebre; Unsane
DIRECTOR	Dario Argento
COUNTRY	IT
SOURCE	Videomedia (UK)
YEAR	1982
TIME	96m48s
CAST	Anthony Franciosa, Christian Borromeo, Mirella D'Angelo, Veronica Lario, Ania Pieroni, Eva Robins, Carola Stagnaro, John Steiner, Lara Wendel, John Saxon, Daria Nicolodi, Giuliano Gemma, Isabella Amadeo, Mirella Banti, Enio Girolami, Monica Maisani, Marino Masé, Fulvio Mingozzi, Gianpaolo Saccarola, Ippolita Santarelli, Francesca Viscardi.
PRODUCTION	Salvatore Argento presents… A Sigma Cinematografica (Rome) Production. [prod] Claudio Argento. © None.
PHOTOGRAPHY DIRECTOR	Luciano Tavoli
MUSIC	Simonetti - Pignatelli - Morante
EDITOR	Franco Fraticelli

DVD Review

When first re-released in the UK by Nouveaux Pictures, **Tenebrae** was originally shorn of about 5 seconds in the arm-chopping scene, which lost the shot of the victim holding the stump whilst it sprayed blood between her fingers. Since then it has been released uncut in Japan on Laserdisc and Australia on video (Palace). It's also currently available uncut on US and UK DVD from Anchor Bay. These are the best versions, containing an audio commentary by director Dario Argento, musician Claudio Simonetti, and journalist Loris Curci. There are also cast and crew filmographies and biographies, a behind the scenes featurette, scenes showing Argento setting up the ambitious crane shot which is a highlight of the movie, and alternate end music credits – plus a theatrical trailer. The disc is presented in 1.85:1 non-anamorphic NTSC/PAL and English Dolby Digital 5.1. Completists may like to note that the Anchor Bay release is missing 10 seconds of footage due to print damage. According to Bill Lustig who supervised the transfer, a tiny bit of dialogue is missing at the end of the scene where Daria Nicolodi and Anthony Franciosa enter his hotel room. This version is also missing a quick insert shot of a stab, which has been 'misplaced.'

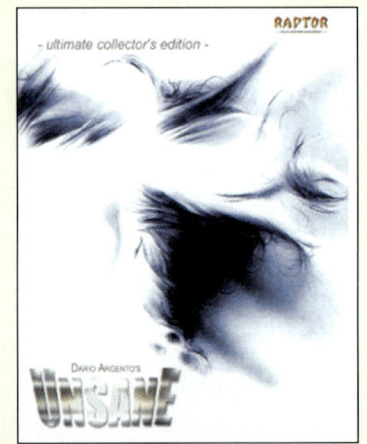

TERROR EYES

step out into the forbidden..... "Terror Eyes" will haunt you long after tonight.....

The young women attending a Boston night school are terrorised by a mysterious killer who performs a bizarre ritual of decapitation on each of his victims. All the evidence points towards one of the teachers, but nothing is what it seems in this chilling story of fear and death.

Starring Leonard Mann, Drew Snyder and Rachel Ward, Burt Reynolds' beautiful leading lady in "Sharky's Machine".

Executive Producers
Marc Gregory Comjean
and Bernard Kebadjian
Produced by Larry Babb
and Ruth Avergon
Written by Ruth Avergon
Directed by Ken Hughes

© Jacket and packaging - Guild Home Video Ltd MCMLXXXIII Your attention is drawn to the copyright warning on the cassette.
A Resource Production   © Lorimar Distribution International Inc.
(R) certificate (X)

RUNNING TIME 1 hr 30mins

VHS FORMAT

Guild

TERROR EYES

LORIMAR presents
TERROR EYES
starring
**LEONARD MANN
RACHEL WARD
DREW SNYDER**
co-starring
JOE SICARI

A Guild HomeVideo Presentation

COLOUR 1 hr 30mins

REVIEW

Originally known as **Night School**, this lacklustre slice 'n' dice opus comes from the same British director who gave us **Chitty Chitty Bang Bang!** It tells the story of a maniac killer (in a motorcycle helmet) who is going around decapitating students at a Boston college, apparently imitating some head-hunting New Guinea ritual. Suspicion falls on a professor (Snyder) who is known to have had affairs with several of the students, but the "surprise" ending isn't that hard to guess. The dialogue is unintentionally funny ("You know, I think you're dealing with a psychotic killer here" muses anthropology lecturer Drew Snyder, who is presumably majoring in The Bleeding Obvious), and severed heads turn up in a pool and a pot of stew. It's quite slickly made, and Rachel Ward looks great in the shower in a kinky scene where her boyfriend rubs red paint all over her. Shame she can't act as well, but I guess you can't have everything.

TITLE	TERROR EYES
AKA	Night School
DIRECTOR	Kenneth Hughes
COUNTRY	US
SOURCE	Guild (UK)
YEAR	1980
TIME	84m56s

CAST Leonard Mann, Rachel Ward, Drew Snyder, Joseph R. Sicari, Nicholas Cairis, Karen McDonald, Annette Miller, Bill McCann, Margo Skinner, Elizabeth Barnitz, Holly Hardman, Meb Boden, Leonard Corman, Belle McDonald, Ed Higgins, William McDonald, Kevin Fennessy, Ed Chalmers, John Blood, Lisa Allee, Elizabeth Allee, Patricia Pellows, J. J. Wright, Ted Duncan, Patricia Rust, Jane-Leah Bedrick, Wally Hooper Jr, Kevin King, Nancy Rothman.

PRODUCTION Lorimar presents... A Resource Production. [prod] Larry Babb & Ruth Avergon. [assoc prod] Leon Williams. [exec prod] Marc Gregory Comjean & Bernard Kebadjian. ©1980 Fiducial Resource International Ltd.

PHOTOGRAPHY DIRECTOR	Mark Irwin
MUSIC	Brad Fiedel
EDITOR	Robert Reitano

DVD Review

When this movie was resubmitted to the BBFC by Guild after the Video Recordings Act, it was passed with 1 minute 14 secs of cuts. If put in again now it would almost certainly be passed uncut, and maybe even with a 15 certificate! Warner in the US put the movie out on tape in 1996 under its American title of **Night School**, but the film remains hard to find here. There are reports that you can get a nice quality widescreen DVD-R bootleg from a UK source, but these remain unconfirmed. Meanwhile, if you're searching for a copy of this, be sure not to get it muddled up with another **Terror Eyes**, a 1988 straight-to-video horror flick starring B-movie scream queen Vivian Schilling.

Video Movies

THE TOOLBOX MURDERS

CAMERON MITCHELL   WESLEY EURE
PAMELYN FERDIN   NICHOLAS BEAUVY

Produced by: Tony Didio
Directed by Dennis Donnelly

Dead, in an incredibly gory multiple murder, are three attractive female victims, all second-floor residents of the same apartment building. One has been killed with a battery-powered hand drill, one bludgeoned to death with a claw hammer, and the final victim stabbed repeatedly with a screwdriver.

The police are baffled. By nightfall there are no clues. Then the apartment of a young would-be stripper is broken into, and the girl is raped before she is brutally murdered by three-inch nails propelled from a nailgun. This is just the beginning.

Colour/93 mins.
Copyright: Hokushin Audio Visual Ltd.
All rights reserved

HOKUSHIN AUDIO VISUAL LTD.
2 Ambleside Avenue, London SW16 6AD.
Printed in England by Robor Ltd.

VHS
PAL
SYSTEM

THE TOOLBOX MURDERS

VM 61

Video Movies

BIT BY BIT... BY BIT HE CARVED A NIGHTMARE!

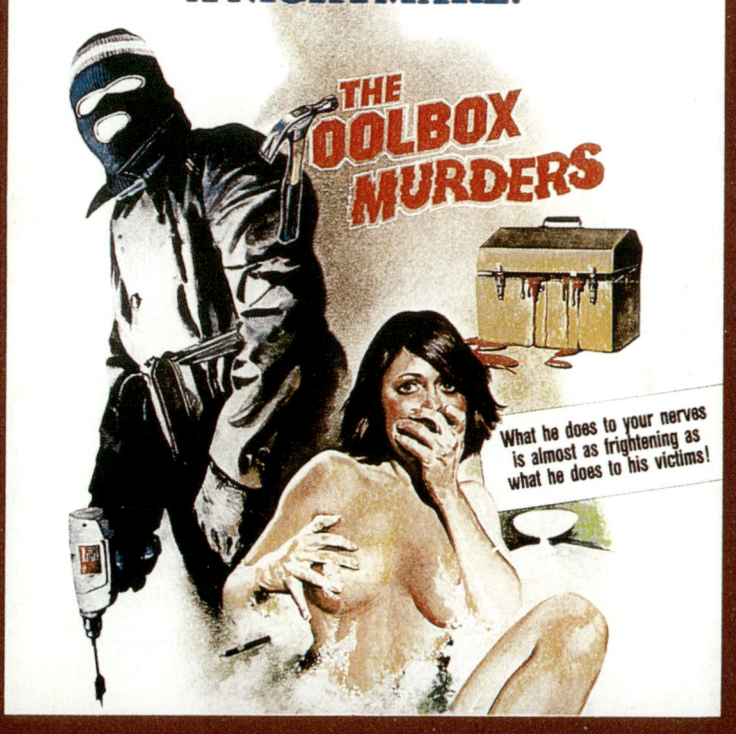

THE TOOLBOX MURDERS

What he does to your nerves is almost as frightening as what he does to his victims!

from Hokushin

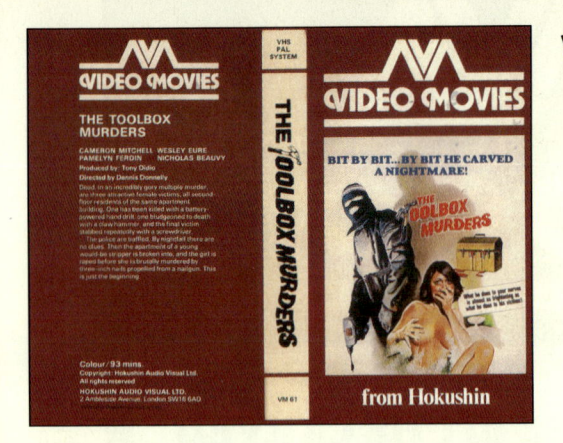

REVIEW

Originally shown at UK cinemas on a double-bill with **Zombie Flesh - Eaters**, this trashy gore opus stars the guy who played 'Buck' in **The High Chapparal** as a deranged building superintendent who kills off his victims with an array of tools (hammer, drill, screwdriver and nail-gun), all the while singing, 'Sometimes I Feel Like A Motherless Child.' This is something to do with him getting revenge for the death of his daughter, but under Dennis Donnelly's suspenseless direction the film just becomes a pointless catalogue of cruelty. It's worth seeing for Mitchell's crazed performance (his character wears a ski mask long before Jason adopted it), and some fairly strong gore murders. Look for porn star Kelly Nichols as the gal who gets the nail-gun treatment. The cast also features Anita Corseaut of **The Blob**. It's supposedly based on a true story. Yeah, right…

TITLE	TOOLBOX MURDERS, THE
AKA	NONE
DIRECTOR	Dennis Donnelly
COUNTRY	US
SOURCE	Hokushin (UK)
YEAR	1978
TIME	83m56s
CAST	Cameron Mitchell, Pamelyn Ferdin, Wesley Eure, Nicolas Beauvy, Tim Donnelly, Aneta Corsaut, Faith McSwain, Marciee Drake, Evelyn Guerrero, Victoria Perry, Robert Bartlett, Betty Cole, John Hawker, Don Diamond, Alisa Powell, Marianne Walter, Robert Forward, Kathleen O'Malley, Gil Galvano, James Nolan, George Deaton.
PRODUCTION	A Cal - Am Artists release. Cal - Am Productions presents... A Tony DiDio production. [prod] Tony DiDio. [assoc prod] Kenneth A. Yates & Jack Kindberg. © 1977 Cal - Am Productions.
PHOTOGRAPHY DIRECTOR	Gary Graver
MUSIC	George Deaton
EDITOR	Nunzio Darpino

DVD Review

This was rescued from the Video Nasties list when re-released in the same heavily cut version that played UK cinemas. VIPCO put out the butchered version in the UK in non-anamorphic fullscreen with trailers and a paltry stills gallery. But then along came Bill Lustig's Blue Underground and did the film proud with a superb Special Edition region free NTSC disc. The extras include an audio commentary with producer Tony Didio, cinematographer Gary Graver and actress Pamelyn Ferdin. Then there's "I Got Nailed In The Toolbox Murders" – a great interview with actress Marianne Walter (aka porn star Kelly Nichols). Lots of other goodies here too. The US disc has a splendid anamorphic widescreen transfer and is uncut, while the UK disc is missing 1 minute 46 secs of violence and gore. Do you really need time to think it over?

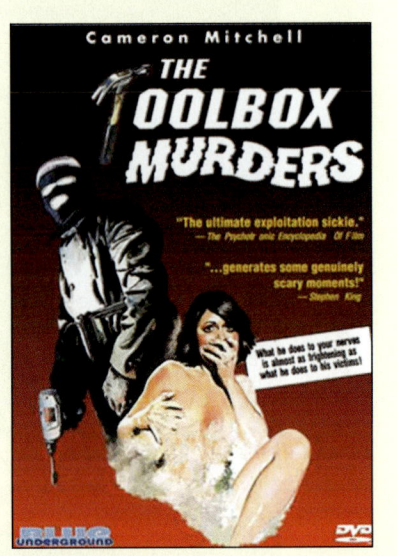

UNHINGED

When Terry, Nancy and Gloria, three pretty young college students crash their car in a driving rainstorm on the way to a rock concert, little do they realize that their troubles are just beginning.

Waking up in a mysterious old Victorian mansion in the middle of nowhere, they find themselves cut off from the outside world.

They are taken in by Marion Penrose, a middle-aged spinster and her mother, Mrs. Penrose, a demented old woman with a pathological hatred for men.

From here unfolds a violent tale of sexual repression turning again and again to savage brutality as it hurls towards its paralyzing climax!

UNHINGED

LAUREL MUNSON · J.E. PENNER · SARA ANSLEY ·
VIRGINIA SETTLE · JOHN MORRISON · BARBERA LUSCH

Produced and directed by DON GRONQUIST Written by DON GRONQUIST and REAGAN RAMSEY
Executive producer DALE FARR · Associate producer DAN BIGGS Music by JONATHAN NEWTON
Director of photography RICHARD BLAKESLEE Editors PHILLIPS BLAIR and FOSTER CASTLEMAN

Colour/Running Time 89 minutes   DOLBY SYSTEM

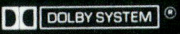

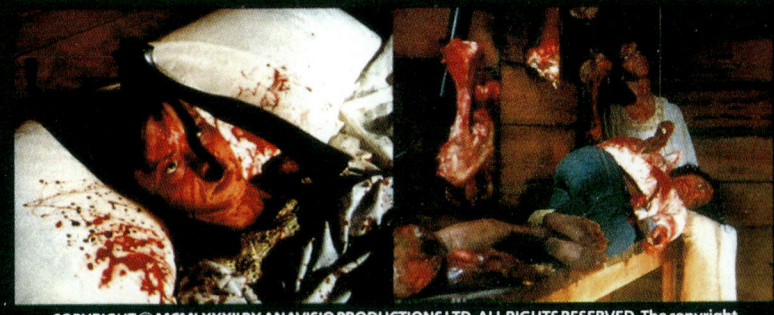

COPYRIGHT © MCMLXXXII BY ANAVISIO PRODUCTIONS LTD. ALL RIGHTS RESERVED. The copyright proprietor has licensed the picture contained in the videocassette for private home use only and prohibits any other use, copying, reproduction or performance in whole or in part. PACKAGING COPYRIGHT © 1983 AVATAR COMMUNICATION LTD; Printed in England. Manufactured and Distributed by CBS/FOX VIDEO, London T.M. designates the Trademark of AVATAR COMMUNICATIONS Licensed by INTER-OCEAN Video Sales Ltd.

VIOLENCE BEYOND REASON. VICTIMS BEYOND HELP....

UNHINGED

VHS 6238-50

AVATAR COMMUNICATIONS

REVIEW

Stop me if you've heard this one before: three college gals on a vacation crack up their car in the wilds of Oregon and end up in a house inhabited by a man-hating matriarch, her persecuted daughter and half-witted son. One sleeping beauty has a hatchet buried in her head. Another character has his brains graphically blown out. And in the **Texas Chainsaw** type climax the last remaining survivor is pursued into a room full of bottled eyeballs, strewn-about intestines and severed limbs. She is then slowly hacked to death, proving once and for all that it's always best to call out the AA on these occasions. The gore effects are pretty effective, particularly a nasty scythe-in-the-stomach sequence. But the acting, photography and direction call to mind the ineptitude of Andy Milligan flicks.

TITLE	UNHINGED
AKA	NONE
DIRECTOR	Don Gronquist
COUNTRY	US
SOURCE	Avatar (UK)
YEAR	1982
TIME	76m08s
CAST	Laurel Munson, J. E. Penner, Sara Ansley, Virginia Settle, John Morrison, Barbara Lusch, Bill Simmonds, Francine Molter, Dave Hood.
PRODUCTION	Anavisio Productions presents… [prod] Don Gronquist. [assoc prod] Dan Biggs. [exec prod] Dale Farr. © 1982 Anavisio Productions.
PHOTOGRAPHY DIRECTOR	Richard Blakeslee
MUSIC	Jonathan Newton
EDITOR	Philips Blair & Foster Castleman

DVD Review

This forgettable low-budget loser of a horror flick was passed with an X certificate for exhibition at the cinema, with cuts. What the paying punters made of it is anybody's guess. It was later removed from the DPP list, but has never been re-released on video in the UK, or on DVD for that matter. We can probably be grateful for that because it's one of the weakest of the Nasties. The movie is only currently available as a cheapie US disc (legal, not DVD-R) in two separate incarnations. One's from a company called Ventura Distribution. The disc is a bog-standard fullscreen edition with not even a trailer as an extra. I've not seen a copy, but I hear the quality is fairly mediocre. Mind you, the VHS tape looked pretty shoddy as I recall. There's another disc out there from Indie DVD. The full screen picture is grainy and not particularly sharp. Colour is generally OK but skin tones waver a bit. It doesn't look terrible though and there is a fair amount of detail in dark scenes. The mono sound is passable with clear dialogue but little else. Extras are an interview with director Don Gronquist and star Janet Penner from an American daytime TV show, trailers for other Indie DVD films, production stills and a comedy audio commentary by 'The Detractors.' The sleeve doesn't have an official certificate but does carry a cross between the American and Australian R ratings. Weird. Completists should be able to track down a copy on the Internet for about a tenner, but you'd have to be a little bit, er, unhinged…

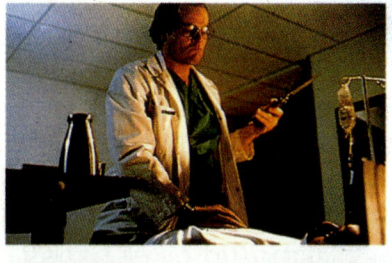

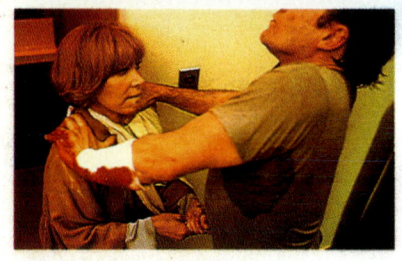

THE HOSPITAL WHERE YOUR NEXT VISIT... WILL BE YOUR LAST

VISITING HOURS

PIERRE DAVID and VICTOR SOLNICKI
Present
VISITING HOURS
Starring
LEE GRANT
WILLIAM SHATNER
MICHAEL IRONSIDE
and LINDA PURL
Screenplay by BRIAN TAGGERT
Directed by JEAN CLAUDE LORD
Produced by CLAUDE HEROUX
Executive Producers
PIERRE DAVID and
VICTOR SOLNICKI
Music by
JONATHAN GOLDSMITH
A FILMPLAN INTERNATIONAL
PRODUCTION

A psychopathic killer viciously attacks a woman journalist when she returns home from a TV broadcast. She survives but the killer refuses to give up. And any girl who stands in his way is in for similar treatment. The trail leads to a hospital where the journalist is at last cornered and finds that she has no-one to turn to for help...

This exciting and superbly constructed exercise in terror stars Michael Ironside as the ripper who likes to photograph as well as murder his victims, Lee Grant as the terrified journalist and William Shatner (of **Star Trek** fame) as her TV producer boss.

Visiting Hours is produced by Pierre David and Victor Solnicki, the men responsible for **The Brood** and **Scanners** and directed by Jean Claude Lord.

Colour/Running time: 105 minutes

Copyright © 1981 Guardian Trust Company. The copyright proprietor has licensed the picture contained in the videocassette for private home use only and prohibits any other use, copying, reproduction or performance in public in whole or in part.
PACKAGING COPYRIGHT © 1983 THE CBS/FOX COMPANY. T.M. designates the Trademark of CBS/FOX VIDEO. Printed and manufactured in England. Distributed by CBS/FOX VIDEO, London.
"CBS"™ is a trademark of CBS INC. used under licence. FOX™ is trademark of Twentieth Century-Fox Film Corporation used under licence.

CBS FOX VIDEO

DOLBY SYSTEM
VHS
1171-50

18

CBS/FOX VIDEO

REVIEW

The only so-called video nasty to have been shown on terrestrial telly in the UK (and no, civilisation did not collapse in the wake of this), **Visiting Hours** is a fairly vicious slasher movie, shot in Canada, that borrows from the usual sources - namely **Halloween**, **Peeping Tom** and **Psycho**. Future heavyweight baddie Michael Ironside (*Total Recall*) is very good as a sleazy psycho who mutilates and murders innocent women, photographing their broken bodies afterwards. The dime store psychology of the piece informs us that it's because he was abused as a child by his swaggering white supremacist father that he now hates independent, successful women. After picking up biker babe Lenore Zann and slapping her around a little, Ironside develops a particular fixation on investigative reporter Lee Grant, who is a TV celebrity at the studio where he works as a cleaner. He breaks into Grant's house, but after failing in his attempt at killing her he looses his fury on the hospital where she has been taken to recover. The bedpan bloodbath continues until Grant, who proves to be a resourceful character, turns the tables on her attacker and washes him out of her hair with an acid facebath. The movie is actually very well made, with good performances and much more depth than usual in the dialogue and characterisations.

TITLE	VISITING HOURS
AKA	NONE
DIRECTOR	Jean Claude Lord
COUNTRY	CAN
SOURCE	CBS/Fox (AUS)
YEAR	1981
TIME	99m24s
CAST	Desbois, Yvan Ducharme, Sarita Elman, Kathleen Fee, Domenico Fiore, Tali Fischer, Richer Francoeur, Lorena Gale, Angela Gallagher, Judith Gay, Isadore Goldberg, Dean Hagoplan, Victor Knight, Sheena Larkin, Sylvia Lennick, Frances March, Steve Michaels, Kimberley McKeever, Bob McKeowan, Malcolm Nelthorpe, Roland Nincheri, Mary Rathbone, Ron Robbins, Robbie Roberson, Danielle Schneider, Lisa Schwartz, Danny Silverman, Marty Starr, Jerome Tiberghien, Katherine Trowel, Len Watt, George Zeeman, Linda Singer, Michaelle Viau.
PRODUCTION	Pierre David & Victor Solnicki present A Filmplan International Production. [prod] Claude Heroux. [exec prod] Pierre David & Victor Solnicki.© 1981 Guardian Trust Company.
PHOTOGRAPHY DIRECTOR	Rene Verzier
MUSIC	Jonathan Goldsmith
EDITOR	Jean Claude Lord & Lise Thouin

DVD Review

Who would have thought that Captain Kirk would have made the DPP list! **Visiting Hours** was originally passed X at the cinema with cuts. It was re-released after further BBFC cuts by CBS/Fox. Then ITV accidentally broadcast the uncut version in 1989 and got rebuked by the ITC. Anyone who taped it then had a result! If you want to find the film nowadays then you are going to be spending a lot of your own visiting hours at car boot sales and Cash Converters. Even with the cult value of William Shatner nobody has bothered to resurrect this boring and generally goreless slasher for a DVD release, and even the Fox VHS has long been out of print. Keep watching the TV schedules…

CV 005

THE WEREWOLF AND THE YETI

STARRING

Paul Naschy · Grace Mills · Gil Vidal
Silvia Solar · Luis Laduni

There is no substantial proof that the Yeti exists, this strange link between man and animal that has eluded all scientific investigation.

Professor Lacombe sets out to find the Yeti and organizes an expedition to Tibet. A member of the team is attacked by strange creatures and is turned into a werewolf.

The expedition is slaughtered by bandits, with Silvia, the professor's daughter the only survivor escaping to hide in the mountains.

It is here that she is witness to a life and death struggle as the Yeti and the Werewolf demonstrate their savage ferocity in a bloody battle to the finish with herself as the victor's prize.

DIRECTED BY M. L. BONNS
COLOUR ● 84 MINUTES ● CERT 'X'

WARNING: The copyright proprietor has licensed the film contained in this video cassette for private home use only, and any other use including making copies of the film, causing it to be seen or heard in public or broadcasting it or causing it to be transmitted to subscribers to a diffusion service or otherwise dealing with it in part, is strictly prohibited without the prior written permission of CANON VIDEO LTD.

VPD

VIDEO PROGRAMME DISTRIBUTORS LIMITED
BUILDING No. 1, G.E.C. ESTATE, EAST LANE,
WEMBLEY, MIDDX HA9 7FF.

VHS

THE WEREWOLF AND THE YETI

TWO BLOODTHIRSTY BEASTS IN DEADLY COMBAT

CANON VIDEO

REVIEW

Paul Naschy's eighth outing as the joke shop wolfman Waldemar Daninsky opens to stock footage of Westminster Bridge with, for some inexplicable reason, "Scotland The Brave" playing on the soundtrack! Then we're off to a studio-bound Tibet, where Count Waldemar helps conduct a search for a monster who's even sillier than he. Naschy wanders off into the snow in search of the scriptwriters and is rescued by two scantily-clad cave-dwelling bimbos who are quite taken with our barrel-chested hero. "He will be a good companion and a passionate lover…" says one of the (obviously short-sighted) females. After a quick round of kinky nookie our hero discovers that the girls are cannibals, so he is obliged to whip out his stake and convert them into smoking skeletons. Meanwhile the rest of the low budget expedition has been captured by a horde of Tartar roughnecks, whose evil leader has a fondness for skinning young girls alive - these scenes probably account for the film's nasty status. The Yeti turns up at the end to wrestle with Naschy, but the film itself is even more abominable.

DVD Review

It's hard to believe, we know, but **The Werewolf And The Yeti** remains banned in the UK. Giving this a certificate would obviously bring about the downfall of society as we know it. Or something like that. Luckily we still have the Internet, and the advent of DVD-R. One American company calling themselves Monsterland Films have released a bootleg disc of the uncut movie under the title of **Night Of The Howling Beast**. I haven't seen it, but the distributors describe the quality of the fullscreen print used as being OK, which is not a good sign! Usually they tend to lavish superlatives on anything that's even barely watchable.

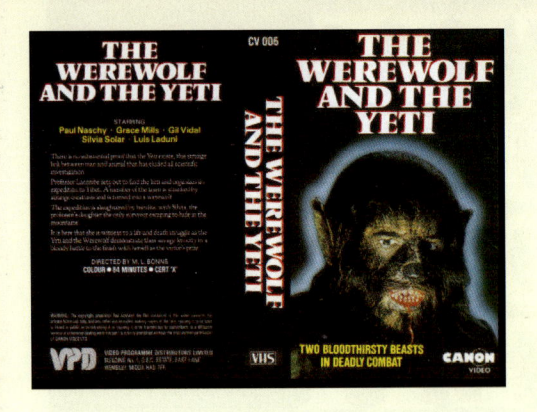

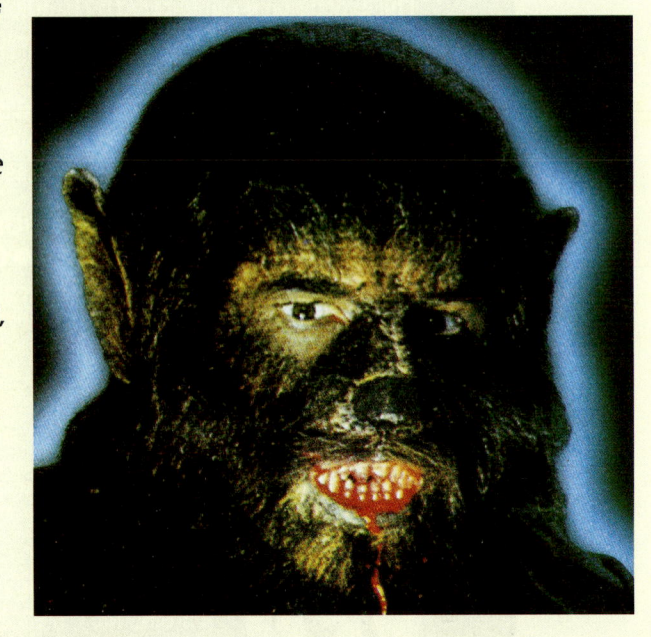

TITLE WEREWOLF AND THE YETI, THE

AKA La Maldicion de la Bestia; Night of the Howling Beast

DIRECTOR Miguel I. Bonns (as M. I. Bonns)

COUNTRY SP
SOURCE Canon (UK)
YEAR 1975
TIME 83m43s

CAST Paul Naschy (Jacinto Molina), Grace Mills, Silvia Solar, Gil Vidal, Luis Induni, Castillo Escalona, Ventura Oller, Veronica Miriel, Juan Velilla, Carmen Cervera, Pepita Ferrer, Jose L. Chinchilla, Fernando Ulloa, Juan Oller, Ana Maria Mauri, Indio Gonzalez, Victor Israel, Eduardo Alcazar.

PRODUCTION Profilmes, S.A. presents… [prod] Not credited.1975 Profilmes, S.A.

PHOTOGRAPHY DIRECTOR Tomas Pladevall

MUSIC Not credited
EDITOR Carmen Fabregas

THE WITCH WHO CAME FROM THE SEA

Starring:
MILLIE PERKINS, LONNY CHAPMAN,
VANESSA BROWN, PEGGY FEURY
Directed by
MATT CIMBER

Molly has a way with razors! She uses them with devastating effect. She cuts men down to size in an effort to revenge herself of her father's sexual perversions.

VTC Plc
14 Suffolk Street, Pall Mall, London SW1.

WARNING
ALL RIGHTS OF THE PRODUCER AND OF THE OWNER OF THE WORK REPRODUCED ARE RESERVED. UNAUTHORISED COPYING, HIRING, LENDING, PUBLIC PERFORMANCE, RADIO OR TV BROADCASTING OF THIS VIDEO RECORDING PROHIBITED BY LAW.

Colour 88 minutes
VTC 1019

ADULT HORROR

THE WITCH WHO CAME FROM THE SEA

VHS

VTC
VideoTapeCenter

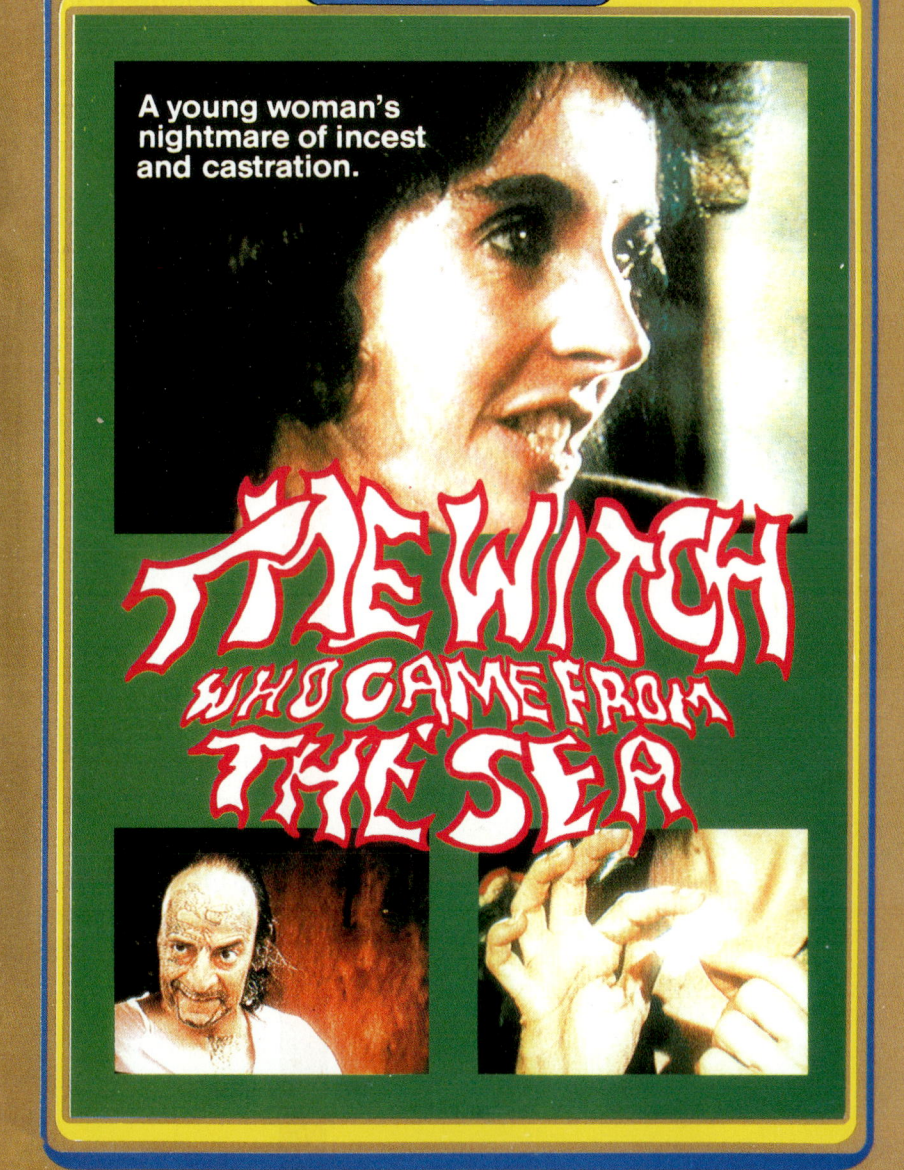

A young woman's nightmare of incest and castration.

THE WITCH WHO CAME FROM THE SEA

Colour 88 minutes
VTC 1019

REVIEW

A really bizarre movie from the writer of the cult youth movie **Wild In The Streets**, Robert Thom (who died in 1979). Thom was married to the star, Millie Perkins, and a certain amount of his screenplay seems to have been based on real-life incidents from his wife's childhood - some life she must have had! Perkins plays Molly, a troubled barmaid who has sex with a number of different men and then castrates them with a razor! In one scene she gets a mermaid tattooed on her chest by a completely tattooed man named Jack Dracula (played by Stan Ross of **Beyond The Valley Of The Dolls**). Director Matt Cimber was previously a porn movie director (which probably explains the 'guest appearance' of porno star Serena in a party scene). He was also married to Jayne Mansfield, and went on to direct some pretty lousy Pia Zadora flicks like **Butterfly**. This is surely his best film to date, featuring a terrific performance from Perkins, (who starred in the Hollywood epic, **The Diary Of Anne Frank**), and some very graphic bloodletting - watch out for the bit where Perkins gets high, ties up two musclebound football stars, and starts using her razor on them. As she runs around all naked and bloody, having a great time, it's easy to see why our prudish censor was offended! Having said that, **Witch** is not your standard exploitation thriller. Too bizarre and slow-moving for popular taste, it has a definite art house feel about it.

TITLE	WITCH WHO CAME FROM THE SEA, THE
AKA	NONE
DIRECTOR	Matteo Ottaviano (as Matt Cimber)
COUNTRY	US
SOURCE	VTC (UK)
YEAR	1976
TIME	84m05s
CAST	Millie Perkins, Lonny Chapman, Vanessa Brown, Peggy Feury, Jean Pierre Camps, Mark Livingston, Rick Jason, Stafford Morgan, Richard Kennedy, George Flower, Roberta Collins, Stan Ross, Lynne Guthrie, Barry Cooper, Gene Rutherford, Jim Sims, Sam Chu Lin, Anita Franklin, John Goff, Verkina.
PRODUCTION	MCI presents... A Matt Cimber production. [prod] Matt Cimber. © None.
PHOTOGRAPHY DIRECTOR	Ken Gibb & Dean Cundey
MUSIC	Herschel Burke Gilbert
EDITOR	Bud Warner

DVD Review

Another film that was quietly removed from the DPP list and disappeared into (probably well-deserved) obscurity, this arthouse oddity has only recently resurfaced as a DVD-R. The bad news is that the disc in question looks like it was transferred - very badly - from the original tape master. While the tape never looked that good, the DVD-R is almost unwatchable. There is also a VHS tape of it, but only on NTSC, and even that is hard to find. I guess that some movie buffs might like this one for its cheap and sleazy milieu, depicting the grungy bar scene, tattoo parlours and beaches of California, and of course there's also Millie Perkins' committed performance to recommend it. Good hunting.

WOMEN BEHIND BARS

starring
Lina Romay

The lure of stolen diamonds -- millions of pounds worth -- is overwhelming for luscious Shirley Field who shoots her lover for possession of them, then gives herself up pleading crime passionel.

Given the mandatory short sentence, however, she has not bargained for the violence and sexual practices that make up everyday life in Central American women's prisons. She may know where the diamonds are hidden awaiting her release, but will she ever possess them..?

GO VIDEO LTD.,
P.O. BOX 4BT, 35-37 WARDOUR STREET, LONDON W1A 4BT
WARNING: All rights of the Producer and the Owner of the work reproduced reserved Unauthorised Copying, Hiring, Lending Public Performance, Radio or T.V. Broadcasting of this Video Cassette prohibited.

GO128

WOMEN BEHIND BARS

REVIEW

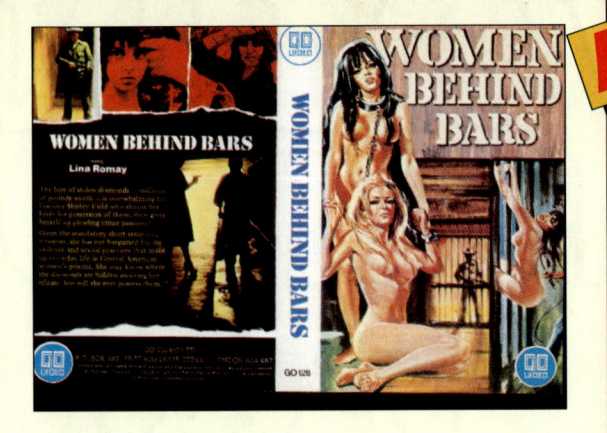

TITLE	WOMEN BEHIND BARS
AKA	Des Diamants pour L'Enfer; Visa pour Mourir; Prison Sado pour Femmes; Punition Cell
DIRECTOR	Jesús Franco (as Rick Deconnink)
COUNTRY	FR, SP
SOURCE	Go (UK)
YEAR	1975
TIME	75m12s
CAST	Lina Romay, Martine Steed (Martine Stedil), Nathalie Chapell, Roger Darton, Ronald Weiss (Carlo de Bries), Denis Torre, Frieda Altstadt, Ramin Ardid, Clifford Brown (Jesús Franco).
PRODUCTION	Brux International Pictures & Eurocine presents... A co-production of Brux International Pictures - Eurocine. [prod dir] Pierre Querut. © None.
PHOTOGRAPHY DIRECTOR	Gérard Brissaud (Jesús Franco)
MUSIC	Daniel White
EDITOR	Raymond Dubois (Jesús Franco)

Another Jess Franco abomination, this inept Women In Prison saga is set in an extremely ramshackle jungle jail where most of the female inmates lounge around naked complaining about the heat: "It's so muggy, it's keeping me awake…" Sexual assignations with the warden help relieve the boredom for the cast, if not the viewer. The star of the show is Lina Romay, Franco's real-life missus, who has been banged up for murdering her faithless lover at a dive called The Flamingo Club. As part of her rehabilitation treatment she is hung naked in chains, whipped and electrocuted. She accepts all this with remarkable lack of animosity, saying "Why should I hold grudges against a little punishment?" But eventually Lina breaks out and marches the wicked warden off into the forest where he is shot dead by Franco himself - who obviously couldn't think of a better way to end the film. This is a typically poor effort with all the usual Franco trademarks: an excess of pointless zooms, awful canned music and scratchy travelogue stock footage - some of which has been "borrowed" from another Franco nasty, **Cannibal Terror**. "It is true we have committed murder," muses Jess at the end. "But who were the victims? People who deserved to die." The movie does not deserve its place in the nasties list though - a dustbin might have been more appropriate.

DVD Review

This doesn't look too shocking these days, particularly in the light of some of the WIP flicks that are available on German labels. In fact **Women Behind Bars** is generally just your typical softcore romp with some sadistic treatment, such as electric shocks administered to the breasts and genitals of Lina Romay. Being married to Jess Franco, the gal has had to be a trooper! Anyway, the movie was eventually released from the Nasties list and packed off into obscurity. It has never been released on disc in the UK or America, but you can get an uncut European disc under the title of **Women Of Cellblock 9**. The quality of the transfer is mediocre, and fans of Franco/Romay prison movie mayhem would be better advised to check out **Ilsa The Wicked Warden** (aka **Greta The Mad Butcher**) or some of the other productions put out as part of the Erwin C. Dietrich Collection.

A brutal excursion in terror.

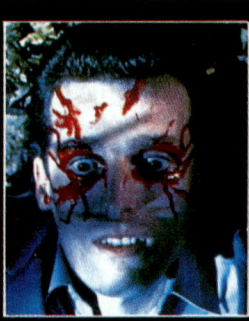

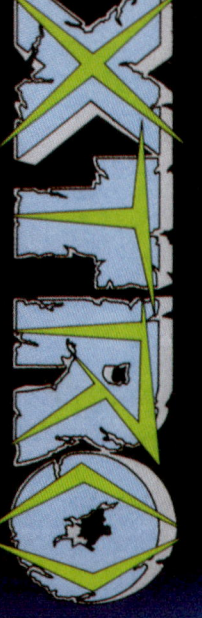

XTRO

The night sky is filled with a blinding light. Sam is relentlessly drawn towards the beam.

Three years later.
Sam returns home. Things... have changed. But more importantly, he's changed. And now he's come for his son. What follows is a brutal blood-bath as a rampaging alien stalks its human prey.
Running time: 82 mins approx.   Colour

STARRING
BERNICE STEGERS • PHILIP SAYER
SIMON NASH • MARYAM D'ABO • DANNY BRAININ

Special Effects by: NEEFX. Special Effects Makeup by: Robin Grantham. Director of Photography: John Metcalfe. Associate Producer: James Crawford. Written by: Robert Smith & Ian Cassie. Executive Producer: Robert Shaye. Producer: Mark Forstater. Directed by: Harry Bromley Davenport.
© MCMLXXXII Ashley Productions Ltd.

PolyGram Video
1 Rockley Road, London W14 0DL

WARNING: All rights of the producer and of the owner of the work reproduced reserved. Unauthorised copying, hiring, lending, public performance, radio or TV broadcasting of this video prohibited.

790648 2

VHS PAL

Passed only for persons of 18 years and over. **18**

REVIEW

The pre-production title for this British-made sci-fi shocker was **Judas Goat**, the significance of which is not really worth pondering on. It's a dreary exercise in grotesque special effects which borrows elements of **Close Encounters**, **Alien**, and cross-breeds them with **Kramer Vs Kramer!** Dad Sayer is kidnapped by aliens one day and returns to his family three years later in the form of a four-legged crablike monster - don't you hate it when that happens? He assaults a gorgeous blonde and the next day explodes from her womb, a full-grown human, later returning home to his wife to battle for custody of their son. The effects are impressive in places, but the plot is so ridiculous - and hard to follow - that the film very quickly becomes wearisome. Several unrelated sequels followed, none of which made the nasties list.

TITLE XTRO

AKA Monstromo (shooting title)

DIRECTOR Harry Bromley Davenport

COUNTRY GB
SOURCE Polygram/Spectrum (UK)
YEAR 1982
TIME 82m03s

CAST Philip Sayer, Bernice Stegers, Danny Brainin, Maryam D'Abo, Simon Nash, Peter Mandell, David Cardy, Anna Wing, Robert Fyfe, Katherine Best, Robert Pereno, Tok, Tik, Susie Silvey, Arthur Whybrow, Anna Mottram, Robert Austin, Vanya Seager.

PRODUCTION Amalgamated Film Enterprises Ltd & New Line Cinema Corporation present... [prod] Mark Forstater. [assoc prod] James M. Crawford. [exec prod] Robert Shaye. © 1982 Ashley Productions.

PHOTOGRAPHY DIRECTOR John Metcalfe

MUSIC EDITOR Harry Bromley Davenport

DVD Review

There seems to be some confusion about whether or not this movie was ever an official Video Nasty. It was later removed from the list and passed uncut for video and cinema release. A slightly cut version of the film shows regularly on the Sky Cinema channels, while 2003 saw the release of a 2-disc box set by the Dutch-based Marketing Film label. This gives us two versions of the movie: a Director's Cut and the original version. Neither transfer (fullscreen) is particularly good quality. In fact the Sky print looks ten times better, and that one's in widescreen too. But we get the full rape scene here and an alternate ending too. The disc has a 5.1 Dolby Digital soundtrack, but only for the Dutch release – the English is in 2.0 mono.

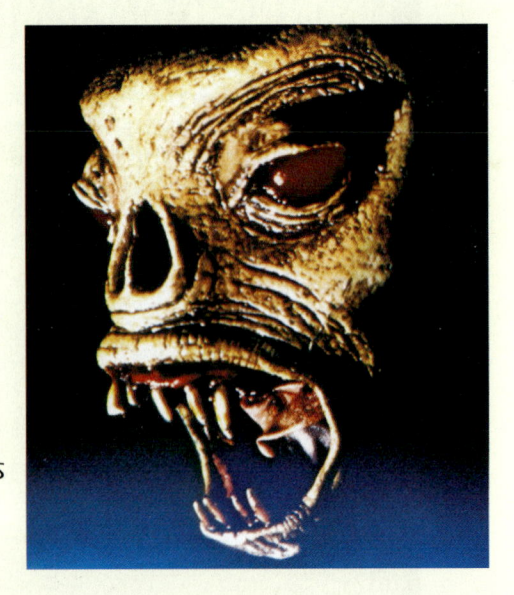

ZOMBIE CREEPING FLESH

A centre producing synthetic nourishment for the Third World is rocked by a huge explosion. A cloud of toxic gas fills the air and asphyxiates the workers.

They return as flesh-eating zombies — destroying villages and quenching their thirst for blood on the inhabitants..... DEVOURING THEM ALIVE!
A Special Squad is sent — their mission is to destroy the energy formula..... and end the blood-crazed zombies reign of terror.....

Approximate running time 81 minutes – M264D
© Merlin Video
Distributed by VCL Video

VCL

WARNING
Copyright subsists on all recordings issued under this label. Unauthorised broadcasting, public performance, copying or re-recording in any manner whatsoever is prohibited. Not to be resold, hired out or leased without the prior permission of VCL VIDEO.

ZOMBIE CREEPING FLESH

M264D

VHS

Merlin VIDEO

When the Creeping Dead devour the living flesh!

ZOMBIE CREEPING FLESH

Starring
Magrit Evelyn Newton, Frank Garfeeld,
Robert O'Neil and Selan Karay

Directed by Vincent Dawn   Produced by Sergio Cortona

WARNING: X Certificate – Not to be rented or sold to persons under 18

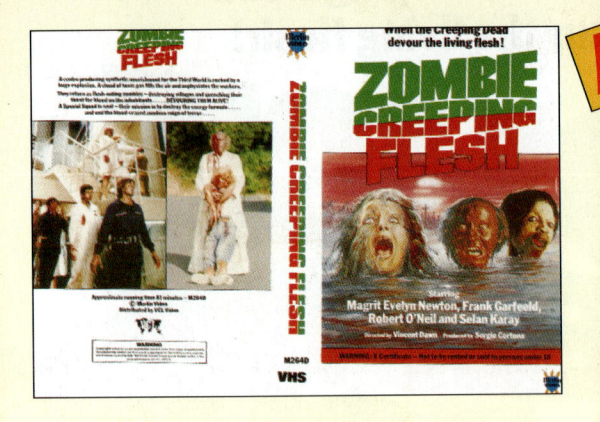

REVIEW

"What's eating you?" asks one jungle mercenary of another in this routine addition to the zombie/cannibal series. The answer is a motley assortment of grotty-looking living corpses that have been set in murderous motion by a gas explosion at a chemical plant deep in the jungles of New Guinea. Scientists have been beavering away trying to stem the tide of world hunger, but instead they've created a bunch of murderous zombies with hefty appetites. A commando team has been sent in to clear up the chaos (a nod to Romero's **The Crazies**?) and manages to rescue some journalists - among them pretty Newton - before gradually being wiped out in a suitably grisly fashion. Though you could at a stretch consider this to be an allegory on what might happen if we let the Third World problems get out of hand (the ultimate success of the hunger project is that human beings become a recyclable commodity - mankind eats itself!). The film is bluntly predictable in its approach and the effects are not on a par with those seen in Fulci movies. Gore highlight: the scene where Newton has her eyeballs pulled out through her mouth!

TITLE ZOMBIE CREEPING FLESH

AKA Inferno dei morti viventi; Virus; Apocalypsis Canibal; Hell of the Living Dead

DIRECTOR Bruno Mattei (as Vincent Dawn)

COUNTRY IT, SP
SOURCE Merlin (UK)
YEAR 1981
TIME 81m35s

CAST Margit Evelyn Newton, Frank Garfield (Franco Giraldi), Selan Karay, Robert O'Neil, Gaby Renom, Luis Fonoll, Piero Fumelli, Bruno Boni, Patrizia Costa, Cesare Di Vito, Sergio Pislar, Bernard Seray, Victor Israel, Pep Ballenster, Joaquin Blanco, Esther Mesina.

PRODUCTION A Beatrice Film (Rome) - Films Dara (Barcelona) co-production. [exec prod] Sergio Cortona. © None.

PHOTOGRAPHY DIRECTOR John Cabrera

MUSIC Goblin
EDITOR Claudio Borroni

DVD Review

This one was finally passed uncut in 2002 and there are plenty of good quality DVDs available. The best is Anchor Bay's version. It's region free and titled **Hell Of The Living Dead**. The film is presented in 1.85:1 anamorphic, NTSC. The extras include a nice featurette, Hell Rats Of The Living Dead, featuring a video interview with director Bruno Mattei - in Italian with English subtitles. We also get a poster and still gallery, a theatrical trailer, cast and crew biographies and filmographies, plus a collectable booklet. VIPCO's UK disc is also uncut, but is lacking extras (apart from a still gallery and trailers from **Cannibal Holocaust** and **Shogun Assassin**. The print used here isn't too good – cropped in the ratio of 1.66:1 non-anamorphic PAL. There's also a region 2 German disc from Laser Paradise.

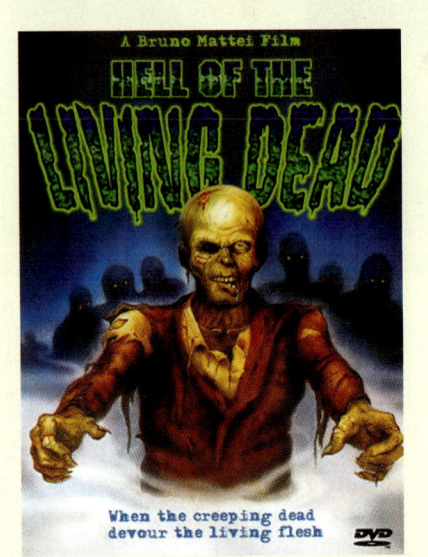

ZOMBIE FLESH EATERS

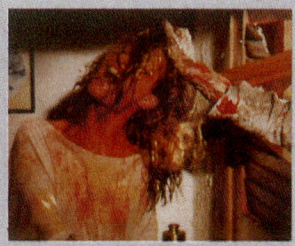

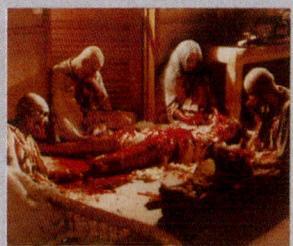

Starring
RICHARD JOHNSON
TISA FARROW
IAN McCULLOCH

When the earth spits out the Dead...

they will return to tear the flesh of the Living...

ZOMBIE FLESH EATERS

RUNNING TIME 89 MINUTES, COLOUR
SEE WARNING ON REVERSE

STRONG UNCUT VERSION!!

VIPCO

In Hudson Bay a sailing-boat that has a neglected appearance is drifting slowly out to sea. A coast-guard boat draws up alongside and a policeman goes into the cabin. His colleagues do not see him come out again and one is about to go into the cabin when a terrifying sight appears out of the hatchway — a man, covered in blood, walks towards him menacingly. Only after being hit repeatedly by bullets from the policeman's gun does he fall overboard and disappear amid the waves.

This news causes a sensation and panic in the whole of America, also because the sailing-boat belonged to a famous scientist who disappeared rather mysteriously in the Caribbean. The scientist's daughter Ann together with Peter West, a famous American journalist, set out to look for him. The two of them set sail on a schooner belonging to Brian, a young American ethnologist, and Susan, a young underwater photographer. Far out at sea, Susan dives to take some photographs, but is attacked by a huge shark; however, she is saved by a Zombie who unexpectedly appears out of the depths of the ocean. In the meantime, on Matul Island, in the Antilles, Professor Menard is carrying out strange experiments.

What follows in the Caribbean and later in New York is terrifying — ZOMBIE FLESH EATERS are here!!

WARNING
The copyright proprietor has licensed the film contained in this videocassette for private home use only. Any other use including making copies of the film, causing to be seen or heard in public or broadcasting it or causing to be transmitted to subscribers to a diffusion service, letting on hire or otherwise dealing with it in part or any kind of exchange scheme is strictly prohibited. Any breach of the above conditions render the offender liable to prosecution by Video Instant Picture Company Limited".

REVIEW

Fulci's celebrated gorefest borrows the rules of zombie-lore set up by George Romero ('Beat 'em or burn 'em - they go up pretty easy…) and grafts them on to an EC comic book storyline set on a remote tropical island in the West Indies. It is there that sweaty professor Richard Johnson has been trying to deal with a voodoo-induced plague of zombie flesh-eaters by shooting all of his dead patients in the bonce! Soon after arriving on the island of Matoul, four tourists (Farrow, McCulloch, Gay and Al Cliver) are chased around the island by the shuffling, glassy-eyed living dead, who move so slowly they are lucky their victims obligingly stand there and wait to be eaten. This widescreen feature is vividly photographed and has some impressively nasty set-pieces bolstered by excellent special effects. A highlight is the surreal scene where the lovely Auretta Gay goes skinny scuba-diving and encounters an underwater zombie and a shark! Elsewhere the flesh-eaters make a spectacular entrance, clawing their way out of the ground in an ancient graveyard for Spanish Conquistadors. This scene looks like it might have been inspired by a similar sequence in Hammer's **Plague Of The Zombies** (1966). The gore is typically excessive, with lots of cannibal movie-type pulling out of stringy entrails and munching on sweetmeats. Probably hardest to take is the bit where Olga Karlatos gets her eye punctured - in extreme close-up - on a wooden splinter. This sequence is conspicuously absent from the cut version, which is basically the same as the prints that went round cinemas with an X certificate in the early 80s. One of Fulci's most entertaining films (he appears in a cameo as a newspaper editor), it's marred slightly by a rather lacklustre ending.

TITLE	ZOMBIE FLESH-EATERS
AKA	Zombi 2; Zombie
DIRECTOR	Lucio Fulci
COUNTRY	IT
SOURCE	Vipco (UK)
YEAR	1979
TIME	87m01s
CAST	Tisa Farrow, Ian McCulloch, Richard Johnson, Al Cliver (Pier Luigi Conti), Auretta Gay, Stefania D'Amario, Olga Karlatos [and uncredited] Ugo Bologna.
PRODUCTION	Variety Film. [prod] Ugo Tucco & Fabrizio De Angelis. [prod man] Antonio Mazza. © None.
PHOTOGRAPHY DIRECTOR	Sergio Salvati
MUSIC EDITOR	Fabio Frizzi & Giorgio Tucci Vincenzo Tomassi

DVD Review

When originally released to UK cinemas with an X certificate in 1979, this Fulci favourite had 14 cuts totalling 1 minute 41 secs. These included a 15-second cut of Olga Karlatos having her eye pierced by a splinter of wood, then the deletion of almost all shots of Olga being eaten by zombies. All shots of blood gushing from Auretta Gay's throat after being bitten were also taken out, and various other bits of zombie mayhem. An additional 26 seconds were missing from the prologue showing a zombie being shot, but this was probably down to the distributor. In the pre-VRA days, VIPCO released the above version on video. Later on they issued the uncut version at a premium price, which then got on the DPP list. After the VRA, VIPCO re-released the cinema version without any further cuts (cert18). They misleadingly described it as complete, as it was uncut compared with the cinema version. The uncut version was finally made available a couple of years back. VIPCO have an uncut version now, but it's not as good quality a transfer as Anchor Bay's region free US disc. This has a great 2.35:1 anamorphic transfer, a remastered Dolby Digital 5.1 soundtrack, audio commentary with actor Ian McCulloch and lots more goodies. The title of the US disc is **Zombie**.